THE
BIG DROP

Classic Big Wave Surfing Stories

EDITED BY JOHN LONG
AND
HAI-VAN K. SPONHOLZ

FALCON*

Guilford, Connecticut
An imprint of The Globe Pequot Press

A FALCONGUIDE®

Copyright © 1999 by John Long
Published by The Globe Pequot Press, Guilford, Connecticut

Falcon and FalconGuide are registered trademarks of The Globe Pequot Press.

Map illustrations by Gardner Heaton.
Front cover: Kaipo Jaquias at Pipeline. Photo by Rob Gilley.

Grateful acknowledgment is made to those who granted permission to reprint the selections in this book. A complete list of copyright permissions can be found on page 244.

Library of Congress Cataloging-in-Publication Data
The big drop!: classic big wave surfing stories/edited by John Long with Hai Van K. Sponholz.
    p.   cm.
    ISBN 1-56044-917-9 (pbk.)
    1. Surfing. 2. Surfers Anecdotes. I. Long, John, 1953-. II. Sponholz, Hai Van K.
GV840.S8B44   1999
797.3'2—dc21   99-33815
                                                      CIP

Manufactured in Canada
First Edition/Ninth Printing

CAUTION
Outdoor recreational activities are by their very nature potentially hazardous. All participants in such activities must assume the responsibility for their own actions and safety. The information contained in this guidebook cannot replace sound judgment and good decision-making skills, which help reduce risk exposure, nor does the scope of this book allow for disclosure of all the potential hazards and risks involved in such activities.

Learn as much as possible about the outdoor recreational activities in which you participate, prepare for the unexpected, and be cautious. The reward will be a safer and more enjoyable experience.

CONTENTS

BIG WAVES OF THE WORLD

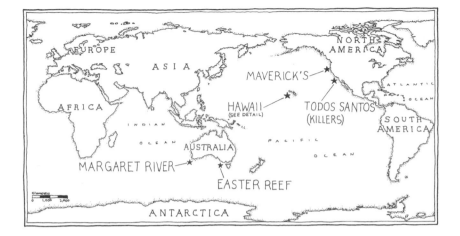

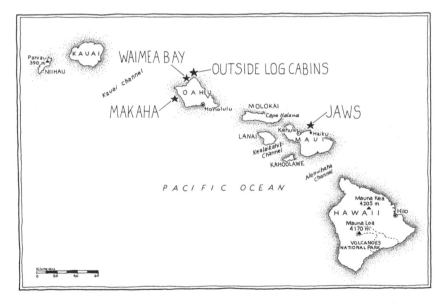

A map of the world's big wave venues can be misleading. You could go to all the places shown above and never once see a big wave—it's not like mapping out the topography of Mount Everest or El Capitan—these are moving mountains, products of location, bottom contour, and climatic conditions. There are many other spots on the world that get big surf, but this map represents the places that are famous among surfers for breaking in the 15-foot-plus range. The one thing all spots have in common is access to the mighty big bit of ocean that's necessary to generate the huge swells that are ultimately responsible for these adventure stories.

Map note by Marcus Sanders.
Map drawn by Gardner Heaton.

INTRODUCTION

John Long

I'd gone to Hawaii's Oahu Island to film the opening to a movie. One night, about a week after I arrived, the late-night news reported waves of 25 feet at Waimea Bay. The following morning we bailed on work and drove flat-out from Waikiki up to the North Shore. Born into the Southern California surf culture, I'd grown up hearing about legendary big wave venues like Waimea and Pipeline and Sunset. Several times as a kid I'd paid a buck to get into funky old auditoriums and listen to famous surfers and watch grainy films of men shooting down titanic waves on surfboards. I'd waited my whole life to see this business firsthand and was smacking the driver—a local surfer—to step on it. When we got within a mile of the Bay the clear dawn air suddenly filled with mist and my friend said, "Oh, it's gonna be *big!*" A little farther and I started hearing the percussion of mortar fire, or perhaps carpet bombing. I wanted to duck. "That's the waves making that sound," my friend corrected. I laughed in his face.

When we screeched into the parking lot, I stopped laughing. I jumped out of the car and stared out at the ocean in disbelief. What I saw out there I couldn't call waves, at least not as I understood them. More like liquid mountains—hissing, spitting, and unloading like neutron bombs. *"Damn!"*

Waimea Bay describes a horseshoe roughly a half-mile deep and a mile across. The waves steam around the right-hand edge of the bay, where the shoreline cuts abruptly inland and is girded by enormous, mottled boulders. We scrambled out onto these and watched the monsters smoke past so close it seemed I could reach out and touch them. When a 30-foot wall of water curled over and broke, the earth shook, spume shot 50 feet in the air, and the ocean convulsed with currents and boiled with sand churned up from the floor of the sea. It seemed impossible, insane that any human would challenge these waves—but there they were, a group of perhaps two dozen, careening down the

Taylor Knox riding the wave that won him $50,000 in K2's 1998 Big Wave Challenge. Location: Todos Santos, Mexico.
PHOTO BY LES WALKER

vertical faces of these great walls of water. It was a little like trying to outrun chain lightning.

For an hour we stood there, drenched to the bone. Everything looked so exaggerated, it felt like the landscape of a dream. With that dizzy mixture of fear and excitement, I wondered if these waves and these surfers were made for each other and found completion together. For one of the few times in my life, I wished I'd gotten involved in a sport other than climbing.

The next thing I saw made me *glad* I was a climber.

During a previous lull, four or five surfers had hit the water running and started paddling out to the lineup. The leaders were already cresting the first wave of the new set, catching air off its backside. A second later, their arms a furious blur, the others paddled up the mounting wall. Everyone cleared—but one. A grisly green beast reared before him like the face of Half Dome in Yosemite. He stood up on his board and dove, but it was too late. My stomach turned to stone as I watched his dark profile drawn up inside the curling wall and then torpedoed over the falls. Splinters of his shattered board shot into the air and bobbed atop an avalanche of foam. Minutes seemed to pass before he surfaced, pushed a hundred yards inside, and thrashed around the chop like a rag doll. Then the shore break caught him and dashed him onto the sand, where he lay limp until several lifeguards sprinted over and beat the water out of him. I couldn't believe it when he finally staggered to his feet and stumbled away.

"That guy better find another line of work," I said.

"Naw," my friend said. "He just needs to find another board. He'll be back."

Sure enough, in about 20 minutes the guy returned with a new board and paddled back to the lineup. Riding these waves was so special that even the worst imaginable thrashing was considered fair tradeoff for the experience.

Big wave surfing ranks among the greatest adventure sports in terms of its rich history, classic milestones, colorful characters, controversies, all-time performances, startling innovations, hilarious and tragic events, and the vein of true grit that runs through all top performers. Technical surfing on small waves is not an adventure sport because, barring fluke, there is little penalty for a mistake. The constant with all adventure sports is a simple and final one: a break in form or an error in judgment can kill you. And there's also the real chance that nature will serve up something for which no amount of judgment or technique can compensate. There are simply forces at play far beyond anyone's ability to control them. When you're out in the lineup and a 40-foot rogue wave jumps up from the deep, skill and experience only count for so much. The world champion might be carried away while the terrified rookie might survive. Once the adventure starts pushing the envelope, there's no foretelling the outcome, a fact borne out time and again in the following stories.

Given the sheer volume of material written about big wave surfing, it was difficult to select the "best" stories with any certainty. It was also impossible to provide a cogent history, to cover all bases, and to do justice to the many pioneers and champions past and present. I simply tried for balance and selected those pieces that refused to be excluded, stories that sparked a special excitement and that were, most of all, unforgettable. A glaring and regrettable gap concerns the complete lack of stories by or about women. We looked high and low and couldn't find a single piece about women riding huge surf. We do know that Layne Beachley has been towing into some mackers lately with Ken Bradshaw. A few other names come up—Margo Olberg in the early days at Sunset, Jeannie Chesser, Rell Sunn, and others—but their stories, if written, escaped us. At press time, *SurferGirl* magazine reported that Sarah Gerhardt, a 24-year-old chemistry Ph.D. candidate, broke into the exclusive, so-called Maverick's Men's Club when she rode three waves at Maverick's just 24 hours after a storm that produced some of the biggest waves ever photographed there. With women kayaking the meanest rivers, climbing the steepest rocks, and summiting Mount Everest, true big wave surfing would appear to be lagging behind other adventure sports in terms of women's involvement, but obviously that is changing even as we speak.

Other omissions exist simply because it was impossible to fit everything in. There's a strong big-wave community in Australia but their main venues—Easter Reef and near the Margaret River—are not represented in these stories. It should also be mentioned that Taylor Knox, 26 (photographed by Les Walker), won the inaugural K2 Big Wave Challenge in 1998 for a monster wave he surfed at Todos Santos in Mexico. The prize is $50,000—not bad for a guy who suffered a skateboard accident at age 15 that threatened to end his shot at a surfing career. Peter Mel is also unfortunately absent except in passing, but it should be noted that he significantly pushed the cold-water envelope last year at Maverick's.

But who can complain about a sport with so many excellent stories that it's impossible to collect them all? Compiling and editing this collection has been a remarkable experience. I'm reminded of what Ricky Grigg said of his surfing career: "It's been one hell of a ride." I trust that everyone who reads on will feel the rush of plummeting down a wave that rears like a beast and crashes like thunder.

In the Beginning . . .

Ricky Grigg

*R*oughly 50 years old, big wave riding is a relatively new adventure sport compared to, say, mountaineering or river running. The colossal waves at Makaha on Oahu's west shore—questionably the birthplace of big wave surfing—were essentially unridable until the late '40s, when lighter balsa boards came to replace the solid wooden behemoths of previous eras and surfers began adding fins. Ricky Grigg was not at Makaha in the '40s, but his mentors were and he knows their story well. When Grigg first ventured to Hawaii in 1958, he immediately joined the budding big wave crusade and helped establish the standards at classic big wave venues such as Sunset and Waimea Bay. Like most big wave pioneers, Grigg possessed the essential qualities of the master "waterman": paddle champion, small wave shredder (1967 international champion), inveterate big wave junkie, accomplished scuba and free diver, and ultimately an oceanography professional. In short, the ocean was Grigg's life. Through the lens of Grigg's personal story, the following account helps put in perspective all stories that follow.

‡   ‡   ‡

In the early 1950s, I was in my middle teens in California and just beginning to tempt big waves along the West Coast. Every winter we typically had waves 10 to 12 feet. Then one incredible day, on January 10, 1953, the surf went ballistic. Rincon, a favorite surfing spot near Santa Barbara, was 15 to 18 feet, and Overhead Ventura was even bigger. When I woke up that morning and looked out our second-story beach-house window in Santa Monica, giant waves were rolling in half a mile offshore. The surf was breaking beyond the Santa Monica Pier by the breakwater, where it is about 15 feet deep. The waves must have been at least 20 feet high, surf twice as big as I had ever seen. Before I got out of the shower, the phone was ringing off the hook. Charlie Reimers, Peter Cole, Buzzy Trent, Joe Quigg, Matt Kevlin—everyone was headed north for Santa Barbara to surf Overhead and Rincon.

That day at Rincon I caught my first triple overhead wave. I also got pounded, squashed, rolled underwater, and terrified; by day's end, I felt like a drowned rat. Despite the wipeouts, from then on I was absolutely hooked on becoming a big wave rider. Nothing I had ever experienced felt so dramatic. The huge waves were as magnetic to me as they were beautiful, and I was drawn to them like an enchantment. The waves were huge and I was scared, but sliding down those great silver faces at Rincon was pure joy. It was a fleeting emotion, and like an addiction it would remain something I would have to recapture again and again, never getting quite enough. That day changed me forever. Big waves were in my blood. The early pioneers of big wave riding in Hawaii felt the same way about giant surf: They were addicts.

In the early 1950s, a small cult of Californians lived in a Quonset hut at Makaha Beach on the northwest coast of Oahu. Their names are legendary: Buzzy Trent, Jim Fisher, Walter "Flippy" Hoffman, and Woody Brown, along with George Downing, Wally Froiseth, and a few other locals who grew up in Honolulu. Jim Fisher was a daredevil who gained fame for riding giant combers and surviving horrible wipeouts. Buzzy Trent and George Downing, though, were the first to successfully tackle the really big waves, those in the 25-feet-plus range. They were the first masters of Makaha, the original top guns. While in one sense they were rivals and occasionally clashed in the water, they were also the best of friends, motivating and inspiring each other. Bud Browne has some footage of Buzzy Trent in 1953 sliding so fast on what appears to be a 25-foot Makaha wave that his board left the water several times before he finally got the axe. Trent was known for his power and high trim. He would never back down if properly lined up for the takeoff.

Buzzy Trent was eight years my senior as I was growing up in Santa Monica. In high school he was an all-state fullback. In track he ran the 100-yard dash in 10.1 seconds. Buzzy began surfing in the mid-1940s, when he was in his teens. His board was a 10' 6", double-fin, square-tail concave, a Bob Simmons masterpiece of Styrofoam sandwiched between plywood. The nose consisted of a huge spoon so pronounced that you could have mixed a salad in it. It was on this board that I caught my first wave.

Ricky Grigg surfing pipeline in the early '60s surf movie Cavalcade of Surf.
PHOTO BY BUD BROWNE

After high school, Buzzy went to USC on a full football scholarship. In his first year he got clipped and broke both legs. USC withdrew his scholarship, and the next thing Buzzy knew he was out of college. He became a boxer in the Golden Gloves tournament, but again he met disaster. This time it was the other guy. He hit an opponent so hard it killed him right there in the ring. Next, Buzzy became a bullfighter in Tijuana, then a lifeguard in Santa Monica, and, finally, the master gladiator in big surf at Makaha.

Actually, with Buzzy you can't say "finally." After pioneering big wave riding, he then became a hang-gliding fanatic. He once jumped off the mountains above Makaha during a Kona storm and was blown so high he almost froze to death before floating back to earth in Wahiawa, nearly 25 miles away. Buzzy ended his hang-gliding career by hitting a water tank going 50 miles an hour. He lost his kneecap on that one. Next he took up cycling, but no sooner had he begun than he had a serious head-on with a parked car. Later he was playing with his pit bull when it suddenly, for no apparent reason, bit him in the mouth and jaw and wouldn't let go. Buzzy had to strangle the dog to get it to release him. In 1998, at age 69, Buzzy was walking 20 miles a day, every day. You could see him any day of the week, with hat and shades, head down, walking straight ahead along Kalaniana'ole Highway, perhaps still dreaming of 25-foot waves at Makaha.

While Trent was power, daring, and athletic grit, Downing was smooth and stylish. He had impeccable judgment and seemed always to be in the right spot. In the '50s, George was known as the Desert Fox, named by Buzzy after Rommel, the famous German general in World War II in the North Africa theater of operations. Intense, intelligent, and proud, George has the best wave judgment of any surfer I've ever known. No matter what the topic, if it's on the ocean—sharks, pollution, currents, sand erosion, you name it—George has an expert opinion. At Point Surf, Makaha, there is no one I'd rather surf with.

Downing and Trent were not only the first true matadors of big surf, they perfected the equipment and the technique for big wave riding. With help from Joe Quigg, they invented the first "elephant-gun" surfboard, a stiletto tear-drop machine shaped like a spear, which would hold in on giant watery faces up to 30 feet high. Downing invented a bailout off the back of his board, a rapid sinking maneuver that helped avoid the horrendous wipeout of not making 25- to 30-foot waves. Trent exhibited the willpower, stamina, and boldness to take the wipeouts head-on. On land, he could hold his breath for minutes at a time. In big surf, he could survive two-wave hold-downs. By the time I reached Hawaii in 1958, Downing and Trent had set the stage for us to tackle even bigger surf on the North Shore of Oahu. We simply followed their lead.

North Shore surf had been ridden occasionally in the 1940s and early 1950s but never on a consistent basis and virtually never when it was truly big. An exception was a December day in 1943 when Woody Brown and Dickie Cross went out at Sunset Beach. For several hours the surf continued to build, and in the late afternoon it broke loose with waves upward of 40 feet high. The ensuing epic cost Dickie Cross his life and postponed a full-scale assault of surfing on the North Shore until the late 1950s.

By the winter of 1957 a small group of Californians, including Greg Noll, Pat Curren, Bing Copeland, Del Cannon, Mike Stang, and Mickey Muñoz, had migrated to the North Shore. Makaha was getting crowded, and they figured with caution and training they could handle North Shore waves. A small clan of Hawaiians led by Henry Preece had set up a grass shack on the beach at Haleiwa and were regularly surfing there. Surfing the North Shore was an idea whose time had come. One day, the California crew was watching Waimea Bay. It was just starting to break at 10 to 12 feet. Greg Noll was convinced it could be ridden, and before long he was leading the pack paddling out. When they got to the lineup, though, there was more talk than action. Everyone agreed it was much bigger than it had looked from the beach—maybe 15 feet or even bigger. There were lots of wipeouts that day. No one was riding a board designed for high speed. None of the boards had cords. No one knew anything about the currents, the bottom depths, or whether the surf was coming up or going down. A few great waves were ridden that day, one in particular by Mickey Muñoz. It was about 18 feet, and Mickey, who had been one of the shortest guys in high school, was suddenly 9 feet tall. That day Mickey made varsity.

The following year, 1958, the campaign to conquer the North Shore began in earnest. As luck would have it, it was my first year in the Islands. I had graduated from college and was on my surfing sabbatical. I was ready to ride anything—well, almost anything. My first day out was with Peter Cole, who also had just arrived from California. The rain and cold of Northern California had gotten the best of him, and like me, the stories of big surf in Hawaii had fired his imagination. On that first day, Peter and I were out at Sunset, where it was 6 to 8 feet and about as big as I could handle. Late in the day, a few 10- to 12-foot, eye-popping sets came in. Later that winter Peter and I would surf 12- to 15-foot waves with impunity, putting in six- to eight-hour days in the water. Peter once made nineteen swims for his board (no leashes) in one day, and I was right behind with seventeen. By the end of the year, we were in top shape.

About two dozen of us were surfing big North Shore on a regular basis that year. The most respected were Greg Noll, Pat Curren, Peter Cole, Kimo Hollinger, Henry Preece, Buzzy Trent, Jose Angel, Paul Gebauer, Joey Cabell, and George Downing, to name a few. We decided Waimea could be ridden up to 30 feet. Bigger than that, the bay starts to close out. The rip currents turn into rivers too strong to swim against. The only way to get to shore during close-out conditions is to swim in hugging the right side of the bay. Buzzy Trent used to say, "Stay in the whitewater—it's your lifeline to shore." If you drifted left toward the middle of the bay, a rip current tearing out to sea would greet you. In minutes it would transport you back outside the lineup on the far west corner of the bay. The only way to get in was another round-trip, but this time hugging the whitewater.

Peter Cole was one of the few guys with enough guts to try catching waves over 30 feet, although he always maintained it was extremely difficult to paddle into waves that big. Waves travel at a speed proportionate to the depth of the water where they break; thus, a 30-foot wave breaking at a depth of 30 feet is traveling at more than 20 miles an hour. To paddle into a wave moving this fast is very difficult, but Peter has ridden a few. Back in the late 1950s, when Peter was in his prime, he took off on 25-foot waves without even thinking about it. This was before leashes, and Peter still refuses to wear one. It was also before he lost sight in one eye after his board skegged him one day at Sunset Beach. But even this couldn't diminish the big wave appetite of Peter Cole, the most stoked surfer I have ever known. At 69 he is still in the lineup at Sunset Beach. If there is surf, no matter what the conditions, he will be there. I can remember dozens and dozens of times when the wind was howling sideshore or even onshore and no one was out at Sunset, and Peter would say, "That can be surfed." Sure enough, out he'd go. Of course this attitude was in part owing to Peter having been an all-American collegiate swimmer who only missed making the U.S. Olympic team by a fraction of a second. Peter could survive any wipeout, any hold-down, any swim. Given the 40 years that he has put into the lineup at Waimea Bay, he must have ridden more big ones than anyone else, including all the modern guys. Today, when Peter paddles out at Sunset Beach, everyone cheers. He truly is the oldest and grandest man on the North Shore. In the old days Peter's strategy was always to catch the biggest wave. And when it came, it was usually him or Pat Curren who caught it.

Pat Curren was always a man of few words. His motto was not to talk about it but just to do it. And what he did was ride the biggest waves. He experimented with boards, perfecting Downing's guns, and his own, for the bigger, bumpier faces of Waimea Bay and Sunset Beach. Many of us in the original crew used his boards. Board builder Dick Brewer picked up where Pat Curren left off. Pat was a leader in other ways, too. He always sat at the head of the Viking table when dinner was served in his Quonset hut at Makaha. He pounded on the table and uttered monosyllabic cries: "Food! Beer! Women!" But alas, there were no women. Several seasons came and went, and one day Pat did find a woman. Her name was Jeanine. Petite, quiet, and lovely, she seemed to exert a magical control over Pat. They were married and had a son, Tom. Twenty-five years later Tom was the best surfer in the world.

Greg Noll is another guy who has tested the limits of riding the biggest wave from a paddling takeoff. One of the great legends of big wave surfing concerns a wave Greg rode at Makaha on December 4, 1969. That day brought the biggest surf in the history of surfing in the Pacific Ocean. Waimea Bay was reported to be 40 feet, Makaha was 35 feet, and Kaena Point was 50 feet. The storm that produced this swell had a wind fetch of 1,800 miles. The winds in the fetch were 65 knots, and it sat stationary in the North Pacific 1,000 miles northwest of Hawaii for 48 hours. Property damage caused by high waves to homes on the North Shore exceeded $1.5 million. Only a couple of people went surfing in Hawaii during the peak of the swell. Greg Noll tells me his giant wave at Makaha was the telling moment in his big wave riding career. It was perhaps 35 feet high, a quantum leap bigger than anything he had ever laid eyes on. In his mind, he knew this was it. Now or never. Thirty years of training had gone into the buildup for this moment, and he said to himself, "Now." And what he did made history—the biggest wave ever ridden up to that time.

We called Greg "The Bull," and no one has ever been more appropriately named. The name came from Greg's stance on his board. He was like a Sherman tank; once he was on his feet, there was no moving him. The Bull could plow through tons of whitewater without so much as a wobble. Knocking him off was like overturning a rhino. But it had not always been like that. Greg and I grew up together in Los Angeles Bay, Greg in Manhattan Beach and me in Santa Monica. Greg was tall and skinny and had arms as long as a chimpanzee. In paddling races, he was tough to beat; pumping up and down from a kneeling position on the board, he was like an oil well, never tiring, as relentless as he was confident. Greg was a super hotdog surfer. His back turn was snappy, he hung ten, and he was the man on wheels before Dewey Weber. But then Greg began to grow, and he became heavier and thicker and stronger. During his years pioneering the North Shore, he was a force to be reckoned with. We all respected his power. Knowing he was in the water somehow helped us overcome our own fear. Though Greg kept surfing for many years after the epic '69 wave at Makaha, that moment was his ascent to the mountaintop, his moment in time. The beast within him had been conquered.

The 1960s were the years when the North Shore surf pioneers completed their study. Jose Angel, who had absolutely no fear of gigantic surf, became the first surfer to ride giant Backdoor at Pipeline. Jose lived on the beach at Pipeline, and when the surf came up it seemed to energize him, pulsing through his veins. At night, while he was sleeping, the pounding roar of wild waves seemed like an electric current charging his batteries, and when he woke up in the morning, there was no stopping him. And not just at Pipeline. Jose would paddle out at Waimea and take off on anything. Left of the peak, sometimes too soon (under the falls), sometimes too late (over the falls), but always in a supercritical position. He seemed to revel in surviving the most horrible wipeout possible. Jose even trained for a time to challenge 40-foot waves at Kaena Point. I called him Iron Man. When I surfed with Jose, I never worried about drowning because I figured he would somehow be there to save me. Over the years, we rode hundreds of days together at the Bay and at Sunset. Tragically, Jose, one of the greatest watermen of all times, died in a scuba-diving accident in 1976. I've never gotten over my despair about losing him, but I know he is at peace. Memories of Jose still inspire us all.

Outer Reef Pipeline was one of the last places to be conquered. Most memorable was Greg Noll's famous ride, filmed in slow motion by pioneer surf photographer Bud Browne. Greg kept going and going and going, and the wave kept getting bigger and bigger and bigger. Finally, it catapulted him off the nose as his board reached a point where it couldn't go fast enough to keep up with the wave.

The Next Generation

As the 1960s gave way to the '70s, a new era of big wave riding emerged. The pioneering years, when the challenge was simply "survival," gave way to more stylish big wave surfing. New moves, such as radical bottom turns, clean S-turns, and some serious tube riding previously accomplished in surf only up to 12 feet, began to show up in 20-footers. This increase in maneuverability was made possible by breakthroughs in board construction and design, particularly with the advent of lighter boards. The invention of the thruster (three fins) gave surfers an enormous increase in maneuverability. The equipment was honed by such master shapers as Greg Noll, Dick Brewer, Randy Rarick, and Pat Rawson.

This second era of big wave surfing lasted through the 1980s. The surfers who impressed me most were Jeff Hakman, Jock Sutherland, Eddie and Clyde Aikau, Nat Young, Mark Richards, Ian Cairns, Mike Doyle, Barry Kanaiaupuni, Gerry Lopez, Reno Abellira, and Shaun Tomson. They were more athletic than their big wave forebears, representing the elite of tens of thousands compared to the several hundred contenders in the pioneering era. Waimea Bay remained the capital of big wave riding, with Makaha taking over top billing only once or twice a decade when Waimea Bay was totally closed out and unridable at 30 feet plus.

The 1990s ushered in a third era of big wave surfing, with major new technology—Jet Skis, restyled guns, foot straps—and the exploitation of the outer reefs, such as Jaws on Maui. The third era also includes an ongoing search around the world to discover and conquer the ultimate ridable wave, what Mark Foo called "Discovery of Destination X."

While big wave riding today has become high-tech, the hearts of the players remain the same. Having lived in Hawaii during most of the early years of big wave surfing, I recognize a few men as outstanding among the best of the first. All possess distinctly different talents, but what they share in common is rugged individualism. Looking back, I see them as completely comfortable with themselves. To a man, they did things their way. Strong, sometimes stubborn, unique, unconcerned with group values, often alone but never lonely, these were men you respected for their power. Most were all-around watermen—swimmers, divers, paddlers, sailors. They rode huge waves because they were drawn to them naturally. And like my own obsession with surfing, they did it for love.

The names and faces of the day's greatest big wave riders have changed many times, but one aspect has not changed and never will: the fear element. No invention, no high technology, no future trick will ever take the place of guts. Buzzy Trent said it best while talking about Waimea Bay in an interview in *Surfer* magazine in 1966.

As Buzzy said, "You either have it, or you don't."

Amen.

THE DEATH OF DICKIE CROSS

Bruce Jenkins (as told to him by Woody Brown)

*I*n the early '40s, Woody Brown lived above the Waikiki Tavern, the
epicenter of island surf culture and craziness. He began shaping boards,
experimenting with designs, and soon joined Wally Froiseth, John Kelly,
Fran Heath, Rus Takaki, and younger homegrown surfers such as George
Downing to begin exploring winter surf potential on the North Shore of Oahu.
"Nobody went to the North Shore," said Woody. "We were the first. Froiseth
and Kelly told me there were big waves at what's now Sunset Beach." On
December 22, 1943, Woody and a young friend named Dickie Cross were pacing
around the beach at Waikiki, " . . . where there was no surf at all. So, we got
bored. Finally we said, 'Let's go over there and try.' So we went up the North
Shore." Once there, Brown and Cross paddled out at Sunset on a rising swell.
Sunset had rarely been ridden and it was only Woody's third or fourth time
surfing the North Shore. The epic that ensued—relayed in the following story
from Brown's raw perspective—cast a pall over North Shore surfing for nearly
15 years.

‡   ‡   ‡

A bunch of us surfed Sunset in the early '40s. We were the first ones. The
day my friend Dickie Cross lost his life was one of the biggest I'd seen, a
swell coming up to 20 feet or more. As it turned out, this was one of the
biggest swells ever. It washed out the old Haleiwa Restaurant and did a
lot of damage on both sides of the highway. But we didn't have any idea
it would escalate like that. The channel at Sunset looked negotiable in the
middle of the bay, so we figured it was safe to go out. This was late afternoon, and we were all alone out there.

Just when we got out beyond the break, a tremendous set appeared on the horizon, maybe a mile out. It looked to be over a hundred feet of water. It was just one wave, all the way from Sunset down toward Waimea, as far as we could see. Here we are, sitting outside a 20-foot break but inside this wave. Dickie and I just said to ourselves, "This is it. It's all over."

The wave came in, but it turned out there was a great, deep hole in the reef out there. The wave dissipated in the middle. Now we realized, "Hey, we're still alive. Let's get the heck out of here." We figured if we lost our boards coming in through the whitewater, we'd never make it in, so we're digging like mad in the channel, for maybe 20 minutes. Finally Dickie sat down on his board and rested. "You know where we are, don't you?" he said. And I knew. We hadn't moved an inch. We were in the exact same place where we started. And it was starting to get dark, with huge sets coming in every 10 minutes. We didn't know what to do, so finally we decided to wait until the next huge set went by—which would be about 10 minutes—and then paddle like hell to get outside of them, paddle down the coast, and come in at Waimea. We remembered that when we went by Waimea before we went out, the waves were only 20 feet. The whole bay was open, right? It was just breaking on the point, more or less. We thought we could come in over there, on the big beach break.

But it didn't work that way.

As we started the 4-mile paddle to Waimea, it kept getting bigger and bigger. The surf went up on the Haleiwa Restaurant and wiped out the road at Sunset. It was the biggest surf they'd had in years, and we were stuck out there. George Downing swears the waves were 40 feet high that day, breaking over a shelf in 80 feet of water, and I think they were easily that big.

Anyway, we got out okay, past the big sets at Sunset, and started to paddle down the coast to Waimea. Dickie was only around 17—he was just a gutsy young guy. We paddled down and Dickie kept working his way in! I'm looking in as we're paddling the coast and saying, "Look! The surf is breaking right along a line where we are, ahead and behind us. We're right in the line of this killer break. We better move out more, yet."

"'Nah, nah, nah!" Dickie said. "That's all right."

He wouldn't move out. I could see we were in a boneyard, so I pulled and said, "Well, I'm gonna move out. Come on!" I went out about a hundred yards farther than him, and we paddled down like that, side by side.

Then what I was afraid might happen did happen: A set came right where we were—a big, tremendous set. Outside of us there was just a big, blue stepladder as far as you could see, all going uphill. Oh, man! I scratched for all I was worth. You could paddle 10 hard strokes and you'd still be going up the face of the wave.

I got over them—I got over all the sets—and I sat down and looked for Dickie, because he was inside of me! But I couldn't see him because the waves were all in the way. And then, on the last wave, I saw him come over the top, and it was so steep he and his board just flew off the backside—his board must have flown 60 feet in the air.

Dickie grabbed his board, then he paddled out to me and I said, "Dickie, you really think you could have lived through that?" He said, "Hell no!" Then I said, "How big do you think these waves are out here?" We agreed on 60 feet.

We kept going down the coast, and Dickie was right there with me. But as we got close to Waimea, he started going in again, and I said, "Hey! Hey! No!" because we had agreed we'd go out in the middle of the bay, where it was safe, and sit there and watch the sets go by and see what it looked like. Then we could try to judge where to get in.

But no! Dickie started cutting in, and I hollered at him, "Hey, hey, don't go in there. Let's go out in the middle!"

"Nah!" he said, and kept going.

He just wouldn't pay any attention. It seemed like it was his time—just like something was calling him, you know? Look at how he was acting: He had almost got caught inside and admitted he couldn't have lived through it, and still he insisted on cutting in. Again.

When we got to the point, there were 20-foot waves breaking. Big sets would come every 10 minutes. Time and time again I'd see Dickie go up over these swells and come back out off the top. The next one would come and he'd disappear and then I'd see him come up over the top, and it looked like he was actually trying to catch them. That was the only thing I could think of.

Finally, he came up over the top of this one monster and lost his board. "Oh, boy!" I thought, "two of us on my little cut-down board!" I was exhausted. Two guys on one board? What chance do we have now? I wondered. "Come on out!" I yelled at him. He answered and it sounded like he said, "I can't, Woody. I'm too tired." That's what it sounded like. But then he started swimming out toward me, so I started paddling in to catch him, to pick him up on my board. At a time like that, with those big waves rolling through, you're watching outside all the time. Your eyes are always out there, and you never feel safe. So I'm paddling in and one eye's out there and one eye's on Dickie. All of a sudden, we saw the darn mountains coming outside in the blue water, just piling one on top of another, way out there.

I turned around and started paddling outside for all I was worth because I figured if I lost my board, too, we'd have no chance at all. Two guys swimming in those conditions? Our only hope was to save our only remaining board. So, I turned around and paddled out toward the first wave and it kept getting bigger and steeper and higher and getting a little white on the top. Well, I saw that I just wasn't going make it—you know, the wave was cresting already. Later, the people on the beach said it was 40 feet high. I threw my board and just dove down and headed for the bottom. That's your only chance in a wave that size—get down in the deep water.

I could dive 30 feet easily in those days. I did it regularly, diving for fish. But this was a new experience. I was in clean, blue water, but it was pulling me toward the bottom. It was so deep, I saw whitewater coming up below me. Eventually, I got to the surface. I really have no idea how. The whole set was that way; they all broke in roughly the same place. I looked around frantically for Dickie, but there was no more Dickie. That's the last I ever saw of him.

It was getting dark, and I was thinking about sharks. I figured, what the heck, I'm gonna die anyway, might as well try to swim in, and I took off my shorts to reduce the drag. I mean, sharks? At that point, what difference did it make? Another set came in, breaking maybe 100 yards outside of me. I got another terrible beating. I was just down there, you know, underwater where you don't know what's up, down, sideways, anything. But as the set went on, I dove a little shallower each time. I found that it was pushing me in that way.

When I got inside, I saw the way the current was running—just like a raging river, so fast, along the beach. I knew if I got too far over (toward the rocks), it would pull me right back out. I just battled for all I was worth. Somehow, barely conscious, I got to the sand and crawled up the beach on my hands and knees.

We never found any part of Dickie. He just vanished. We did find the board, just shattered to pieces. I talked to an army guy who had been on the beach that night, and he told me, "We never did see that other guy after he got wrapped up in that last big wave." Those were his words: "wrapped up in that last big wave." Based on that, I figured Dickie—who had so much guts—tried to bodysurf the wave. The fact that he got "wrapped up" could only mean that he was up in the curl, right? How else would you express it? So, I figured he tried to bodysurf in. To this day, the thought of that gives me chills. Why didn't he just dive down under the wave? I will always wonder . . .

I was never quite the same after that. It was a month or two before I could even go out surfing at Waikiki, and from that point on, I found Makaha a lot more to my liking. Sure, I went back to the North Shore, but never with the same old fire.

PLEASANT SKIES

Mike Stang

*A*t the outset, big wave pioneers had no idea how to negotiate huge Makaha. The boards were crude and the techniques were revised after most every session. During early encounters, when making a wave was the exception and wipeouts were the rule, the only things keeping the learning curve from flattening out altogether were drive, faith, athletic ability, and, most of all, guts. But as the following account illustrates, to the '50s big wave rider, simply getting to the venue could require an act of nerve.

‡   ‡   ‡

As big wave surfers in the '50s, I guess you could say that we lived a much different lifestyle and experienced a side of Hawaii that most never imagined. Airfare to Hawaii was always the biggest outlay for us California-based surfers. Once you got to the islands, there was usually a friend there you could stay with. Either that, or several guys would rent a place together.

For a few years, surfers used an airline called U.S.O.A. It was founded by a crazy old lobster fisherman, Frank Donahue. The airfare was cheap, something like $75 one way, and the flight was horrifying. Those old DC-8s sounded like doom and looked like they had been glued together with flour paste. It took forever to get to Hawaii. Guys would be crapped out in the aisles. You'd spend a week recovering from one of those flights.

I was publishing a surfing annual at the time, and I gave Donahue an ad in exchange for a free ticket. I'm not sure now if that was a fair trade or if he got the best of me. I had to wait two days in the airport for the flight finally to take off. It wasn't so much that the flights were unscheduled—Donahue just wouldn't let his pilots take off until there were enough passengers to make it worth it.

One flight stands out in my mind. One of the regular U.S.O.A. pilots got drunk and couldn't fly. Donahue knew something about flying, but he didn't have a license—to say nothing of having the credentials to pilot a commercial airliner. Since he couldn't afford to give back everybody's money, Donahue just climbed into the pilot's seat and took off for Hawaii. I guess the regulations were pretty thin in those days, especially regarding these rubber-band airplane flights.

In the winter of '56, several of us decided to pass on Donahue's outfit and take a cruise ship home from Hawaii. The cruise lines were offering ridiculously low fares to compete with the increasing number of airline companies that had begun to fly to the Islands. Mickey Muñoz, Bruce Brown, Bob Sheppard, Jack Haley, and I traveled on the S.S. *Leilani*. The dinner menu offered five courses, all you could eat. We wiped them out every night.

The first night, when the waiters came to our table, they asked each one of us, "And what will you have tonight, sir?" Each of us said, in turn, "Everything you've got on the menu." They brought us food by the tray and cartload until we finished it all off.

During the day, we did calisthenics on the deck. It was a seven-day trip and there was nothing else to do. We did calisthenics for hours, working up appetites for dinner. Then we'd eat every entrée—mahi mahi, steak, chicken, lobster—all the side dishes, then dessert. Toward the end of the trip, the waiter would come to the table and politely say, "I suppose you all want everything on the menu . . . again."

THE LIFE AND MYSTERIOUS
DEATH OF JOSE ANGEL

Bruce Jenkins

*I*n *every adventure sport, each generation produces someone so bold and talented that when he sets to work, all bets are off. Jose Angel was such a man, a big wave kamikaze whose courage was so great and actions so perfectly outrageous that his peers could only gaze at his stunts and yell, "There ain't no way I'm trying that!" While even the boldest surfers engaged colossal waves with a sense of awe, Angel seemed to ride an invisible current of fearlessness, meeting both the mackers and the ocean herself as a kind of aquatic crony—often in situations that came close to killing him. The following is the story of this once-in-a-lifetime big wave "hellman" whose fearless style encouraged and astounded the old, and whose legacy has inspired a whole new generation of surfers. The adventure world owes a great debt to surfer/writer Bruce Jenkins, who in this article (and several others herein) has used his award-winning skills as a sportswriter to capture the essence of one of surfing's genuine icons.*

‡   ‡   ‡

Jose was not frightened by the sharks. He shouted at them. They left him alone. Adrift between islands, swimming for his life, Jose knew the strength of his will would carry him through any obstacle. He would swim the full 13 miles, and he would make it to shore alive.

Of all the stories told about Jose Angel—diver, educator, family man, legendary big wave surfer—this one stands alone. He was diving for black coral off Maui that summer day, and when he surfaced he found himself a half-mile from the spotting boat. They never connected. With the cur-

Jose Angel dropping at Sunset. This photo appeared on the cover of Surfer *magazine's first issue, 1960.* PHOTO COURTESY OF *Surfer* MAGAZINE

rent running strongly toward Oahu, Jose knew there was no turning back. So instead he put his head down and swam—thirteen miles, to the island of Molokai.

"Jose Angel Feared Lost at Sea," the headline read that evening. But Jose was just fine, churning his way through the channel, then hiking 4 miles to the nearest telephone. Back home on the North Shore of Oahu, he couldn't understand what all the fuss was about.

"I swam to another island," he said cheerily.

Three weeks later, Jose Angel was dead.

On July 24, 1976, he went back to that same diving spot off Maui, near the city of Lahaina. There was another miscalculation, but this one was fatal. He dove into 340 feet of water, thinking the depth was only 240. Nobody comes back from 340 feet, not even Jose Angel. One of the world's great watermen—perhaps the bravest big wave rider of all time—was lost. He was 41 years old.

They speak of Jose Angel to this day, his friends from the North Shore's glory years. They remember his almost superhuman feats in the giant waves of Waimea, Sunset Beach, and Pipeline, and they debate the circumstances of his death. Like the great Eddie Aikau, who died just two years later, Jose remains the topic of lively conversation. In the kind of vague, mystical sense that befits a legend, he is still with us. Greg Noll calls him "the gutsiest surfer there ever was," and both Gerry Lopez and Billy Hamilton feel there is no comparison between Angel and "us normal guys."

Lopez and Hamilton? Normal guys?

"This was a true man among men," says Peter Cole, still a big wave rider at 61. "There's nobody like Jose—today, back then, any time. He was the most go-for-it guy I've ever known. Noll was the same way, but with Greg, it was almost a job. With Jose, it was just fun. He'd ride 25-foot Waimea waves, backside, take the worst wipeout you've ever seen, and come up laughing. He'd get held under two waves and come up completely stoked. It was just no big deal for him."

Angel was one of the first surfers to ride outer-reef Pipeline. He was a Sunset regular no matter what size the waves were, the more horrifying the better. And he handled the wildest days at Laniakea and Avalanche. But Angel's signature move, the one that truly captured his spirit, was at Waimea Bay.

"He used to have this thing," said Ricky Grigg, "where he'd paddle outside and wait for the biggest, gnarliest, meanest wave of the day. He'd take an unbelievably hairy drop, make the hard part of the wave and then just step off the rail and let the wave blast him. He'd kind of stick his chest into it to challenge the strength of the wave and feel its power. He would simply let it destroy him. That was his life."

Sometimes he wouldn't merely step off the board. "I was paddling out at Waimea with Jeff Hakman one time," recalls North Shore underground rider Bill Sickler, "and we saw Jose do a backflip off his board—right in the pit of this massive wave. This is before leashes, of course. We finally got up to him, and Jeff goes, 'Jose, what the hell were you trying to do?' And he says, 'Well, I thought I'd see if I could jump back over the lip.' It's like riding a wave wasn't quite the thrill for him. If a wipeout looked good, he'd stick himself in the worst spot. Try to imagine that kind of consciousness."

Nobody could have imagined it back in San Francisco, where Angel grew up. The only child of a British mother and Filipino-Spanish father, Jose was quite an athlete during his boyhood and collegiate days at San Francisco State. He was a swimmer, wrestler, boxer, scuba diver, and tennis player, aside from being an excellent student—but he wasn't much of a surfer. That changed the day he met Mozelle (Mo) Gooch, a strikingly attractive tomboy from the farmlands of Tennessee.

As Mo tells it, "I had just graduated from UCLA, and I went up to teach phys ed at San Francisco State for a couple of years. I had my little Ford woody and my surfboard, and we started going surfing together in Santa Cruz. I was five years older than Jose, but we were very much alike. Couple of crazy Virgos with the same birthday (September 2). Couple of mavericks just crazy about each other."

Mo was on her way to a teaching job in New Zealand when she stopped in Hawaii during a layover. "It felt like home to me," she says. "I canceled everything, just to stay a while in this wonderful place. When I called Jose, he said, 'Well, I'm coming over there, too.' That was 1955. We got married that year, and we never left Hawaii."

For a while, Mo was the surfing star of the family. "She was just guts-up, going wild, surfing Makaha and Haleiwa and big Publics," says Fred Van Dyke, one of the most accomplished North Shore pioneers. "There was something very conservative about Jose, but when he moved out to the North Shore a couple years later, his true nature came out. He became the most courageous surfer I ever encountered."

More than anyone, Mozelle knew what drew Jose to the water and what drove him to greatness. "He suffered from skin allergies, especially when he was a kid," she says. "Wool, alcohol, certain kinds of foods, all kinds of stuff would get to him. Early on, he realized he'd get the most relief in the water. I think it became a psychological thing. He felt the water was his friend, that it wouldn't hurt him. It was home."

Throughout the 1960s and early 1970s, Angel was among the most respected men in all of Hawaii, let alone the surf community. He was principal of Haleiwa Elementary School, imparting knowledge and common sense to North Shore kids. In the days before lifeguards, he rescued countless tourists who ventured too far into the raging surf. He and Mo raised four children, all of them athletic and charismatic, from their house near Log Cabins. But his fame among surfers was immediate and wide: When the first *Surfer* magazine was published, back in 1960, there was Jose on the cover, dropping into a classic Sunset peak.

"He was a really polite guy, very gentle, very easy to talk to," says Clyde Aikau, who, like his brother Eddie, worshiped Jose. "All I know, man, is he rode big Sunset. Totally fearless. And he seemed to fall down a lot (laughs). Didn't matter if the wave was gonna close out. Jose would take off. Guys like Greg Noll and Jose are still superheroes for me."

While he never achieved the fluid surfing style of a Paul Strauch or

Joey Cabell, Angel left an indelible mark as a backside Waimea surfer. "Since Jock Sutherland, I don't think there's been anyone close to Jose backside at Waimea," says Randy Rarick. "Marvin Foster probably comes the closest today, but the whole nature of the thing has changed. Back then, with that equipment, it was like jumping off a cliff." Other names were mentioned—Sammy Lee, Adam Salvio, Ronnie Burns—but Cole scoffed at the comparisons. "Backside at Waimea," says Cole, "nobody touched Jose. Then or ever."

Angel was just 5' 11" and 170 pounds, but his body appeared to have been chiseled from stone. On land, he was the voice of reason. In the water, he seemed very nearly insane—in the manner only surfers understand. A few stories from his friends:

Gerry Lopez: "For a couple of winters, there were a lot of unreal days at Outside Pipeline, the only place besides Waimea that was surfable. All of a sudden, here'd come Jose, paddling out from his house down by Log Cabins. I mean, it was hard enough to get out by Pipeline—I can't even imagine it down there. A big set would come in and clean everybody up, and while we're all floundering and swimming around, here comes Jose, bodysurfing over the falls on a 20-foot wave. He was just laughing at us! This guy could hold his breath longer than anyone. I don't think he ever thought about a wave harming him."

Laird Hamilton: "Both of us got pounded on a wave at Waimea one day, probably around 20 feet, and we were down there for quite a long time. I came up first, and I'll never forget when Jose came up. His head was kind of bent to the side. He'd been hit directly by the impact. Really shook him up. And he looks at me and goes, 'You all right?'"

Greg Noll: "I remember a day way back, when we were all just feeling our way around Waimea, and Jose swam all day long. Paddles out, takes off, goes on his ass, swims in, heads right back out. Time after time. And every time, he's more stoked than the time before. I knew there was something different going on with this guy. By the end of the day, you saw tire tracks going up the side of the hill, but he's still there, just excited as hell. Never made one wave. I'm thinking, this guy's definitely got balls of granite."

Cole: "Jose liked guys that were sort of macho, like himself. One day Gary Speece took a bad wipeout at Pipeline, cut his head wide open, and when he got to the beach, Gary got a needle and stitched himself up—right there on the spot. Jose couldn't get over it. He talked about that for days. He's like, 'You can't believe this new guy. He got all screwed up and stitched his own head. You gotta see this guy!'"

Ricky Grigg: "One day we surfed Waimea all day long at 20-plus, and that night we got on Jose's boat in Haleiwa for a black-coral campaign. We left around midnight, and when we got out into the lineup at Avalanche, the engine crapped out. We were just terrified. One of the stern lines got tangled in the prop, and we were drifting toward some 25-foot sets in the middle of the night. Jose dove into the water, got down underneath, unwound the thing, scrambled back in, and started us up. I'm still not sure how."

Ken Bradshaw: "One of my first winters on the North Shore, a couple of military guys got trapped outside on a really huge day at Sunset. A big rescue took place—lifeguards, helicopter, the whole shot. All of a sudden, here's a guy on the beach, putting on his swim fins and jumping into the water, without his board. Jose Angel. He went all the way out there into 15-foot surf to help out, then just quietly swam back in by himself, right through the break. That was like a measuring point for me. I said to myself, if you can pick off a wave like Eddie, surf like BK and Hakman, and take the beatings like Jose, you're ready."

It's not surprising that some of the most eclectic North Shore surfers— Trevor Sifton, Laird Hamilton, Phil Perry, and Jose's own son Johnny—grew up around the Angel household. "You spent enough time around Jose, and you were ready for anything," says Sifton, notorious for his outer-reef expeditions. "He'd surf Waimea on the day of a contest and tell the guys to buzz off. The waves don't happen that often, go buzz off. They're not gonna tell Jose Angel to get out of the water. He's been out there his whole life. He was surfing Waimea when those guys were in diapers."

Thanksgiving Day of 1974 brought all-time conditions at Waimea. The now fabled 1974 Smirnoff Championships contest was on that morning, and Jose was out early with Grigg, Cole, Mike Miller, Kimo Hollinger, and James Jones. "The contest organizers came out on a boat and told us to clear the water," Jones recalls. "A guy named Marshall Rosa was driving. He's probably the finest physical specimen in the Islands today, now that Jose is gone. He's a big guy, and real tough. Marshall asked Jose to go in, and Jose said no. Marshall kind of circled him with the boat, and they kind of went eyeball to eyeball for a couple of seconds. Then Marshall drove away and let Jose surf. You really had to meet Jose in person to get a feel for the kind of power he had."

No one remembers Jose getting into a fight. "That's because nobody screwed around with him," said Grigg. "One time, a big local guy tried to break into his garage. Jose calmly went downstairs, grabbed a three-pronged spear, pulled it back, slipped open the door, and flipped the lights on. Jose said, 'I'm gonna spear you right in your eye.' The guy whined, 'Please, please spare me, I'll never come back!' Jose just stood there and laughed."

Cole, who spent as much time around Angel as anyone, recalled only one time he really got angry. "Nat Young was over one winter, and he was really a jerk. He's real mellow now, a much nicer guy, but back then he was real arrogant and cocky. So they're out at Pupukea and Nat said a couple of things that really made Jose angry. Next thing you know, Nat did a bottom turn into Jose and pushed him into the whitewater.

"Jose just flipped out. He grabbed Nat, kind of tussled him around, and told him to go to the beach. Then Jose went straight in and waited. He was so mad, he was ready to kill the guy. Nat got a little panicky. He paddled up the coast, and Jose jogged along the beach. Nat turned back the other way, and Jose just kept following. Nat didn't come in for like three hours. Jose finally gave up and went home, but the point was made. I don't think that story was in Nat's book (laughter)."

Jose had no problem adjusting to the North Shore summers. He simply went diving, with his customary maniacal frenzy. It was legal to catch turtles in the '60s, and Jose was part of a regular crew including Warren Harlow, Jeff Johnson, Pat Curren, and Neil Tobin, diving off Jose's 13-foot Boston Whaler in the waters between Waimea and Haleiwa.

Most of the guys were bringing up turtles in the 160- to 200-pound range. Jose, of course, topped everyone one day with a 300-pounder. "I really think Jose loved diving more than anything," Johnson recalls.

For Jose's friends, things started getting a little scary out there. There were times when Jose went down so deep, for so long, he'd actually pass out before reaching the surface. On a black-coral dive off Kauai in the summer of 1974, he stretched the limits of his equipment and suffered a severe case of the bends, leaving his right leg partially paralyzed.

"It reached the point," says Johnson, "where his friends didn't want to go down there with him. He was getting too far out. He found a guy who was a U.S. Navy SEAL diver, Jack Thomasson, and they started going down to 300 feet, where the air becomes poisonous. Well, Thomasson didn't come up one day. They never found him."

As it turned out, Jose's life on land wasn't going too well. The details of his private life were—and are—the province of his family. Nobody else's business. But Mozelle, now 62 and still teaching at Kahuku High School, was quite willing to talk about it.

"I've been thinking about it for 16 years, and there are times when I feel Jose took his own life," she said from her North Shore home. "I have no proof of that, but there were things he said and did those last few years that made me wonder. It started with that terrible case of the bends he got. We had four kids and not enough money, and he was taking all kinds of chances down there, just to help make ends meet. There was another shocker that same summer, when his mother came down with stomach cancer. The doctors told Jose she wasn't going to live. She'd been separated from his dad for about 10 years, and the doctors left it up to him: keep her alive or just let her go. He made the decision to let her go, and it just tore him up inside."

The story was getting grim for Mozelle now, but she continued: "He met another gal in San Francisco while his mother was ill. He told me all about meeting her. Next thing I know, he asked for a divorce and jumped into another marriage. And she had four kids, too. It was a big mess. I took our kids back to Tennessee for a while, to let Jose sort this out. He and this woman, they were only married a short time, from May until December 1975. But he was never himself after all that. He started diving more and more, deeper and deeper, and he couldn't really surf all-out with the bad leg. I think he was scared to death, knowing he wasn't going to be himself again. I remember the time he told me, 'Nobody can see how crippled I am if I'm diving.'"

Jose was now supporting two families, and he was in debt. There were plenty of hints that he was losing the old spirit, but then again, how do you explain the swim to Molokai? That goes down as a survival effort for the ages. "A little 13-mile swim didn't bother him a bit," said Johnson. "He told me the sharks started coming up and circling him. So he went down and yelled at them. Amazing story. But things didn't get any better for him. He told me he was gonna hang it up—go to Maui, make one more dive, and that would be it. Turned out that was the last dive he made."

Jose and Ricky Grigg had been black-coral diving partners for more than two years. They had explored virgin reefs off the islands of Kauai and Maui, Jose leading the way with his brute strength and fearless demeanor. He'd jump off the boat with a 20-pound rock under his arm, quickening his descent, and routinely bring 6- to 8-foot trees to the surface.

July 24, 1976, brought a slight change in the routine. Grigg needed some photos of a diver decompressing for one of his research projects, so he was going as a cameraman. They were 5 miles off the coast of Maui, at a place Jose called Shark Ridge. "He was about as happy as I'd ever seen him," Grigg recalls. "It was a beautiful, calm day, and I remember him saying, 'I'm so stoked. Every single day is like my whole life. I live it that way. I live each day like it's the last.'"

With his tank and his float bags and his 20-pound rock, Jose rolled over the edge of the boat. Suddenly, the wind came up. The postcard-perfect ocean turned to heavy chop, and after about 12 minutes there was no sign of Jose. "Another three minutes went by, and I started getting panicky," said Grigg. "Three minutes is the ball game out there. I'd been getting my cameras ready and the boatman—Robby was his name—was in charge of the fathometer. I went over to check the thing, and it said 340 feet. I started yelling at the guy— 'Look at this!' He said it was 240, no problem. I said, 'Read the damn thing.' He looked at it and said, 'Oh, my God.'"

Grigg knew he couldn't go after Jose. "It's just not humanly possible," he says. "I figured Jose got to 250 feet, where his depth gauge reached its limit, and went another 25 to 30 feet before he dropped the rock. I'm guessing he was around 300 feet before he figured out what was going on, and if I went down under those conditions, I'd be dead. I also knew I had to explain this to Jose's family, and at the same time deal with my own grief about Jose. It was a horrendous, crushing sort of feeling."

Grigg's only hope was to find Jose alive. They circled the area for six hours, joined later by helicopters and about 20 other boats, including some from the Coast Guard. The search lasted three days. Nothing.

Grigg and Cole deeply doubt Jose committed suicide. They are joined by John Severson, Bud Browne, and Don James, among others who had known Jose from the late 1950s. But Mozelle isn't so sure. Neither are Harlow, Johnson, Hamilton, Fred Hemmings, or Van Dyke.

"I would never accuse Ricky of anything," says Van Dyke, "but I think he knows more than he's willing to tell anyone. Ricky's a damn good scientist, and I've never really gotten a straight answer on this. But I did know Jose, and I know he was worried about his virility, longevity, and the possibility he'd be handicapped the rest of his life. I wouldn't call him a macho man, but he was like a bullfighter. I think he'd rather go in style than sit around being half-ass the rest of his life. I don't know if he went out that day to take his life, but I think when he got down there, he just said, 'Screw it. This is beautiful.' Just took off his mask and went into the sunset."

More than anyone else, it is Angel's oldest daughter, Shelly, who offers the most interesting perspective. Now in her thirties, she's had a rich, wildly diverse life as a policewoman, Hollywood stunt performer, volleyball star, competitive swimmer and surfer. She was just 12 the day her father died. This is how she remembers it:

"I'd been out there countless times on my dad's dives. I always drove the boat. But that particular day, he didn't let me go. He squatted down, looked me in the eye and told me this was gonna be his last dive. I remember saying, 'Oh, good, Mom will be glad to hear that.' I didn't realize what he was really saying. But he told me, 'Too many people on the boat today. Stay here and take care of your sister. And if you need to call Mom, use the phone down at Tobin's shop.' All of that was strange, completely out of character for him.

"When Ricky came back that day, he started crying. But I didn't. I knew what was going on. I knew from the beginning that my dad was never one to grow old gracefully. He just couldn't have done it. I can remember him lying on the carpet, paying us a penny for every gray hair we could pull out of his head. He should have been proud he had white hair, but he wasn't. He needed to go out with a bang. I'm glad it happened, as I look back. I personally feel he planned it that way."

Any disagreement among Jose's old friends, she feels, is completely unnecessary. "They say he passed out, or he misgauged his depth. Hey, he knew where he was," says Shelly. "He always knew exactly where he was down there. I feel sorry for Ricky, because there wasn't a thing he could do, and he's probably pissed at my dad, because he put him in a no-win situation."

Like Eddie Aikau, Jose represented the essence of the Hawaiian surfing spirit, and it seems little coincidence that so many things in surfing changed after they died. "For a lot of people, that was like the final straw," says Jones. "There was a dramatic shift right then, around 1976, '77, '78. Professionalism came around. Sponsorship and money came in. The focus left Hawaii. It's really never been the same. It's sort of eerie, in a way."

Like the greatest of legends, Jose Angel remains the subject of rumors, visions, and hallucinations. One story claims he surfaced that day, swam ashore, dropped everything, and hopped a plane to the Philippines. He was reportedly spotted in Australia, and again in Mexico. Jeff Johnson got the chills when he heard that a live, deep-sea nautilus shell—the type that lives at 1,200 feet—washed up on the beach at Makapuu, then mysteriously disappeared from its temporary home at Sea Life Park. "I'm not superstitious," he says, "but that was a mystery. Just like Jose."

And the Aikau connection perseveres. In February 1986, the first Eddie Aikau contest went off at maxed-out Waimea Bay, and even Clyde (who would win the event) was a little nervous. "The turtles got me past the fear," he recalls. "There were two of them. They kept popping up, rising from the depths, right there in the waves. Sometimes it was just one, sometimes two. In my mind, I saw Eddie and Jose that day."

As for Mozelle Angel, she still lives in the old house near Log Cabins. Wouldn't think of moving, she says. When they held the Fourth of July paddleboard race this summer—Jose's event—she stunned everyone by grabbing a board and heading out there. It was Mo, at the age of 62, and her son Johnny, 22, sharing the entire 3-mile paddle in a 5-foot swell that seemed to appear from nowhere. Perhaps they felt Jose's spirit, too, for he may still be out there, at peace in the ocean, diving the deepest, laughing the hardest, and yelling at the sharks. Still at home.

BANZAI PIPELINE

Sam Moses

While most all the stories in this collection are told from an insider's point of view, the following account by renowned sportswriter Sam Moses examined, in 1982, surfing from the perspective of big-time professional sports. The result is a unique take on both surfing and one of its most storied big wave venues: Pipeline.

‡   ‡   ‡

They call the North Shore of Oahu "Country." Lush dairy farms abut the ocean, and the smells of manure and sugarcane rise from the furrowed fields along the narrow Kam Highway. The North Shore catches the northeast trade winds, which blow in from North America to sway palm fronds and erase footprints on the beach at night, leaving fresh windrows in the sand by morning. In the dark, the whoosh of the trades can be mistaken for the sound of the breaking surf, which rumbles like a distant train. It's the rumble that reminds one: More than country moods, more than warm winds, the North Shore is big waves.

The North Shore lures surfers the way Hollywood lures actresses, their heads full of dreams of glory. The surfers get off the plane in Honolulu in December and, with their boards under their arms, head for the North Shore. There they rent beach houses along the 12 miles from Kawela to Haleiwa, less for the pleasures of oceanfront living than for the utility of it: To check the surf each morning, all they have to do is raise the bamboo blinds. They don't need cars, are indifferent to phones, and avoid shoes. They take only night jobs or those with employers who accept the Six-foot Rule: When the surf hits six feet, the employee hits the surf. They may do it at Sunset Beach, with its classic waves; Waimea Bay, with its towering surf; Rocky Point; Velzyland; Off-the-Wall; Pupukea; Gas Chambers; or others. For more than 20 years, North Shore winters have been a rite of surfing. The surfers keep coming back, year after year, in search of the perfect wave. If it exists, it will break somewhere on the North Shore.

Some surfers believe they've already found the perfect wave. They call it the Banzai Pipeline—Banzai for the attitude one must adopt to surf it, and Pipeline for the long, hollow tubes it forms as it breaks. People line the beach just to watch the Pipeline roll in, and they stay until sunset, because it's difficult to turn away. One starts to go but then looks back for just one more wave. On a good day 8- and 10-foot tubes tumble in hour after hour. The Pipeline's waves erupt just 75 yards from shore with manes of spindrift that become miniature rainbows and make the surf seem to sizzle like a good fire. On a spectacular day the waves are twice that high and may peel off for 100 yards or more, the disintegration of the curl chasing the formation down the coast. And if a wave "closes out," or collapses, it looks and sounds like an avalanche.

Other waves around the world form tubes—Uluwatu, near Bali, has cleaner curls than the Pipeline does. The surf at Sunset—and Waimea and Haleiwa and Kaena, all on the North Shore—is often bigger than at Pipeline. But no place else has the Pipeline's combination of form and size, and no other wave matches Pipeline's power in winter. There isn't a significant piece of land in the 2,000 miles between the Aleutians and Oahu, so every North Pacific low-pressure system is felt on the North Shore, which is canted toward the stormy Alaskan archipelago. The tidal wave that killed 159 people on the North Shore in 1946 resulted from an earthquake in the Aleutians.

Because there's no continental shelf around the Hawaiian Islands, ocean swells are untempered as they approach the shore. At Pipeline, traveling at an open-water speed of 25 miles per hour, they meet a fossilized coral reef a mere 500 yards from land. Oceanographers call this spot the "10-fathom terrace," and it trips the swells, shaping them and causing them to lunge forward until they hit the inside reef, which is only 100 yards offshore and a mere 10 feet below the surface. This second reef curls the swells into the tubes that about 15 seconds later come crashing down— after having provided surfers with the momentum for their ride. The challenge of riding a board while completely enclosed by the tube is what surfing Pipeline is all about.

"I've surfed the best waves all over the world and there's nothing as awesome as Pipeline," says Mark Richards of Australia, the champion professional surfer for the last three years. "It completely closes over you and you're inside this huge, green barrel. Water is rushing and gurgling over your head and the whole ocean is shaking. All you can see is a little hole of sunlight at the end of the tube and you just hold your breath and pray it doesn't close before you get there."

Surfers are rarely so reckless as to charge into the tubes without watching them a while—mind surfing, they call it. Early on a Pipeline morning they'll squat on the beach, their boards stuck tail-first into the sand. The surfers quietly study the waves—how they break, the time interval between them, the frequency of the sets, the onshore and offshore currents, the riptides, the configuration of the coast that day. And because the currents are so strong at Pipeline, even getting out to the lineup, the area where the swells begin to curl and the surfers straddle their boards as they wait for rides, can be difficult. There's no channel, so the surfer must wait for a lull between sets to paddle to the lineup. If the lull isn't quite calm enough or it doesn't last, whitewater will hit the surfer head-on and steal his board from under him. Often he must compensate for the current by paddling out diagonally to the lineup. Once there, he may wait 10, 20, even 30 minutes for the wave he wants or can catch. "Outside!" a surfer cries when a big set approaches, the way whalers used to cry "Thar she blows!" Then he flops on the board and paddles as hard and fast as he can, trying to match the wave's speed so they unite gently, like relay runners making a smooth baton pass. He must be at the lip of the wave at the moment it curls. If he's too late, it will roll past him; too early, it will break on top of him.

A Pipeline wipeout isn't the same as falling from a diving board into a swimming pool. For one thing, because a steep wave sucks the water off the already shallow bottom, the depth in the trough may only be 3 feet—the Pipeline's greatest danger, for another wave will almost certainly come crashing down on the surfer, at a force estimated at 1.4 tons per square foot for a 15-footer. Surfers call the falling lip of a wave the guillotine. It can snap surfboards in two, crack necks, spines, and femurs, and slam bodies against the coral bottom.

And once a surfer survives the free fall, the guillotine, and the coral, then, pinned to the bottom, he faces the scariest part of all: those desperate seconds of black and airless turmoil as the surf thunders over him. He is unlikely to be held down more than 10 seconds, but it will seem like an eternity. The turbulence rasps him against the coral, and while his arms protect his head, his torso is churned and whipped, like a rag doll with a fire hose trained on it. After the wave passes, the surfer still isn't

Derek Ho on a classic Pipeline drop. PHOTO BY ROB GILLEY

home free. When he explodes frantically to the surface, the foam may be too thick for him to get his head into the air. Many are the surfers who have survived the free fall, the guillotine, the contact, and the crush, only to suck in a lungful of foam.

The coral at the Pipeline isn't jagged—9,000 years of swirling sand have rounded the edges—but it has craters and nooks that can snatch at limbs and trap bodies. Surfers have been crammed into holes and shoved underneath ledges by the turbulence. Disoriented, they lose track of which way is up. That's the Pipeline at its most terrifying. Thus the expression "planted by the Pipe" is almost literal; the churning water displaces tremendous amounts of sand, which may swirl over anything wedged under a ledge, performing a sort of burial at sea. North Shore surfers whisper about strange disappearances at Pipeline and imply that the bodies are still down there.

Ghoulish Pipeline stories, many exaggerated, abound. Some are light: the sandbar called Gums, so named after a surfer lost his teeth to it; the legend of the phantom board, found one glassy summer day floating outside the 10-fathom terrace, covered with seaweed, as if its rider had vanished seasons ago. Others are heavy: the 16-year-old whose board washed ashore one night in 1981 and whose mangled body floated ashore two days later; or the 1975 incident in which four girls were standing too close to the shoreline when a huge set of waves sent a wall of water surging up the beach, knocking the girls down and carrying them out to sea. None survived. And then there was Shiggy, the popular Peruvian, who went back for one more wave after he had just gotten the best tube of his life. They had to pry his corpse off the rocks.

Says Steve Pezman, publisher of *Surfer's Journal* and a Pipeline watcher for 25 years, "Pipeline has such a presence; it's so intimidating, so ominous, that it's like cheating nature when you survive. It takes some kind of animal drive to surf it. You've got to want it bad—more than anything else in the world. You just grit your teeth and paddle out into it."

Fred Van Dyke, 52, an English and swimming teacher, has been surfing big waves for 35 years. He listens to the Pipeline at night. His small house, a sort of A-frame on stilts with a sign on the steps that says "OLD SURF STAR'S HOME," is on the beach. Van Dyke doesn't surf much anymore, but he remembers. "When the big waves come, they're at 15- to 18-second intervals," he says. "Boom! Shakes your house. Boom! Shakes your house. The humidity is usually high, and you sweat: You sweat all night, through two or three pillowcases. Your whole body's wet. You know you've got to get some sleep, but you can't sleep because you hear that pounding, and you know you've got to meet it in the morning. When you get up you look out there and see those huge curls, and you look for excuses: It's too big, it's too windy, it's too choppy. But you know inside that it can be surfed. So, naturally, you paddle out, and you're committed. You knew you had to do it.

"Once, after a day of surfing with a buddy, we were walking out of the surf and we looked at each other, and he said, 'Wow! this is great.' I said, 'Yeah, this is great. What is it?' He said, 'You know.' And I said, 'Yeah.' It was that we were safe on the beach and had another night to drink beer and go to sleep. That's it. The best part about riding Pipe is the end of the day when you're walking up the beach with your board under your arm and you're safe for another day. That's the ultimate thrill, and I'm not the only one who feels that way."

Possibly the best indication of the allure of Pipeline is that many of its pioneers still live near it; not only Van Dyke, who has the body of a well-muscled teenager and plans to live to be 106, but others, all in their forties and early fifties, like Peter Cole, 51, a computer systems analyst for the federal government in Honolulu. Cole lives on the beach, too. Before wet suits were invented, he and Van Dyke surfed in one-piece long underwear they bought at Goodwill Industries for a quarter. Cole was the one who would look at a monstrous wave and say, "That can be ridden," when everyone else was saying "No way," and then paddle out and prove it. Some say Cole can still swim against the riptide the way others swim with it.

Many of the young surfers on the North Shore today have never heard of Van Dyke or Cole or the others, nor have they heard the stories of the high times these men had back in the '50s and early '60s. "We all had old panel trucks with mattresses in them," says Van Dyke. "We'd camp at the Pipeline in the trucks, sort of park them behind a dune, but the surf would come up and wash under the trucks, and sometimes in them. So we'd take the mattresses out and get out mosquito nets and climb up into the trees and build a little platform with two-by-fours. We'd sleep up there, and the surf would come up to the trees. You could feel the surge when it went through, see the whole tree sway. We used to sit up there and watch the tubes at the Pipeline and say, 'Jeez, maybe in 2,000 years guys will be surfing these waves.' We lived in those trucks and the trees for the whole winter of '57, and no one thought of riding a board there."

It didn't take 2,000 years for someone to ride the Pipeline; it was more like four. His name was Phil Edwards. That first ride in 1961 was historic, but not spectacular. The boards were much longer then—about 10 feet compared to the current 7-footers used at Pipeline—which made turning difficult and getting tubed all but impossible. What Edwards did was make the wave: paddle out, take off down its face, turn in, and ride it to the beach. Some even suggest Edwards's wasn't even the first ride there; after all, when Captain Cook "discovered" the Hawaiian Islands in 1778 he was greeted by surfing natives on huge teak boards. There are even Polynesian surfers immortalized by petroglyphs in the lava rocks near Pipeline. Who's to say that none of them ever surfed Pipeline?

Says Edwards, "For 20 years people have been saying to me, 'You weren't the first. Some ancient Hawaiian king probably rode it on a log centuries ago.' Well, fuck them: I was the first. I dragged a bunch of guys down there that day. I wanted someone to hold my hand and I admit it. They all had the chance. They were all tougher guys than me. I don't claim to be a macho man, but I did it and they didn't, so there.

"I had an experience recently that made me realize how much that day is still with me. I walked into this store, and a guy ahead of me just let these double doors slam in my face. He was burly and had a beard, you know—Mr. Tough Guy. I just thought, 'Oh brother—one of those.' Then I thought, 'You're not so tough. I was the first guy to ride the Pipeline.'

"We thought surfing Pipeline was a death-defying deal and kids now surf there for fun. Just the same I'm amazed more surfers haven't died there. The last time I surfed Pipeline was 1969. I was glad when I was finally getting too old. I could say, 'I'm not going to risk my life like this anymore.'"

In the late '70s, Australians, New Zealanders, and South Africans arrived and went crazy at Pipeline, surfing with an aggressiveness some regulars resented. And with the trepidation barrier broken, the Pipeline was being surfed in droves. Because there isn't room for two surfers on any one pipe, competition for the waves was intense and often unfriendly. Intimidation, both psychological and physical, became a part of surfing Pipeline.

The toughest and smartest surfer got the waves, the way the biggest pup in a litter gets the bone; in fact, "dog" became the tag for a surfer who stole waves by taking off in front of another. "Idiots were falling out of the sky on top of you," says one surfer, "and it got so if you stole anyone's wave, you'd better be prepared to be worked over." There were even fistfights in the water, the surfers straddling their boards while they duked it out. And there were racial overtones: locals, the euphemism for Polynesian-blooded Hawaiians, versus haoles (pronounced HOW-lies, meaning outsiders or whites). Pipeline feuds contributed to the already sorry North Shore crime rate. The situation saddened the pioneers, who could remember the days when there were enough waves to go around and there still was camaraderie in the water.

But such goings-on weren't inconsistent with the surfers' casual every-man-for-himself approach to life. They have always seen themselves as escapists and mavericks. Timothy Leary, the drug culture guru, once said, "Everything is made of waves, and surfers are mutants, throwaheads of time," and the surfers liked that. They are fond of saying they are like the waves themselves: No two are the same. But it's not really true; it just seems that way because they're too drifty to get it together. Ironically there's a disdain for competition among many surfers, who see their sport as a sort of free-form artistry.

The first surfer to stand clearly above all the others at the Pipeline was Butch Van Artsdalen, although overall he wasn't nearly the surfer Edwards was. "During my time Butch was really the King of the Pipeline," says Edwards. "He had it all over me because he was self-destructive. I was a chicken, but he had the kamikaze attitude you need to ride Pipeline."

They called him Black Butch. He liked to bar-fight, and he liked to take direct hits on the head from 20-foot waves—at least he would surface smiling. He became a Pipeline lifeguard and saved many lives. Unfortunately, his own wasn't one of them. He died in Wahiawa Hospital in 1979 of cirrhosis of the liver caused by alcoholism. He had his friends with him when he went out, smiling, into a hepatic coma, a beer in hand. His ashes were scattered in the Pipeline lineup. A funeral train of 40 surfers on their boards circled the floating ashes and tossed flower leis on the spot.

For a couple of years in the late '60s, Jock Sutherland was the undisputed ace of the Pipeline. Raised on the North Shore, Sutherland, a switch foot, was more than a Pipeline specialist; in fact, he was the first surfer since Edwards to be considered clearly the best in the world. Sutherland was known for dropping acid before he took on the Pipeline, but he was also intelligent and somehow stayed in at least tentative touch with reality. Says his brother-in-law, Mark Cunningham, a Pipeline lifeguard who is most likely the best bodysurfer alive today, "Other guys would lose it for a while, but with Jock it was controlled craziness. He always knew what he was doing."

Sutherland enlisted in the army in 1969, and after he came back to the North Shore in 1971, he never regained his form. He spent the season of

1982 in a cast from hip to ankle, after breaking his femur on the rocks at a spot called Jocko's, named after him. He was the first to surf against those rocks.

Then there was Jose Angel, the most fearless if not the most skilled Pipeline surfer. Of Filipino-Chinese-Spanish-British ancestry, Angel was an elementary school principal in Waialua and a semiprofessional boxer and wrestler. He didn't get high on drugs; he got high on nitrogen. He was hooked on scuba diving for black coral, which lies 150 and more feet down.

Angel first came to the North Shore in 1955 from Santa Cruz, California, with Van Dyke. For the first few years, Pipeline scared Angel. But then he seemed to change. "He was the guy the photographers started following," says Van Dyke. "There was no limit to what he would go out in. There wasn't a wave he wouldn't take off on. He would wipe out in all of them, and it wasn't with grace or finesse. He had a way of bailing off the board, doing a backflip, and falling 20 feet to the trough. People still talk about his wipeouts."

Most surfers are followers. The Pipeline went untouched for years. After Edwards surfed it, he looked over his shoulder and saw three of his buddies paddling toward the lineup. It's the same today. On a particularly nasty morning the Pipeline may be empty. Finally, one surfer will screw up the courage to tackle it. Then there will be a swarm.

Once in a while a surfer like Edwards comes along with the perfect style—just the right blend of easy skill in the water and laid-backness on land. The other surfers want to be just like him. Edwards's guru is the irascible North Shore character Flippy Hoffman, who has surfed the 40-foot waves at Kaena Point, or so the story goes.

Gerry Lopez, 33, of mixed Japanese, German, and Spanish descent, is considered the best surfer ever to come down the Pipeline. Like no surfer since Edwards, Lopez, who is 5' 8" and 140 pounds, has become a cult figure. He's the only surfer to have parlayed Pipeline into a living, and a handsome one at that. Lopez, too, has his idols: the North Shore pioneers. "I look at those guys and think how great they were," he says. "They remind me of the mountain men of the Old West. Those North Shore guys were real watermen."

Lopez, a goofy foot, is the only surfer ever to make the Pipeline look easy. Never the most radical, he's still the best when the tubes are 10 to 12 feet and perfect. He has a remarkable ability to stay cool in the pocket. He has been filmed inside long tubes casually wiping the spray from his eyes. "The faster I go out there, the slower things seem to happen," he says.

But Lopez has taken his lumps. His board once gave him two black eyes, and another time he was unable to walk for two weeks because his tailbone was cracked after a free fall that ended in 2 feet of water in the trough. He laughs at the notion that he's the all-time king of the Pipeline. "The king of the Pipeline is the wave," he says. "The best anyone can do is survive it."

But that's exactly it: What makes Lopez different from the other Mr. Pipelines is that he got away with it. Says Edwards, "I know Gerry. I see him all the time, and we don't even talk about that place. But he must have some secret. He doesn't seem to me like any daredevil. I think he must have figured out something nobody else ever knew."

Lopez chuckles at that notion. "The whole trick is catching the wave at the right place at the right moment," he says. "It sets up the whole ride. If I've figured out anything different, that's it. It seemed obvious to me. It's just a matter of being in touch with it. There's virtually an 'X' out there in the water to tell you where to catch the wave. I paddle around, and when I see a swell coming, I go right for the X. The wave and I meet right there, and I take off and catch it, while the other guys turn and see that I'm gone and just say, 'That @#$%!'"

"But what really makes the difference," he adds, "is learning to keep your perspective and staying away from the waves that can hurt you." North Shore pioneer Fred Van Dyke agrees: "Fame and fortune at the Pipeline. That's what lures a lot of kids out there, and they end up getting drilled."

Equipment and attitudes change with time, and the champions come and go; but the peerless Pipeline wave remains the same. And when the Aleutian swells hit the reefs just right, and Pipeline rears up in all her ferocious majesty, even the greatest of watermen are walking on quicksand.

OUTSIDE PIPELINE, 1964

Greg Noll and Andrea Gabbard

"I looked out the window as we banked over Honolulu and I felt like a warrior being carried into battle by the wings of an eagle. When I stepped off that plane and that warm island air hit me, I had all the goddamned confidence of a rhinoceros. I think if Kaena Point had been breaking 40 that night I'd have gone out and ridden it in the dark."

So wrote Greg Noll, patron saint to every surfer who has paddled into a big wave. Throughout the '50s and '60s, Noll was the man at Waimea and Sunset; to this day Noll remains the quintessential, go-for-broke big wave pioneer. Bolstered by countless photos, films, and anecdotes of fellow big wave riders, Noll's image is indelibly stamped on surfdom: a 6' 2" 230-pound warrior, clad in black and white striped trunks, seemingly welded to his board as he hurtles down the face of a 30-foot leviathan, forever charging, forever tracking the most critical line.

Phil Edwards tagged Noll with the nickname "Da' Bull." "One time," says Noll, "when we were at Pipeline, he accused me of being bullheaded because I knew I was going to get wiped out on this one wave, and instead of ejecting like I should have, I just squatted down and got eaten alive. Afterward, Phil said, 'You bullheaded sonofabitch. I think I'll just call you Da Bull from now on.'"

The name stuck and the legend grew—a legend earned by such bold performances as the following, at Outside Pipeline, the place where "Da Bull" earned his name.

‡   ‡   ‡

In all the years I've been going to Hawaii, I've only seen the far Outside Pipeline reef break a few times. It's a rare, white-elephant break. Everything has got to be just right for it to work. The swell has to be really clean and the direction absolutely precise to hit those outside reefs.

I'm talking way outside. First, there's Inside Pipeline where Phil Edwards was the first to ride and where everyone surfs today. Several hundred yards beyond that is Outside Pipeline, which sometimes breaks when Inside Pipeline gets big and nasty. But this isn't the outside reef I'm talking about. Hell, the monster I rode broke on a reef almost a mile out, on the very edge of the blue water.

It happened in November 1964. Waimea was closing out all across the bay, Sunset was unsurfable, and Inside Pipeline looked like World War II. There's a picture from that day that shows me standing on shore, with my arm around my board, watching the break at Inside Pipe. It was used as a poster for the movie *Big Wednesday*. What many people don't realize is that the wave in the picture is just shorebreak. Horrendous as that shorebreak looked, it was small change compared to the monsters breaking nearly a mile beyond.

It took Mike Stang and me over an hour just to get out. When we were down near the water, we couldn't see what was going on outside because the shorebreak was so huge. So Ricky Grigg spotted for us up on the beach. I knew I could trust Ricky's judgment. He stayed up high and gave us a sign whenever he thought we should go for it.

To get out, we had to get past this killer shorebreak and through a vicious lateral current. After watching it for a while, we noticed that there was one spot where an incoming current hit the lateral current and formed a saddle, a slot where we might be able to take advantage of the current and possibly shoot through the shorebreak. Trouble was, we had to start about 300 yards up from this spot and drift along with the current, timing it perfectly so that we'd get sucked out through the slot rather than slammed back on the sand.

We got worked at least four times before we finally made it out. We had started early in the morning and ended up spending over eight hours in the water.

When we got outside to that far reef, there were no lineups, nothing to indicate what our position should be. Only four sets broke out there all day. We'd watch a wave break, then paddle like hell to get as close to the whitewater as possible, to determine our lineups. The next wave would break maybe a quarter of a mile away so we'd paddle hard to get there before the whitewater subsided, desperate to try and establish another point of reference. Then we'd sit there for a couple of hours until another set came along and we'd go through the same routine until we felt we'd tightened up on the lineups.

There were six to eight waves in each set. The sun hit the face of these long, colossal walls that faded out toward Waimea Bay and made them breathtakingly beautiful. It was a surreal day. I was so mesmerized I'd stop paddling just to watch one of those beautiful waves move through. They were like pure, liquid energy. Then I'd jerk myself back into reality and say, "You'd better wake up, Pal. This thing breaks on you, you might end up sucking suds."

Despite its immense size, the outside wave was still one hell of a tube, much the same as Inside Pipeline. But unlike Inside Pipe, which tends to peak, the outside break rolled in as a long, long wall. Mike and I chugged up and over these waves feeling like tiny freighters, dwarfed by the huge seas. Now and then we'd paddle for one. They were almost impossible to catch. They were so big and moving with such speed that we couldn't paddle fast enough to get established on the face of the wave. You really had to windmill to have even a prayer of catching one.

To establish our lineups we worked off Kaena Point and back up on the hill behind Pupukea, taking three or four azimuth measurements, until we finally got our lineups in late afternoon, just as this one particular wave came through. It was the only wave I caught that whole day, and it's permanently etched in my mind.

In a 20-foot wave at Waimea, the shoulder drops off. The wave I caught at Outside Pipeline that day walled up 25 feet high about half a mile in front of me. It broke to the left, so I was riding with my back to the wave, goofy foot, and it was a god-awful uneasy feeling. Instead of getting smaller as I rode it, the sonofabitch grew on me.

It just kept getting bigger and bigger, and I started going faster and faster, until I was absolutely locked into it. I felt like I was on a spaceship racing into a void.

At first, I could hear my board chattering across the face of the wave in a constant rhythm. As my speed increased, the chattering noise became less frequent. Suddenly there was no noise. For about 15 or 20 feet, I was airborne. Then I literally was blown off my board.

When I hit and went underwater, I thought I was certainly going to drown. I got pounded good before I popped up and started sweating the next wave. It was a huge one, too. I saw Mike paddling for it, but he had a shorter board than mine and couldn't get into it.

Said Mike, "It was heart-wrenching to watch Greg catch that wave, because I knew he had probably wiped out and got washed inside. In desperation I decided to paddle to the inside reef. Inside Pipeline is unique in the way it breaks in shallow water. There's a hell of a lot of water in the waves, and it moves incredibly fast, bottom to top. When the wave breaks, it snaps like a peal of thunder. I paddled in and took off on a wave. I was only halfway down when it sucked me right back up to the top and threw me over the falls. I hit so hard that when I came up, I wasn't seeing double, I was seeing triple! I was standing in waist-deep water. Greg, who had just finished dealing with his own wipeout, came running off the beach toward me with a real concerned look on his face. He figured I was going to get ground up on the lava rocks and coral. I was lucky that I didn't."

A guy has to get over some real fears to get to the point where the decision to either go or not go becomes automatic. You have to decide how much you're willing to risk, how much you're willing to give up. Your life, maybe? It depends on how badly you want that wave.

THE LAST WAVE

Greg Noll and Andrea Gabbard

S *ome 30 years later, people still talk about the swell of 1969— how it washed out roads and swallowed houses on the edge of the sea, how mountainous waves fired off various outer reefs, a spectacle old-timers had never seen in their lifetimes. And they still talk about Greg Noll, who on that winter day in '69 quite possibly rode the biggest wave any surfer ever paddled into, a Makaha beast estimated at 35 feet plus. Noll's ride has been captured in murals and song, written up a hundred ways by a hundred people, argued about endlessly—some insisting the wave was a legitimate 50-footer, others saying "no more" than 30. In any event, Noll's adventure at Makaha has become legend, arguably the most famous big wave ride of them all.*

‡   ‡   ‡

In many ways the winter of '69 was the peak of my life. I was 32. I had built a successful career of surfing and making surfboards. That winter I returned to the Islands and, as usual, stayed with Henry Preece in Haleiwa. I had stayed at Henry's house nearly every year since I first met him and Buffalo Keaulana in the '50s, when I'd first started coming to the Islands. Here I was, 15 years later, still coming to the Islands each season for the big winter swell.

Henry's little wood-frame house is about four blocks from the water, where you can hear the surf and feel it when it gets big. About two o'clock one morning, I woke up to the sound of a far-off rumble and the rattle of dishes in the kitchen. Half asleep, I thought, "Hell of a time to run the tanks through." Every once in a while, the army would drive its tanks

Greg Noll and Mike Stang, big wave pioneers, at Waimea Bay. PHOTO BY BUD BROWNE

down from Wahiawa, through Haleiwa and out to Kaena Point. I got up to take a leak and suddenly realized there were no tanks. It was the rumble of huge surf breaking from the horizon.

I started pacing, tried to sleep, paced again. By sunrise my stomach was full of butterflies. My adrenaline was pumping. I was ready to go take a look at Waimea Bay. As soon as my wife, Laura, and I got there, I could see that the whole North Shore was closed out. Solid whitewater as far as you could see. You can't go out when it gets that big.

Laura and I decided to go take a look at Makaha—just for the hell of it. Every once in a while, when the North Shore closes out, Makaha Point still has ridable surf. Far less often, when the North Shore closes out, Makaha does this wonderful, magical thing that I had heard about over the years from older surfers like George Downing and Buzzy Trent. If God sees fit to have that north swell come in at an absolute, perfect direction, Makaha gets unbelievably monstrous swells, as big or bigger than the ones that attack the North Shore, except they're not peak breaks. These Makaha giants peel off from the Point in precise, seemingly endless walls.

In the 15 years that I had been coming to the Islands to surf, I had never seen Makaha do its magic. Sure, I had ridden a number of big Makaha Point days when the waves were breaking 20 feet, but compared to

Waimea's hang-on-to-your-balls super-drop, Makaha Point surf just didn't have it for me. I had heard the stories. Supposedly the really huge surf at Makaha only happens about once every dozen or so years. I had missed the day in '58 when Buzzy Trent and George Downing rode some monster surf at Makaha. I was convinced that Waimea was where it's at, the ultimate go-for-broke spot. There's not a bigger place on the face of God's earth to ride than Waimea. That's the way it is and always will be, world without end—at least that's what I thought.

Was I wrong!

We headed to Makaha, taking the road that led around Kaena Point toward the North Shore. We figured the worst thing that could happen is that it would become a good excuse to see my old pal Buffalo, do a little beer drinking, and talk stories Hawaiian style.

I felt the intensity of 20 years of surfing bigger and bigger waves pent up inside me that day. As we approached Kaena Point, we noticed several places where gigantic storm surf had already washed across the road. I told Laura to walk across the bad spots while I drove the car. I held my door open, ready to bail out if a wave hit the car.

As soon as we reached Kaena Point, I knew this day was going to be different. Terrifying waves of 50 feet or bigger were pounding the end of the island. We stopped at a couple of places to take pictures. One memorable photo from that day shows a giant wave dwarfing a couple of beach shacks in the foreground. *Surfer* magazine printed it in its March 1970 issue with the description, "Kaena Point at 40, 50, 60, or 70 feet." That day, the waves demolished several shacks on Kaena Point and nearby areas as well as most of the road. As we got nearer to Makaha Point, I said, "Holy shit. It's happening."

Makaha was doing its magic.

Usually, no matter how big the north swell is, by the time it gets around to the Makaha side of the island, it dissipates or you're looking at full-on stormy, windy, nasty weather. The horizon off Maili Beach, south of Makaha, becomes what the old-timers call a "cloudbreak." The rate of speed of big swells creates wind and spray that rain down on the ocean. On this day, the water was nearly as smooth as glass, beautiful, and the waves were so big that they literally put the fear of God in me.

The radio began to broadcast evacuation orders for people in homes on Makaha Point. The police had just started to put up barricades on the road, but we made it through. And there it was, not just ridable Makaha— great, big, horrifying Makaha.

You couldn't even see the break from the normal place on the beach.

You had to get back up on the hill above. On a normal, smaller day the break comes off an inside reef. On a big, 20-foot-plus day the break comes around the Point in a long wall and forms into a huge section referred to as the Bowl. The unique thing about Makaha is that under perfect conditions, waves will hold their shape at 25 feet or—so the stories go—bigger. Today that's what it looked like: bigger. *Much* bigger.

The waves were breaking on a set of reefs I didn't even know existed, just inside where the blue water began. They looked like they were breaking out twice as far as usual. I started going into a mental freeze-up and a haze settled over my brain, like I was in a dream.

There was just a handful of guys out in the water. Along the shore and on the hill above the beach, people were already lining up to watch. With the break so far out, it was almost impossible to see the surfers in any detail, let alone take clear pictures.

I got my board waxed up and started looking things over, setting up a plan. I saw that the crosscurrent was raging, so I knew that, to survive, I would have to swim like a sonofabitch for the Point or I would end up way down the beach, past Clausmyer's house. This house marks the place that is your last hope of getting ashore in one piece before the shoreline turns to solid rock. On a giant day like this, if you don't eat it in the surf the rocks can easily get you.

I waxed my board some more and headed into the water. It was surprisingly easy to get out. People have asked me, "How in the hell did you even get out?" Most of the breaks that would have been normal Makaha waves were just backed-off soupy slop and not that difficult to paddle through. It was like that almost out to the Point. Beyond the Point is where the waves were actually breaking.

I paddled way over to the left of the bowl, then headed straight out for a long ways past the break before I could paddle over to where a group of guys was sitting. They all were well-known big wave riders, including Fred Hemmings, Bobby Cloutier, Wally Froiseth, and Jimmy Blears. I had surfed different places with these guys for years. You could tell that this was no normal day. Usually we're out there laughing, joking, giving each other a hard time. When the surf gets really big, all that bullshit goes out the window. At Waimea, for instance, when the surf starts coming up, guys' attitudes would change. Peter Cole would get a little more hyper, Buzzy Trent would start talking faster, Pat Curren would get quiet. Peter likes to joke about how I'd start hyperventilating extra loud as the big monsters started our way.

Today it was serious business. No laughing, no joking. Some of the guys were glassy-eyed and there was talk of calling in the helicopters. Since that morning, when many of the guys had first paddled out, the surf had been steadily building. Now, it was at a size where all but the most experienced big wave riders call it quits.

I sat there with the guys for about 45 minutes, watching these big, thunderous giants coming down out of the north, from Yokohama Bay, toward us. At times they looked so perfect you'd swear you were looking at waves at Rincon or Malibu, only these waves were 30-feet-plus high with a lip that threw out 90 feet or more. At other times the waves broke in sections of two or three hundred yards across. They were horrible, absolutely horrible. As they peeled off toward us, a giant section would dump, and we'd count, "One thousand one, one thousand two, one thousand three . . . ," then boom! The wave would bottom out and, even though they were a quarter to a half-mile away, the impact of the breaking waves was so tremendous that it made beads of water dance on the decks of our boards. I'd never seen that happen before. The whole situation gave me a sick feeling in the pit of my stomach.

And the surf was still coming up!

A few guys caught waves off the backside of smaller sets, hit the channel, and paddled in. Nobody even considered going for the big ones.

The bottom line was obvious to every one of us out there: If you took off on one of the big waves and missed it, and there was a bigger wave behind it, you'd get caught in the impact zone where your chances of drowning were probably about 80 percent or better. If you paddled for one of these monstrous bastards and you didn't get to the bottom, but instead got caught high by catching an edge or hesitating for even a second, you'd tumble down the face of the wave and the whitewater would eat you alive. It would be like going off Niagara Falls without the barrel. It looked to me like my only chance was to paddle as though the devil himself was on my ass, then get to my feet and drive as hard as possible straight down the face of the wave. If I could at least get to the bottom before the lip folded over, then maybe I'd have a chance of drilling myself a hole at the bottom of the wave, and the mass of the wave would pass over me instead of pummeling me along until I simply ran out of air.

I analyzed the situation a little longer and gave myself better than a 50 percent chance of surviving one of these monsters. I figured I had an edge, since all my adult surfing had been devoted to big waves. My motivation was competitive. Deep down I always wanted to catch a bigger wave than anyone else had ever ridden. Finally, after a lifetime of working up to it, the time had come. The chances of this type of surf occurring again might be another dozen years away and out of my grasp. It was now or, quite possibly, never.

I had put enough time into riding big waves to know there was no chance of actually riding one of those waves all the way through. Not the way they were folding over in such huge sections. The best I could expect would be to get down the face to the bottom of the wave, make my turn, then put it in high gear and get as far as I could before the whole thing collapsed on me. Then I'd have to take my chances on the swim in. Getting in would be half the danger. If I survived the deafening impact zone, I'd have to fight my way through that strong side current and into the beach before I reached the rocky shoreline.

By this time the crowd in the water had thinned way down. I paddled about 50 yards away from the other guys to try and think things through. That's my whole deal. I can wait. Like Peter Cole and Pat Curren, I've always been willing to wait for the bigger sets. I always preferred to wait it out, catch fewer waves but, I hoped, bigger ones.

Shortly, everyone else had paddled in during occasional lulls. It felt very lonely out there, but I was working on pure adrenaline. A lot of conflicts raced around my head. My chance of a lifetime—am I going to blow it or do something about it? I've got a family, kids, and people I care about a great deal—is this goddamn wave really worth risking my life? I felt kind of crazy even considering it.

What it came down to was that I realized I'd come all this way, all these years, for this moment. This "Makaha magic" was only going to happen once in my lifetime and that time was now. The next time it happened I'd either be hobbling around on a cane or dead of old age. In either case, I'd forever miss my one chance to catch a wave this large.

I've always had one kind of approach to surfing big waves. That is "Don't hesitate. Once you decide to go, go. Don't screw around." You get into more trouble trying to change your mind midstream—or midwave— than you do if you just make a commitment and go for it.

I spent about half an hour going through this mental battle before I made a decision: "I want to do this. It's worth it to me." Above all, if I let this moment slip by I knew I would never forgive myself. This probably was as close to the "moment of truth" that I would ever get.

I paddled back to the lineup.

I was oblivious to the fact that I was now the only guy left out there. All my thoughts were focused on catching the wave. The wave that might be my biggest—and my last. Finally a set came thundering down that I thought looked pretty goddamn good. "Okay," I said to myself, "let's give this thing a shot."

Surfboards can do funny things at high speeds. If the board isn't shaped right, or the fin is set even slightly wrong, the board can track or catch an edge, sending you ass over teakettle. I was very familiar with my board. I had made it for big waves and used it for three seasons. For me it was the perfect big wave board. At 11' 4" inches long with a one-and-a-half-inch scoop in the nose, it was a big gun for big waves.

The first wave in the set looked huge. Something inside me said, "Let it go." As I paddled over the top of it, I caught a glimpse of my wave. It was even bigger. I turned and began paddling, *hard*. I felt a blast of adrenaline as the wave approached and lifted me and my board began to accelerate. Then I was on my feet, committed.

You could have stacked two 18-wheel semis on top of each other against the face of that wave and still have had room left over to ride it. I started down the front of the wave and my board began to howl like a goddamn jet. I had never heard it make that noise. I was going down the face of the wave so fast that air was getting trapped somewhere and the vibration was causing an ear-shattering WHOOOOOOO!

I flew down the face, past the lip of the wave, and when I got to the bottom, which is where I wanted to be, I looked ahead and saw the sonofabitch starting to break in a section that stretched a block and a half in front of me. I started to lay back, thinking I could dig a hole and escape through the backside of the wave. The wave threw out a sheet of water over my head and engulfed me. Then for a split second the whole scene froze forever in my mind. There I was, in that liquid green room that Simmons had talked about so long ago. I had been in and out of this room many times. Only here the room was so much bigger, more frightening, with the thunderous roar of the ocean bouncing off its walls. I realized I wasn't going to go flying out the other end into daylight. This time I feared there might be no way out.

My board came out from under me. I hit the water going so fast that it felt like hitting concrete. I skidded on my back and looked up just as tons of whitewater exploded over me. It pounded me under. It thrashed and rolled me beneath the surface until my lungs burned and there was so much pressure that I felt my eardrums were going to burst. Just as I thought I would pass out, the turbulence released me. I pulled to the surface, gulped for air, and quickly looked outside. There was another monster heading my way.

There have been many times at Waimea when I've lost my board while trying to catch a wave and had to dive deep to avoid getting caught by the whitewater, or soup, of the next wave. As a big wave passes overhead, it causes tremendous pressure to build in your ears and you have to pop them to clear it.

Here at Makaha I waited for each wave to get within 50 to 75 yards outside me, then I dove down about 20 feet and waited for it to pass. When the first wave broke overhead, I popped my ears and waited a couple of seconds before I heard the muffled sound of rumbling whitewater. The underwater turbulence of the giant wall of whitewater overhead caught me and thrashed me around. These waves were so big and there was so much soup in them that, each time I went under, the pain from the pressure in my ears was almost unbearable. In waves like these, if you can't equalize the pressure by popping your ears, you can lose an eardrum.

I figured the best I could do was try to remain oriented toward the surface and let the turbulence carry me away from the main break. By the time I had cleared the impact zone, the waves had carried me inward about 300 yards. I started swimming for my life, hard for the Point.

The current was like a wild river and my survival now depended on reaching the shore quickly. I reached for every ounce of strength I had left. I was still a hundred yards or so off the beach. I could see Clausmyer's house at the end of the line. I could see the rocky beach coming up. I was a paddleboard champion but never a great swimmer; but on that day I had a real incentive to make it. I swam my ass off.

Even the shorebreak was breaking big. I kept thinking, "If I don't make it to the beach before I reach the rocks, I'll have no place to come in. Did I go through all this hell just to get cleaned on the rocks?"

By now I was swimming almost parallel to the beach. I could see my good friend Buffalo in his lifeguard jeep, following me on shore. The current was so powerful that the beach looked like it was smoking by me. I finally hit shore 50 feet before the rocks began. I crawled up on the sand and flopped onto my stomach, amazed to be alive. Buff rolled up in the jeep, got out, stood over me, and shoved the beer in my face.

"Good ting you make 'em, Brudda," he said. "'Cause no way I was comm' in afta you. I was jus goin' wave goodbye and say 'Alooo-ha.'"

Buff was throwing a big party that evening. Normally I would be up for a party—especially after a day of surfing. But that day I just said no. It was a long time before I ever spoke about that day at Makaha.

I never knew how big the wave was, only that it was easily 10 feet bigger than anything I had surfed at Waimea Bay—and far more dangerous.

From the very beginning, it had always been a joy for me to ride a bigger wave. At one time, a 6-foot wave was terrifying. Then I got comfortable at that stage and an 8-foot wave was intimidating. Then a 10-foot wave challenged me, and so on. At one point I was as comfortable riding a 20-foot as I had been riding 6-footers. And the thrill was always there. Big wave surfing is like an addiction. You always need more size to satisfy you. I think what finally happened at Makaha was that I realized how the addiction was bordering on insanity. At some point a guy has to ask himself, "Are you going to keep this thing in perspective or are you going to slip over the goddamn edge?" After I had analyzed what I'd done, I asked myself, "You're not going to top that, so where do you go from here? What do you do now?"

Hans Hedeman getting ready to take the big drop in Waimea Bay. PHOTO BY ERIK AEDER

WAIMEA BAY

Noted surfing journalist and historian Matt Warshaw wrote that "to surf big waves is to know fear. It's an integral, inescapable part of the experience. Oahu's North Shore is surfing's undisputed capital of fear, and nowhere in the world is more nervous energy, worry, and adrenaline directed toward the deceptively simple act of riding waves."

Since big Waimea was first ridden in 1957, the Bay has accessioned more fear—and naked exhilaration—than any other big wave break on earth. Media attention has recently shifted toward other breaks—Jaws on Maui, Todos Santos in Mexico, Maverick's in California, and the various outer-reef breaks that host tow-in surfing on the North Shore—but Waimea remains the place by which all other big waves are measured, the Mount Everest of surfing. The epics are countless, unforgettable, and occasionally fatal; the proven players are cult figures in their own right.

One thing is clear: No one who ever consistently surfed big Waimea has escaped without a personal epic: cartwheeling over the falls of a thundering 20-footer; getting caught inside, closed out, and hammered by set after set until the world goes black and all seems lost; battling riptides running strong as a river in flood; losing a board and getting drawn into the pounding shorebreak. And yet for all the perils, the payoff remains one of the peak experiences in all adventure sports: taking the big drop down the face of a liquid mountain as the very hand of God closes just behind.

Volumes have been written about Waimea. Many accounts are the kind of verbal narcotic that adventure aficionados can never get enough of. The following Waimea stories are only a taste, but we trust they convey something of the terrible magic of one of the adventure world's great contests between man and nature: surfing the big ones at Waimea Bay.

ALL YOU NEED IS ONE

Greg Noll

*W*iting outside for the biggest wave of the day; never taunting the crashing peak with technical shenanigans out on the shoulder, but dropping into the pit on its own terms; always searching for a deeper line; never backing off, rather challenging the great wave for all its power and thunder and magic; and willing to suffer a ruthless thrashing if the beast came-a-reckoning. Such is the style Greg Noll flaunted at Waimea, a style not geared so much to win contests as to blow his own mind, to squeeze all the ferocious magic from the wave and inspire awe in the hearts of those who knew what an uncompromising business he pursued. In the following short piece, Noll elucidates this style and a few of his early experiences, in plain English.

‡   ‡   ‡

There was a time with Waimea where I felt in my mind like I owned it. First of all, I had a soft spot for the place because after centuries of never being surfed—I mean somebody would have eventually surfed Waimea—somebody had to come along and "pied-piper" the place. In fact, Buzzy Trent called me the Pied Piper for a long time. He'd say that if you guys go out at Waimea Bay with Greg Noll you'll all die like rats, because Waimea couldn't be surfed when it's big. So for three or four years we watched it, and I was trying to get up the balls to go out there. In the process I'd hype other guys. Finally, one day—not a particularly big one—Mike Stang and I were sitting in our car looking at it and we ripped the boards off the car and went out and caught a wave. And that was it.

You know, it was no big deal at the time. But until then, the place was spooky. It was as if it was going to swallow you up—there was the heiau

5 8

up there overlooking the bay, the Hawaiian taboo, and the haunted houses back in the valley. Then you throw on top of that Dickie Cross getting killed there, back in the '40s, and it just had this vibe that if anybody dared paddle out to this place and take off, they would perish. Modern-day surfers can't begin to understand what a dark cloud hung over that place. I feel as though Mike and I—along with our other friends who surfed there that day—were responsible for breaking that taboo. And as the years went by, I got more familiar with it and began pushing the place harder.

Basically, at that stage of my life I lived for Waimea. Sunset was a workout spot for the couple of days a year that Waimea broke. I actually got so cocky at that one stage of my surfing career, I felt that God couldn't produce a wave—in my own way, under my breath, I would almost taunt whoever the wavemaker was to send me something I can't ride because "Goddamit, I can do this!" It was a false cockiness, looking back now, having been humbled by my subsequent experiences at Makaha. But when everything comes together and a guy's 25 or 28, at the peak of his physical being, he's cocky. Like I said, there was a time when I felt like I actually owned the place. Certainly, every once in a while, I ate it. But really, at times Waimea's like a big ol' merry-go-round, and I'd have days when I could ride wave after wave there.

The crucial thing is making that vertical section. After the drop, the rest of the wave is an exit. But remember, when I'm talking about Waimea I'm talking about those days that come every two or three years—and here it's not just the drop. On those days, when the waves come winding down that point, they look like big old gnarly elephants that are lined up and just marching in. For some goddamn reason it usually happens in the afternoon. The sun's on the backside of those things and they get dark and mean. They turn from elephants into prehistoric mammoths. They'll line up across that whole bay and you have to have your brain conditioned to know that they won't close out, and even if they do, you've got to take the chance and get that one ride that's just going to blow your mind. You sit outside of everybody. There were a few of us out there. Pat Curren was one of those who would play that game. And Peter Cole. All you need is one of those and it makes not just your day but your year— I dunno, maybe your life.

1974 SMIRNOFF CHAMPIONSHIPS
JEFF HAKMAN'S STORY

Phil Jarratt

*H*e sits far out in the lineup, scanning the horizon. Other hellmen drift about. It's a closely spaced group, but for their bellies full of fear and anticipation, each man sits alone. And when the ocean rears up into liquid thunder, the surfer makes his move, "dancing on the tightrope strung between critical and perilous." At no time in the history of big wave competitions has the tightrope been strung higher than on the day of the 1974 Smirnoff Championships, held at maxed-out Waimea. Though the recent media crush on big wave surfing has accessioned various dazzling competitions, 25 years ago a contest held in 25-foot surf was unique.

This story follows renowned big wave master Jeff Hakman through the historic day of the 1974 Smirnoff Championships—one of the most extraordinary surfing contests ever—a contest Jeff nearly won.

‡　　‡　　‡

There hadn't been a spectacular winter on the North Shore since 1969. No one knew about the El Niño effect yet, but the consensus among the big wave veterans was that a monster swell was overdue.

"Don't worry," said Peter Cole, sitting out back of his little A-frame at Rocky Point. "It will come. They always come."

Jeff believed him, and when Sunset started to rise during the afternoon before the commencement of the Smirnoff waiting period, he felt that something serious was coming. Jeff surfed until dark, and the last few sets were more regular and more powerful than they had been all day. It was solid and rising, and Jeff anticipated good 15-foot waves the following day. For him this was perfect. He had the boards (Brewers again), he had the experience, he was ready.

Jeff slept uneasily up on Pupukea Highlands that night and was up before first light, peering through the sliding doors at the open ocean. From the house the view of Waimea was obstructed, but you could normally see the swell pattern at Laniakea. On this morning, however, a heavy sea mist clung to the high ground, restricting vision. Jeff pushed open the doors, stepped outside and heard a ROAR as if someone had built a nuclear power plant next door during the night. Jeff couldn't believe his ears. On a big swell he had sometimes heard the howling surf if the wind was still, but this was ridiculous! He dressed quickly, ate some fruit and put his 8' 6" Brewer gun on the roof of his bug.

He drove as fast as the bends would allow down the Pupukea road, then almost drove off the edge of the final U-turn, where there was an unobstructed view of the ocean. He jammed on the brakes and looked out to sea. Holy fucking shit! Jeff had never seen anything like it. Open ocean reefs he didn't even know about were going off all over the place. The lines of swell were stacked to the horizon like blue corduroy. There was little wind and the surface of the ocean was glass-smooth, accentuating the enormity of the waves. It was beyond big—words failed Jeff—and it was perfect.

He swung the little car around and drove back up the hill. Bill Sickler had a 9-foot Brewer gun that Jeff had used before. It was too short, but it was the best thing they had. He woke his roommate. "Bill, Bill, gimmie your gun!"

"Duh, what?"

"Your 9-footer, I need it. Can I borrow it?"

"What, yeah, take the fucker. What time is it?"

Jeff was off down the hill again. He parked at Waimea and ripped the board off his rack.

He recalls, "It was clean and immaculate and, well, Waimea never gets too big if it's clean. Maybe once every 10 years. I didn't really look, you know. There was no one around, it's only just light, so I ran down the shorebreak, waited for my chance, and paddled out. What was going through my mind was 'I'm fit and ready for this contest. If I get a few waves in before it, I'll know the conditions, I'll know where to sit and I'll win.' I figured it was maybe 25 feet on the sets. It was big, but I knew big and I could handle it, and this go-out would give me the edge I needed."

As he paddled out Jeff realized that there was a lot of ocean moving around swiftly. He sat on the outside boil and waited for a set. The first one that came through was the biggest he'd ever seen.

"I paddled over the first two, then turned around and snagged the third. The drop went on forever. I got a little air, but I held on, reached the bottom, and got the hell out of there. Made it. Great feeling. That's the deal at Waimea. If you're out there with no crowd, you can pick your line, set it all up, then you've got maybe an 80 percent chance of making the thing—*if* you get to the bottom. You sort of know the score as you drop down the face, only then it's too late to do anything.

"So I paddled out again and got another one a little bigger, maybe 25 plus. I made that one, too, and now I started to feel really confident. Like I'm cookin'! I paddle out again and sit on the boil, then suddenly the horizon goes black. I was sitting so far out I could see up the coast toward Sunset and I could see this set wrapping. The wave you ride at Waimea Bay is just the tail end of a freight train that shoots right along the entire North Shore, creating havoc and destruction. From out there I could see it coming along the whole coastline. It was totally horrifying.

"I started paddling for the blue water, paddling for my life. When I made it up the face of the first one, I looked over my shoulder before I dropped into the trough and I was in open ocean. When the first wave subsided I looked around again and the whole bay was whitewater. I put my head down and kept paddling over four or five more. I'd already had the biggest wave of my life out here, and these waves were at least 10 feet bigger!"

When the ocean settled and took a deep breath, Jeff paddled into the normal lineup and waited. When a smaller set came through, he caught another wave and made it. He had been back at the boil for about 15 minutes when Sam Hawk paddled out.

"Yo, Jeff! It's good, huh! I saw your last wave, man. How often do those sets come through?"

Jeff said, "Sammy, that's not a set. That's a lull!"

"No waaaaay, man!"

Mike Miller was next to paddle out. He waved to Jeff but paddled deeper inside, out of earshot. Just as he got settled, another throbbing set began its approach. Jeff and Sammy Hawk stroked for the horizon, with Miller way behind them. They scratched over one, two, three . . . then no Miller. He was gone.

Jeff and Hawk moved back into the lineup and finally caught sight of Miller, swimming along the cliff line, trying to avoid the killer rip. They both caught a wave, then looked around to see Miller swimming back out into the lineup.

Jeff said, "Mike, what the hell are you doing out here?"

"Missed the beach. Gotta try again."

The import of what he was saying took a while for Jeff to comprehend. Miller was one of the most experienced watermen on the North Shore. If he couldn't get in, no one could get in. Jeff estimated the size of the killer sets at somewhere between 30 and 35 feet, which was pretty much close-out size for Waimea Bay. When the surf reached these proportions, the amount of water rushing into the small bay was so great that each outgoing wave effectively drained the beach, creating an all-powerful surge of water in a westerly direction, toward the notorious Waimea shorebreak in the middle of the beach. If you were swimming and the surge got you, the only chance you had was to head for open ocean and try again.

Mike Miller appeared in the lineup a second time. "Fuckin' hay! Missed it again."

Jeff said, "You okay, Mike?"

"Yeah, yeah. I'll give it another try."

He swam into the impact zone again for another head clearing. Jeff had had five good waves and judged it time to head in. The next set that came through, he picked off the second, a clean 25-footer. Jeff made it and just as the wave backed into deeper water, he jammed a cutback and proned out, paddling as hard as he could back into the impact zone. This, he knew, was the secret at maximum Waimea. The wave tossed him around like a cork, but he held on and kept in line with the cliff, well away from the savage rip. Then, right before the shore break, he kicked his board away and let the 10-foot surge hurl him onto the beach.

Up in the car park, contest director Fred Hemmings was conferring in hushed tones with the sponsors, the television crew, and the emergency services men. Hemmings felt the contest couldn't go ahead. It was too big; lives would be endangered. Jeff was asked his opinion.

"Well," he said, "I think it's peaked. I think it's on its way down."

Hemmings and the others looked to the sea again and saw that Jeff was probably right. There were now a half-dozen surfers in the water, and they hadn't been hammered by a close-out set for 30 minutes. In all probability, the monster swell had peaked some time before dawn at 40 feet plus. When Jeff had first paddled out, there were perhaps two sets of 35-foot waves. Now they had settled at a consistent 25 to 30 feet. It was probably about 10 feet bigger than any contested surf in the history of the sport, and several of the competitors were all-rounders who had never surfed waves half the size. Hemmings took a very big gulp and called the 1974 Smirnoff on.

Even 15 years later people called the 1974 Smirnoff the most extraordinary surfing contest of all time. Some invitees simply refused to paddle out. Others sat in the lineup and declined to take a wave. The surf roared up over the road at Laniakea, and there was a day-long traffic jam as 5,000 people made their way to standing-room-only Waimea. Some said it wasn't a surfing contest, that it was about something else. Perhaps it was both. Terry Fitzgerald remembers paddling out with Gerry Lopez to start the semifinals. As an enormous set loomed, Lopez said, "If Hakman yells 'mother,' we paddle in."

For safety reasons (allegedly) a water patrol of seasoned North Shore veterans sat outside the lineup all day, marshaling heats and ensuring that no one swimming was in trouble. The patrol included Jose Angel, Peter Cole, Ricky Grigg, and a young wannabe big wave rider from Hanalei Bay, known as T-Bone. How T-Bone got into the water patrol, no one knew for sure (some said he was a protégé of Cabell), but he loved his work.

When Jeff hit the water in the first semifinal, he and Reno Abellira, James Jones, Buzzy Kerbox, Brad McCaul, and a couple of others were corralled just outside the zone while the previous heat dispersed and the water patrolmen caught a wave or two each. Jose Angel and Peter Cole both got the first wave of a good-size set, with Ricky Grigg on the next. Jeff and the others watched as the patrol surfers—most legendary big wave pioneers—nailed a couple of beasts. Then they looked seaward as the last and biggest wave approached. Jeff judged it nearly 30 feet. T-Bone was in the zone, and the semifinalists hooted nervously as the kid from Hanalei started stroking for it.

"The wave just jacked and it was huge," said Jeff. "It started to suck him up the face and he was at that moment of commitment. We were all so close we could see the expression on his face. He just faltered in his paddling rhythm for a split second, and I could tell he was wondering. Then Peter and Jose are paddling out and they're yelling at him to go, go! Suddenly we're all yelling and then he made the decision—he committed. I'll never forget that look on his face, a mixture of apprehension and pride. I mean, what's he gonna do? Every surfer in the world that he respects and admires is watching him. Suddenly he's hanging there in space—only for a split second—where he knew he wasn't going to make that wave and where he could have pulled back but didn't. It was an outlandish act of bravery and commitment.

"That wave of T-Bone's is probably the single most electrifying thing I've ever seen in surfing, because for me it just captures the whole deal," Jeff said. "He pushed it too far, but he knew he had to or nothing was worth a damn thing."

The second semifinal produced the surfing of the day, with Jeff and Reno Abellira going head to head on the biggest waves ever ridden for points.

Says Jeff, "Reno was just brilliant. He was taking off on big waves and getting airborne down the face. As soon as he landed, he'd just jam the thing into the pit, bury the rail, and crank this big, winding turn. I even saw his feet leave the board on one takeoff! In my view he was the surfer of the day in that semi—you just couldn't surf Waimea any better than that. But in the final, I thought I traded places with Reno and surfed above myself. Everything just came together and I surfed way beyond my limits. On one 25-foot wave I was screaming down the face and the nose of the board was suddenly level with the tail. I had to press down on my heels to straighten it. This was a real tribute to Brewer, because on a lesser board I was gone for sure."

World champion Shaun Tomson vividly remembers his epic in the finals. "The worst thing that's happened to me, ever, was getting caught behind this gigantic peak. I had 11 years experience on the North Shore, but the Smirnoff was the first time I'd ever ridden big Waimea. Out of six guys in the finals, four of us had never ridden big Waimea at all. I took off on a good 20-footer and got about a third of the way down before the wave went concave and I free-fell. I landed on my board, bounced off, and skipped down the face. I couldn't penetrate. Then the whole wave converged right on my back. It knocked every last bit of wind out of me. I actually thought I'd broken my back."

The contest Jeff still calls the most exciting of his career came down to half a point difference between him and Reno, and Reno got the nod. Three judges placed Reno first, two in second, and one in third. Jeff was scored first by two, tied for first by another, second by two, and tied for second by the third judge. Under the subjective judging system, no result could have been closer.

OCCURRENCE AT WAIMEA BAY

Mark Foo

*M*ark Foo was among the most influential surfers to ever ride a big wave. Like many others, Foo began not as the big wave radical for which he would later become world famous but as a scrawny 17-year-old clawing up the ranks of the North Shore tournament circuit. He started strong but after several years had not broken into the top 50 in the world professional rankings. Accepting that he would never rule the competitive small wave beat, Foo upped the ante to the big stuff—and quickly found his calling. Foo was among the first to apply slashing small wave maneuvers to big Sunset and Waimea, a bold approach that quickly caught on. He was also one of the first big wave riders to widely promote his achievements, a tactic that rankled some but proved vital in shifting surf industry attention—and sponsorship dollars— to big waves and the athletes who rode them. From the first time he rode big Waimea in 1982, Foo cut a sky-high profile. The following story—a Waimea whopper by any measure—bears out the fact that, while Mark Sheldon Foo might have talked a heroic line, and then talked some more, he definitely put his money where his mouth was. Tragically, Foo died surfing Maverick's in 1994. Surfing journalist Matt Warshaw recounts the events of that fateful day in "Death of a Legend," which appears later in this book.

‡   ‡   ‡

I awoke early on January 18, 1985, unaware that I had a date with destiny. My wake-up surf check revealed 12- to 15-foot waves, too big for anywhere except Waimea (which had been cooking consistently since the beginning of the year) but still not quite large enough to make the Bay break in traditional big wave form. The amazing thing about the Bay is it

Mark Foo dropping into his trademark low-crouch position at Waimea Bay.
PHOTO BY ERIK AEDER

takes so much energy to make it show. Places like Sunset, Pipe, and Haleiwa will all be nothing but maxed-out, second-reef sets—and Waimea hardly dribbles.

By midday the surf met the 18- to 20-foot requirement to become "real" Waimea, and over the next two hours the swell continued to build into 25-foot sets firing at 20-minute intervals. Naturally, guys started to venture out: Ken Bradshaw (of course), Dick Asmus, and a couple of others paddled out in hopes of riding traditional frill-size Bay, but the waves were breaking in an untraditional pattern. Due to the extreme west direction of the swell and the inordinate amount of sand in the Bay from a recent onshore storm, the waves were sucking and pitching like a shallow sandbar. It looked more like Inside Sunset or low-tide Backdoor, except it was massive Waimea—and the riptide was getting serious, too.

The surf continued to increase in both size and viciousness, intimidating everybody until they paddled to shore—all except Bradshaw, who got caught inside on a 30-foot set. He swam for his board but couldn't get to it before the rip pulled him into the danger zone. Knowing what to do, he swam back out all the way into the lineup and tried to stroke it in again; but again the rip pulled him toward the killer shorebreak and again Ken had to swim back out and around. It took three full cycles before he made it to safety. It was an impressive display of water knowledge and stamina—the kind necessary just to survive here. After seeing Bradshaw's ordeal, everyone thought thrice about going out except for James Jones, who paddled out just as Ken reached the beach.

At that point I was unaware of how serious the surf had become. I was on my way back from errands in Haleiwa and I saw there was no one out. I was just shaking the flu and had been in the water only once in the last ten days. I was far from being in the most prepared state, but Waimea was doing its thing and there was only one guy in the lineup. I wanted to get out there.

By the time I got down to the beach, James was already out and had been joined by bodyboarder J. P. Patterson. I finished my stretch just in time for a lull and hit it through the shorebreak without ever getting a good look at it—when there is an opening at big Waimea you have to make your move. Alec Cooke was right behind me. You usually feel a bit apprehensive paddling out at the Bay, so I always take a slow, extra-wide course to properly prepare myself for what's to come. Alec and I were both almost all the way out, but very much in the middle of the Bay when a wave came out of nowhere and cleaned us up. Leashes prevented both of us from swimming, and we soon joined J. P. and James in the lineup.

We all quickly realized that this was no ordinary big day. Most of the waves were too edgy to even consider. All four of us were sitting really wide in the channel, yet waves were jacking up and pitching in a place that normally would be considered the safety zone. Twenty-five-foot waves were breaking where 12-footers normally would and were unbelievably hollow and way too gnarly to ride. I picked up a couple of stock sets and started getting my sea legs back.

The interval between big sets lessened to under 10 minutes. Another set appeared, and one wave was a full-on 30 feet and had us all scratching up the face and looking into the pit of the beast. It was a moment I will never forget. The monster pitched up and out and turned into the biggest tube you could ever imagine. On other days at Waimea, Sunset, Pipeline, or Honolua, I've seen some big holes but nothing like this. It looked like a huge cavern with half the ocean as its roof and sides. With so much power, the water no longer seemed liquid, rather solid and hard, like concrete. At that instant I came to realize that there was no way to ride such a wave, no matter how long a board, no matter how early you got in. There was just too much energy and moving water. The proportions were just far too large. We all made it over that mountainous wave stoked and awed. James told me how he took off on one like that on the morning of the '74 Smirnoff, got pitched, and almost died—and that he'd never do it again. He only half jokingly yelled, "Hey, Alec, if you had caught that one you would have had the record."

The set interval lessened to about five minutes, which meant the 25- to 30-foot waves were only the average ones and the big set waves would show up around every 20 minutes. I didn't know if it was that long, but another set popped up way outside and we headed out over a 20-footer.

Suddenly I could hear screaming from people on the point, but I still couldn't see the next wave. I was the farthest over and inside and I just made it over the last wall to see this beast of a wave fill the entire horizon. I had been looking at waves in the 25- to 30-foot foot range, which were as big as I'd ever seen, but this thing or wave or tsunami was clearly twice as big as anything I had ever encountered. It was standing and feathering a good 200 yards outside, but the only thing I could see was a towering wall of water. No sky; nothing but this massive, angry wave. James, who saw it first, was already digging for the horizon, but there was no way he or any of us would be able to get far enough out, so I decided to bolt for the other side of the Bay, as far into the channel as possible. Of course, I didn't think that this wave would turn out to be a monstrous left that started peeling far, far outside and ended up breaking top to bottom all the way across the Bay. So there I was, having paddled right into the worst place possible. All the other guys were already diving for the bottom as the wave transformed into a thundering avalanche of whitewater—truly awesome. James later called it 48 feet. As far as I'm concerned you could have called it 50 or 60 or anything you wanted.

Bradshaw, who was standing on the beach with Waimea greats Gary Spence, Owl Chapman, Charlie Walker, and Peter Cole, later said, "They're paddling over sets, like 25 to 30 feet, and then this rogue set comes in. And I'm just, 'Wow . . . look at this thing! It's giant!' We were calling this wave 45 feet, conservative. It could have been over 50—who knows. [Bradshaw later called it "the biggest wave surfers had ever encountered."] I'm jumping up and down on the beach, going, 'These guys are history!'"

As destiny or miracles would have it, my leash held. We all surfaced and the other three started swimming. J. P., whose bodyboard leash snapped, asked me, "What kind of leash you got on, a chain?" I was too busy thinking about the next wave to respond.

The lifeguards called in the helicopter as soon as they saw this rogue wave close out the bay. At this stage it was no longer possible to swim in through the rip or the shorebreak. James, with 15 years of big wave experience, didn't hesitate: The moment the chopper was overhead with its dangling basket, James was in it. Alec had just swum into serious trouble and was getting pulverized by the shorebreak. He was in the worst place on earth at that moment and looking like a goner. They kept dropping the basket for him, but there was too much turmoil and roiling water for him to reach it and more close-out sets kept rolling through. As Alec put it, "I was about to become hamburger on the rocks."

At last Alec was able to reach up and grab the bottom of the basket, which was all the pounding sets would allow. As they started pulling him out, another wave smashed into him, rocking the basket and the entire chopper. Heavy drama!

Meanwhile, J. P. had retrieved his board, but he still couldn't beat the rip. He lost his board again as more close-outs poured through and then got plucked out just after Alec.

They left me out there alone, surfing in closed-out Waimea. I realized the seriousness of the situation and my main objective was to get in. The sets just kept coming. I knew that the only way for me to get out of there was to ride a wave into the keyhole in the corner of the beach, and that was what I intended to do. I figured to try and paddle over the huge close-out sets and then try and shoot back into the normal lineup, trying to pick up a 20- or 25-foot in-betweener. The problem was that I couldn't get far enough in before another big set would show and I'd have to hightail it back out. This went on for two or three sets before the helicopter guys came to get me. I waved them off because I still figured I could ride one in.

With the helicopter hovering overhead and another big set approaching, I decided to stay inside and position myself to catch one of the set waves. I was way, way outside and in the middle of the bay as the first wave neared. It looked like a left and I made a serious effort to catch it. I changed my mind because it started sucking out and there was just too much water drawing off the bottom. I knew there was another one behind it, and I figured it would be breaking in deeper water after this first wave and give me a better shot at entry. My theory was correct. It backed off momentarily, long enough to take off and start driving. Then, again, the whole thing started sucking and turning concave. I was already at full speed, but I felt like I was going backward. I saw the free fall coming, but having made a couple free-fall takeoffs earlier in the month, I had the confidence to launch myself over the ledge of what looked like a moving cliff. Technically and mentally I kept it together as I free-fell vertically a good 25 feet on my board. But the flight was too long and the wave too concave and I crashed upon contact with the wave face. The thing about Waimea is that you're going so fast with so much momentum and power that it's not like landing on water; it feels more like pavement. The worst part is, you bounce and skip, instead of penetrating the surface, leaving your body at the mercy of the wave, which usually results in a journey over the falls. This time I hit so hard I saw stars, then I started bouncing down the face as a good portion of the Pacific started to collapse on top of me. I felt the explosion of the lip; I heard my board snap like kindling; I felt my watch break away from my wrist and then felt myself get sucked up and over for another thrashing. Things turned pretty gray for the rest, and when I resurfaced the helicopter was waiting. I had given it my best shot. The bay was whitewater from end to end. I jumped into the basket for the ride home.

For all of us who lived through the experience, life and waves took on a new perspective. I will never forget that monster tube or that monster closeout and especially that takeoff. I believe much more in destiny now. The series of timing, circumstance, and events that resulted in me being out there with the others, and then alone and surviving, makes me know it was meant to be for me, and telling the story is part of that fate. Thank God we're all still alive.

Epilogue

In the aftermath there has been much hoopla and controversy surrounding the question of who has ridden the largest wave ever. The answer? Nobody. Several men hold the record and have successfully made truly huge waves, the type you could safely call 30 or 35 feet. Now that I have seen even larger waves firsthand, I do not believe it is possible to ride them. There have only been rare times when such waves, the ones above all the rest, have even been seen, let alone attempted. Those waves remain in another realm . . . the Unridden Realm.

KEN BRADSHAW INTERVIEW

Bruce Jenkins

Who is the best big wave surfer? The question is impossible to answer, though occasional competitions can showcase a given surfer getting the best rides on a given day. What separates a big wave surfer from the rest of the pack is consistency in big surf - the man who is always there, always charging for the gusto. And also the man whose judgment matches his courage. A reckless charger is not a master, just a daredevil. The short list of master big wave riders is perhaps two dozen deep, but Kenny Bradshaw is at the top of most everyone's list. Bradshaw's amazing career has always personified the core values of the classic big wave waterman, committed, self-contained and self-motivated, dauntless, assertive and entirely addicted to riding the biggest waves on earth. The following interview illuminates facets of this amazing athlete, but it can only hint at the presence and intrigue of the man himself. Interviewer Bruce Jenkins said, In 20 years of interaction with the greatest stars of baseball, basketball, the NFL, you name it, this might have been the most interesting interview I've had."

(It is crucial to note that this interview took place before Bradshaw became a convert to tow-in surfing, which is the focus of the last part of this book. In 1998, during a historic session at Outside Log Cabins, Bradshaw nailed the biggest wave ever surfed, a beast "in the mythical 40-foot range," as Jenkins later stated.)

‡   ‡   ‡

Bradshaw reminded me greatly of Howie Long, the Los Angeles Raiders defensive tackle: well-spoken, tremendous presence, gentlemanly, yet a savage competitor when necessary. When this guy walks into a room, he takes over. A herd of wild buffaloes could charge the coffee table, and Bradshaw would retain command.

Know this, by way of introduction: Bradshaw was brutally honest—it's the only way he knows—but never bitter, cruel, or mean-spirited. While many of his statements were critical, they were spoken in a tone of amazement. Clear-eyed, animated, and polite, Bradshaw simply laid down the law of North Shore surfing, at least as it exists in his mind. And one thing became obvious: It's not about hatred, rivalries, or making enemies on the North Shore. It's a matter of style. Ken Bradshaw respects everyone who rides waves of this magnitude. It's their style he sometimes can't understand.

And if you challenge him, get him mad, push him a little too far—wow, that's a *bad* idea. This is a man who has taken bites out of surfboards, just to make a point. He's been known to paddle up to another surfer—someone who has flagrantly broken the code of ethics—and simply rip out a fin with his bare hands. If an old-fashioned brawl is the last alternative, Bradshaw couldn't be more ready if it comes to that. "Ken Bradshaw will survive," he says. "I don't care what you do, who you bring, or how many. I will match whatever you give me."

Considering that Bradshaw rides the biggest, most frightening waves in the world, it is nothing short of amazing that he grew up in Texas. It's one thing to make the jump from California—countless big wave riders have done that, from Buzzy Trent to Sam Hawk to Richard Schmidt—but *Texas?!* "It all comes down to desire," he says in his earnest, high-pitched voice.

He'd been an all-city linebacker in high school, probably bound for greatness at some big university, "and it was fun, no doubt about it," he recalls. "I loved head-huntin'. You know, roving monster man, just search and destroy." He was a formidable 5' 10", 165 pounds in the tenth grade (compared to 6', 185 pounds today), and he probably could have written his own ticket by his senior year. But when Kenny discovered the waves at Surfside, Texas, near Galveston, he realized that nothing else really mattered in life. He had found his calling.

"It was about a 75-mile drive from Houston, and my sister started taking me down there when I was about 13. People give Texas a hard time, but there was a lot of surf then. Not fantastic, but big, long, mushy peaks, where you could get some paddling experience and wave knowledge. There was no intimidation factor, no overpowering situations, so I did nothing but conquer the waves. I conquered every wave I came across in Texas, so that's all I knew.

"I'd be out surfing all day—just 10 straight hours in the water. My sister literally had to come out and say, 'We're leaving without you.' I got so into surfing a couple of summers, my parent's just couldn't handle it. I didn't want to play football any more, and for them, that was it. We had a big war. I ran away from home—twice."

The second time was for good. Bradshaw, now 17, had graduated from 9-foot boards down to 7-footers in a very short time. He entered a Surfside contest and reached the semifinals. He had conquered Texas, and he was ready for California. Imagine his good fortune—it was the winter of 1969 to '70, one of the biggest in recorded history.

"I found a place in Encinitas and spent that whole winter surfing Swami's, Windansea, and Trestles. It was huge, incredible. That was my first winter in California, so that's what I thought surfing was. It's big. Every day's big! I'm out at Swami's, and I'm out in the kelp beds! This is great! By Christmas, I was surfing as well as most of the guys around: Cheer Critchiow, Alf Laws, Tom Ortnen. In any size I could get my hands on. It was a whole new world, and I was on fire."

Eventually, he caught wind of the real California: 0- to 1-foot with possible 2-foot sets. Blown out by noon. Interminable boredom. Find a job, and fast. Catch the surf movies, and dream of Hawaii. "I was 19, it was the winter of 1971 to '72, and there was no surf. I was living alone in an apartment, just ready to break out. I figured I've got to at least see Hawaii. It had a real mystique then. Everybody comes over here now (to Hawaii), but then, you'd see guys get on a plane to Hawaii, and they wouldn't return."

Bradshaw arrived in the spring of 1972, and he did return to California, briefly—just in time to see the 1972 World Contest at Ocean Beach. That was a mind-blowing event, featuring the likes of David Nuuhiwa, Larry Bertlemann, Jimmy Blears (a new acquaintance from Hawaii), and the astounding Michael Ho, reaching the finals at the age of 13. "That was it," said Bradshaw. "About two weeks after that, I packed up for Hawaii—it was the second week of October—and I came to stay."

Bradshaw found a place in Kahala, took a town job, and hitchhiked to the North Shore when he could. "If you didn't make money to survive, you didn't surf," he recalls. "I didn't care if it took me two years before I could go surfing. I knew it was out there. My first experience—you remember it like you remember your first girl. I paddled out at Sunset with a bunch of hot guys out—I remember Sam Hawk, definitely—and it was about 8 feet. I had my California surfboard, and I'm going real fast, wow, and I start my turn—and the tail was just too thin. First time I'd ever been in a real tube in Hawaii. The wave just passed me by and snuffed me. I came up, and I was so stoked. I mean, the power didn't bother me; nothing bothered me. It was just being in Hawaii, being able to do it."

He went after his surfing with a raging aggression, driven to be the most accomplished big wave rider of all time, and unlike so many of today's hotshots, he carried deep respect for the North Shore: its lore, its legends, the surfers who came before him, and the very real mystique surrounding places like Pipeline and Waimea Bay. The sight of a Greg Noll, Jose Angel, or Peter Cole would stop Bradshaw in his tracks, because these were the pioneers, the groundbreakers. In his book, *Da Bull: Life Over the Edge,* Noll wrote, "Every big wave rider I've met is a radical individual. Ken Bradshaw has got the spark. He's intense, he wants it, and he's willing to give up something for it if he has to. Ken Bradshaw spent many years riding big waves before he got any recognition for it. You have to love what you're doing to go out there and do it when the bleachers are empty."

In that same book, Ricky Grigg noted, "Kenny is one of the few surfers at Waimea who does it like we used to, with the same fanatical vigor. The guy claws his way into a wave. There are other guys out there with lots of style, but Kenny has true grit. It's something that comes out of thunder and lightning."

Bradshaw's big wave initiation came on a day in 1976 when the Bay was pushing 30 feet and more. "I went out with Roger Erickson," he recalled. "All morning long it was closing out, 40 feet. Eddie Aikau tried to warn me. 'Oh, brudda Brad, you don't go out when it's this big, brah.'

"But there's waves between the sets that are unreal," Bradshaw told him.

"No, brah. When the waves are hitting the bathhouse (up where the beach meets grass), you don't paddle out."

Bradshaw barely knew Erickson then, but they took on the Bay together. "We stayed out three hours, and I got three or four waves. Then Eddie and Kimo Hollinger came out, and a huge set came in and caught everybody. That was Kimo's last day. A rogue set came in, totally out of time, out of sync."

Kimo Hollinger nearly drowned that day. He was pushed over toward the diving rock, synonymous with disaster on a big day, and it took a human chain of seven or eight Hawaiian watermen, clinging tenuously to the rocks, to haul him out of the water.

"He didn't surf again for like five years, anywhere," said Bradshaw. "I was amazed. But I'm like 22, just amped out of my mind, going (desperately), 'I'm going back out there.' And there's Kimo. 'I don't care,' I'm saying. You think I get fired up now, you should have seen me in the '70s. I was a tyrant. I look at these guys now and think, 'You might have it.' Boy, I had it. I was hell-bent. I'd kill somebody who got in my way."

And he damn near did. Word quickly spread that Bradshaw was not only fearless, tackling 15-foot Sunset and 25-foot Waimea at every opportunity, but a little bit nasty. Not surprisingly, some of the local boys were offended by this brash young warrior. There were violent confrontations, both in and out of the water. "I really got into it with these two guys at Sunset once, and when it was over one of them said, 'Wow, man, you're serious, aren't you?' I said hey, this is my life. You're the one who made it serious, not me."

Mike Latronic, who has shared countless big days with Bradshaw at Sunset, describes him as "really smart, an intelligent guy and very polite. Ninety-nine percent of the time, he's really cool. But if you cross him in the water, he turns into an animal."

I asked Bradshaw if he really did take a bite out of somebody's surfboard.

"Oh, that's commonplace for me. Even today."

"Is that your ultimate statement?" I asked. "I mean, that's a serious statement."

"It is. As much of a brute and bull as people see me, I won't do something unless it's really called for. I wouldn't recommend somebody going after it" would at one when he's in the wrong. I wouldn't suggest that."

Biting a board—that takes some strength." I said.

"It takes desire. Four-ounce surfboards are really easy, though. Thicker ones [laughter]... my teeth were loose the other day. Breaking this is probably more effective, because then they have to leave the water. The runs are real easy. You just bend 'em right off. If you feel bad about it later, you can give 'em 15 bucks. That's what it costs to put em back on. But at least you got the guy out of there."

Bradshaw sees himself as sort of a Sunset caretaker. He watches everything that's going on, who's doing what, and he enjoys being called upon for advice—especially when things get hairy. Latronic recalled one long-ago afternoon when a 4- to 6-foot swell suddenly jumped to 10 feet and beyond, "and there were like 20 waves in the set. I let my board go, and the leash broke, and I'm just, 'Oh no!' I started swimming out, and that was a mistake. I went under about four more waves and just (sound of desperate, heaving breaths)—I'm gettin' scared. Finally Bradshaw says,

'Swim in! Go in!' I was scared to go in, because it was shallow, but you have to, and I learned that. It's the only way."

For years, the Bay was reserved for the big boys, the true emperors of the North Shore. Then came the Eddie Aikau contest, with its $55,000 first prize, and people got a little crazy. Big wave riding made a comeback and a lot of frauds got involved, cluttering up the break when they had no business being out there. "It's turned into a madhouse," says Bradshaw. "There's a whole new crowd at 12 to 15 feet, all these guys thinking they're gonna get rich and be hotshot big wave riders. But when Waimea is really Waimea, there can be 25 to 30 guys out and it's still in the hands of the people who want it. And you've got to want Waimea."

Why does Bradshaw do this? What moves a man to go out there? "I guess it's an addiction," he says. "I have no idea, but it must be like being on drugs. Because when you're not doing it, it torments and eats away at you. When it is happening [long pause]—I guess it's like looking at life itself. For a moment, you've got it all. It's yours. You've gone to the very epitome of what you can do. How many people can say that in this world?

"Yes, there can be more. Is there a bigger one? Will I be in shape? Will I have the right energy level and motivation? But see, there are so few people doing it. There's nobody else to measure up to, but yourself. That's exactly it. Yourself and the next 25-foot mountain.

"I plan to be like [60-year-old] Peter Cole—actually surfing even more than Peter because he's got a job outside surfing. My life is surfing. I bought a house at the end of Ke Nui Road, so I can keep an eye on Sunset forever. I mean, until Ken Bradshaw expires, this is where he's going to live."

The last time I saw Bradshaw, I was out on a pleasant, 6- to 8-foot day at Sunset. In the middle of what looked like a critical drop to me, Bradshaw noticed one of his friends paddling out. "Hey, Bob!" he cried out excitedly, still in mid-descent. "What are you doing out here?" Bradshaw was smiling and waving his hands, like some jovial barbecue host. He did everything but offer this guy the potato chips.

FADE TO BLACK
ONE MAN'S ULTIMATE SESSION
AT WAIMEA BAY

Brock Little

*T*here is nothing small about Brock Little's skill in big North Shore surf,
nor his success at new wave breaks like Mexico's Todos Santos or
Central California's Maverick's. By most accounts, Little was a big wave
prodigy from day one, as if the big grinders rolled in just for him. Always deeper
than the next guy, snagging the biggest waves, scoring the greatest rides. Always
pushing harder and getting away with just a little bit more. As for those bold
enough to follow his lead—well, many felt lucky to survive. But as this story
once again confirms, nobody—even the best in the business—consistently surfs
big Waimea without suffering a personal epic—or, as one author put it,
"confronting death in the underworld."

‡   ‡   ‡

I could hear the surf pounding that morning from my house at Pupukea
Heights, about 2 miles from the ocean. It's a common noise when the
waves are over 15 feet, so I wasn't afraid—just ready to go. I figured the
Quiksilver/Eddie Aikau Memorial contest might be on, so I was stressed
to hurry up and get down to the Bay. I had some cereal, grabbed some
trunks, and jogged to my truck.

Unfortunately, at that time my Waimea boards weren't worth a shit. I
had a couple of new 8' 3"s, and they didn't look right. I don't know—
they were too thin or too light. Something just looked wrong with both
of them. One board was clear, the other green and yellow. I was born on

79

Brock Little at Waimea Bay. PHOTO BY ERIK AEDER

St. Patrick's Day and figured the green would bring me luck, so I went with the green and yellow board.

It was still early when I got down to the parking lot at the Bay. The beach was empty except for meet director George Downing, sitting in the lifeguard tower. He'd been there for the past three years whenever there was a swell, counting and timing the waves. And every time he eventually decided to postpone the contest. He hadn't blown a call yet.

The surf was about 15 to 18 feet—not big enough for the contest but fun-looking, just the same. Darrick Doerner, always the first guy out at Waimea, was picking off some good ones. It's funny: I've always wanted to get out there before Darrick, but I've never come close. He must paddle out when it's pitch-dark. Anyway Darrick was taking off deep as usual and doing all the right things. He's one of the greats at Waimea—and gets very little credit.

I talked to George for a while. He said the waves were supposed to be huge, but clearly the great swell hadn't yet arrived. I told him it was already pretty big and he assured me it was going to get bigger.

"Are you going to have the contest?" I asked. "Wait and see," he replied. I'd been getting that same answer for three years.

More surfers began to arrive: Mark Foo, James Jones, Cheyne, and others—not to mention a bunch of alternates trying to get in the contest. In half an hour the waves had jumped to 20 feet and it began to look like the event was finally on. I grabbed my St. Patrick's board and got ready.

As I walked through the grass to the beach a big grinder came through, at least 22 feet. This is going to be fun, I thought. It wasn't very crowded and Darrick had already come in, so I knew I could get a lot of waves. When I got down to the corner of the Bay I could see the sandbank extended pretty far out, which meant it would be a hassle getting into the channel. But I figured I could just sink under the waves on my 8' 3" and not worry about getting dumped.

The paddle out at Waimea is a lot farther than it looks, and the anxiety and tension build the whole way. I usually feel somewhat calm on the beach, but once I start paddling I realize what I'm getting into. I always try to go alone. On this day the waves had a weird vibe to them—I could feel the power just paddling out. When I got to the lineup my mind sort of went blank. I didn't feel like talking to anyone, plus I didn't see anybody I liked, so I just sat by myself.

I like to sit deep and to the inside. I lined up with the deepest guy. I'm not sure who it was, but I was about 10 yards to his right. The first set went at about 18 feet and I got the first wave. The drop was basic and the wall was easy. Still, my board felt thin and narrow. I can't tell how a board works on its first wave, but I can get a feeling—and unfortunately I was getting a bad one this time. I paddled back out, hoping I was wrong.

After catching a couple of waves the tension I'd felt earlier started coming back. The ocean felt weird—unusually strong and powerful. When a huge set hit the horizon—far bigger than the other sets—I wasn't surprised at all.

When humongous waves move in I can feel anticipation run across my entire body. So much adrenaline pumps through that sometimes I have to yell or shake my arms, legs, and head to try and off-load the jitters. This set was going to be big, but I could tell the waves would be ridable. The first one stood up across the Bay; it didn't look too big, about 22 feet. No one seemed interested, so Michael Ho led the pack over to the next wave, but I swung around and took off on the first one. It was big, but not giant—radical, but not insane. I felt all right when I kicked out.

Then I saw a beast of a wave behind me. It stood up straight, all the way across the Bay, at least three stories high. I wasn't sure if I should paddle in or paddle out. I certainly didn't want this monster breaking on me! Then I noticed someone at the top, paddling and kicking to get into the thing. It was Michael Ho.

Everyone knows Mike's a legendary professional surfer, but he isn't very tall, nor is he known for his Waimea skills. Yet there he was, paddling into one of the biggest waves I'd ever seen. Mike really wanted that bastard. Most anyone else who surfs Waimea would've pulled back, but Mike was going for it.

The wave was trying to break outside the reef, but it just kept feathering. Mike was probably blind from all the spray when he stood up. Lucky thing, too, because he was facing straight down, perhaps 50 feet, to the bottom. Just after Mike got to his feet, the wave slammed into the reef and squared up. He shot down the bumpy face.

He looked uncomfortable on his board, but he rode it like a bull: not sure what it was going to do next and holding on for dear life. About three-quarters of the way down he hit a chop that pitched him off the deck. When waves are that big you're going so fast—and so much water is moving up the face—that it's nearly impossible to penetrate the surface. Not only did Mike not penetrate when he hit, he bounced about 4 feet back into the air—it looked like he could've bounced back onto his board. He skipped a little more on the wave face when he landed the second time, then finally broke through the surface.

I had been yelling my lungs out during Michael's entire ride—I had to yell, I couldn't stop myself. It was a strange feeling. By the time he'd fallen, though, I had begun to laugh like a madman. It was a weird high. Adrenaline is a radical drug.

After all that yelling and laughing I wasn't ready for the wave to hit me, and I was still laughing when it did, so I didn't get much of a breath. Although I was getting worked and didn't really have enough oxygen, I knew it would be fine—compared to what Mike was going through. I was in the channel where it was mushy, not in the pit.

I was done laughing when I came up, and I began to worry about Mike. He surfaced just as I was about to paddle over to look for him. He had a startled look, then broke into a huge smile. He'd just ridden what had to be the biggest wave of his life—the ultimate high.

I paddled back out, knowing the waves were building, hoping I could catch a wave like Mike's. Nothing huge came for the next 20 minutes, however, so I caught a few medium-size ones. Then the horizon shifted big time, and I knew something huge was on its way.

When it arrived in the Bay, the set looked as major as the last one. Once again, everybody paddled over the first wave, so I decided to take it. However, when it was over and I kicked back out, I pretty much freaked: There was a huge, black, monstrous wave, lined up end to end across the Bay, covering the horizon, about to close out. I hadn't yet had the full-on Waimea experience. No question, I was about to get it.

I saw Dennis Pang make it over the top, then it broke right in front of me. I figure the thing was around 35 feet. I took two or three deep breaths, then slid off my board. The wave came over and began to take me for a spin. It wasn't too bad: I was in deep water, and though the wave broke top to bottom, it didn't grab me that hard. When I came up I was feeling so good that when I saw one more, it didn't bother me.

Here we go again, I thought, as I took another deep breath. Behind wave number two, though, I saw another close-out. I was still pretty comfortable, but not quite as happy as I'd been a few moments earlier. Also, until I bailed under the third wave I didn't realize how far I'd been dragged.

I hadn't taken a full-on breath because I was feeling too cocky after the first couple of waves—but now I realized I'd been washed onto a sandbar near the middle of the Bay. After the wave had broken on the outside, all the whitewater had been rejuvenated when it struck the sandbar, and it was taking its newfound energy out on me. I was tired when I surfaced but doing okay. I looked back and saw my board was broken but figured it didn't really matter because the board was crap anyway. I was bummed, though, because I didn't have a good backup for later. Meanwhile I was preparing to get hammered by wave number four. I was no longer enjoying the experience.

The fourth wave worked me harder than the third one—I was really fighting for air. I usually try and cruise underwater for about five seconds then fight for the top, but this fourth wave had me going. I still didn't consider myself in any real trouble after I came up, so I just looked around and analyzed the situation: I was slowly moving in toward the rocks on the Haleiwa side of the Bay. I figured I wouldn't get there for about six or seven more waves, and since I'd probably drown before I got that far, I took off my leash: What was left of my board was pulling me in and holding me back. I began taking deep breaths as wave number five rolled in.

Ken Bradshaw once told me that if a person uses a lot of oxygen going under waves, after about three or four his lungs don't get as much air. I didn't believe him until just then. I thought I was ready for the fifth wave, but I wasn't—I began to get tumbled right after I ducked under. I was trying to stay calm, but after a couple of seconds I started fighting, which just caused my body to use even more oxygen. I couldn't climb my leash, so I wasn't sure if I was struggling toward the surface or diving to my death.

I began to feel real mellow, seeing red stars or dots in front of my eyes. It felt good to relax. I didn't have much power left in me to fight anymore. I knew I might black out, and if I did I would die. It was a weird feeling: I think I know what it would feel like to drown—a desperate fight, then peacefulness as you black out. But I didn't feel like dying. When I tried to go for the surface again, my body had more fight left than I thought. When I came up I saw another huge wave, right in my face.

I've always had this attitude that I would die believing I was going to live. When I went under the sixth wave, I believed I would live. I did everything right: took a deep breath, didn't panic, and started fighting after about five seconds. I saw the same red dots again, but by then I wasn't thinking very clearly so I don't remember much.

The seventh wave closed out the Bay. After what I'd already been through, I prayed this was the last wave of the set. I went under, fighting to stay relaxed. When I came up I was about 30 yards from shore, and although that sounds pretty close, swimming in didn't cross my mind. I took some deep breaths—I wanted to know what it felt like to breathe again. Then I swam out as fast as I could, and stopped when I was far enough out to feel comfortable.

I took another breather, then looked at the surfers across the Bay and at the traffic along Kam Highway. I saw somebody running up the beach with my board, looking around for me. I felt awed. I often get that feeling at Waimea—like some great spirit is out there, watching.

I was in the middle of the Bay with a really good, natural high running through me. I wanted to float around some more, but I knew I should start moving. I swam over to the Sunset side of the Bay and saw Cheyne. We had a quick conversation about how good the waves were, and how I was feeling. I told him I was fine, but it was time to get going.

I began to swim toward the beach, aiming for the Point, and hoped another set wasn't moving in. I've heard stories of Bradshaw having to swim two or three times around the Bay before being able to come in safely. Once was enough for me.

Luckily, the waves were relatively small as they broke behind me and washed me in. I was staying close to the surface and letting the waves roll me to shore. As I passed the Point I was pretty close to the rocks, right where I wanted to be. If I drifted too far the current would take me into the middle of the shorebreak, and that would mean I'd have to swim around again—or try to. I stayed as close to the rocks as I could and made good progress. When I was about 25 yards from the beach I began to sprint. The current was really strong and tried to take me into the shorebreak, like I'd thought it would. I used the last of my energy to fight my way to the beach.

I was barely able to walk up the sand, but my brother was there waiting for me with half my board. I didn't want to fall flat on my face and look stupid in front of him. He began telling me how dumb I was to go out there and how I could've died. I just smiled.

From that day on I was one of the Big Boys at Waimea—or at least that's what people told me. I don't surf to be in the Big Boys Club, and I never needed to be accepted. I just surf Waimea because it's fun. One thing, though: All those years I heard people talking about big waves being a life-or-death ordeal, and you know what? I never really believed it.

Now I do.

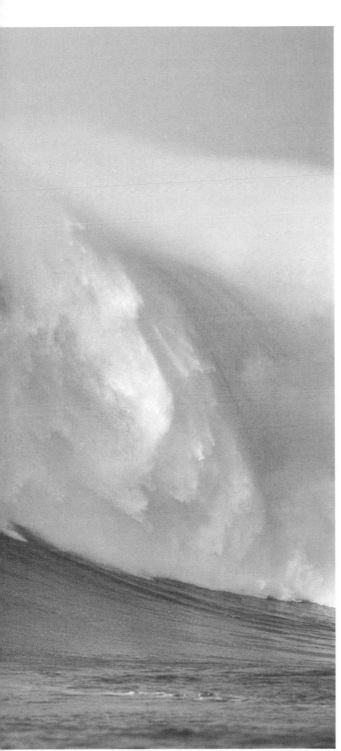

Ken Bradshaw on the biggest wave ever ridden, Outside Log Cabins, Oahu.

PHOTO BY HANK FOTOS

OUTER REEFS

In a December '94 issue of *Surfer,* Mark Foo wrote about "extraordinary waves that were bigger than anything anyone had been able to ride . . . the new frontier of undiscovered and unridden outer reefs—empty, peeling, awe-inspiring cloudbreaks that generations had been watching for years, wondering if they were ridable."

"These," Foo continued, "are the biggest, meanest, most perfect waves you could ever imagine, with nobody out. There now is an underground movement of outer reef explorers . . . guys who live for it. Out there is something so special that some guys, like Jim Broach, who drowned at Phantoms last winter, are willing to die for it."

Everyone knew the dangers of surfing outer reefs. Yet the distant waves were strangely seductive, like siren songs calling—a critical aspect Foo was quick to point out. "While the waves are obviously huge, they also appear deceptively clean and inviting from shore. If you are unfortunate enough to be in the wrong place (which is inevitable, no matter how fit, experienced, and strong you are), there is no way you can make it in unassisted. Jet Skis or boats are highly recommended; the buddy system is mandatory."

Over the years a select few had ventured to the outer reefs, in thumper conditions, and their stories are worth reading. The years 1993 and 1994 simply marked the years when outer reefs caught on and became a special study for big wave artists like Foo. The normal procedure is for two or three surfers to hitch a ride (sometimes up to 2 miles offshore) to the reef break and pick off a few makable beasts while the support boat or Jet Ski lingers on the sidelines, ready to attempt a rescue if all goes wrong or to snag a surfer if he loses his board. And as incurable outer reef surfer Ken Bradshaw says, "At some time you're going to lose your board, no question about it."

Of course, surfers sometimes ventured out with no boat or Jet Ski, simply paddling a mile or so offshore and facing come what may. Doing so required *total* commitment and was a kind of ultimate test in self-reliance. Surfers were bold if they could pull it off, and foolish—or quite possibly dead—if they couldn't. To paddle out (with no support craft) to an outer reef that is really firing is to throw all the marbles, knowing that eventually you are going to face the worse: getting closed out and losing your board. Given that outer reef breaks can form in wildly different locations, and that the peak can shift hundreds of yards between sets, unassisted outer reef surfing remains one of the most perilous adventure sports in the world, comparable to ice climbing without a rope.

The greatest outer reef stories are those that have never been told and probably never will be. Picture the surfer who pulls off the Kam Highway after spotting an obscure outer reef firing 2 miles out at sea. He paddles out and, totally unseen, catches a few mountains, then strokes the long way back to shore and simply drives off, never mentioning the experience to anyone. Or how about if the solo reef surfer gets ruthlessly worked, his board snaps in two, and he has to swim a couple miles back through churning currents, eventually crawling onto the sand more dead than alive? Whatever the outcome, it's hard to imagine a practice more solitary, committing—and terrifying. Solo outer reef surfing, in truly huge surf—is there any arena where man could wield less authority?

Under the best circumstances, where a cadre of expert big wave riders venture out with all possible support, the dangers of surfing big outer reef waves are considerable. To face such dangers, the rewards must also be significant. Said Foo of the experience, "How can I describe the feeling of gazing into a 30-foot-square tube from the shoulder, seeing through the peak like a hole in the ocean, with the pit framing one of the North Shore's tallest buildings, miles away? How do I convey the sights, sounds and sensations that only a handful of humans out of the billions of humans, past, present, and future, will ever experience? What's it like to walk on the moon, Mr. Armstrong?"

SPEAKING OF OUTSIDE REEFS

Fred Van Dyke

*T*o read the magazines one would think that surfing outer reefs was a routine invented just last week. This story, by big wave pioneer Fred Van Dyke, says otherwise. It also says that legendary surfer Flippy Hoffman had a fancy for tackling the outer reefs alone—over 45 years ago. In the meantime the techniques and mind-set have changed considerably, but the great challenges of surfing outer reefs remain the same. The game, it seems, is for keeps.

‡   ‡   ‡

Flippy Hoffman loves the outside reefs. He is a surfer who has always sought the lone wave, the place where he can ride freely, get that fantastic drop, and not have to think about someone paddling up the face as he angles across the wave. Flippy has probably ridden more outside reefs than any other rider, many times alone.

When I first came to the islands, I did not know there was a difference between an outside reef and the inside lineups where most surfers rode—except for Waikiki, which has many outside reefs that you see breaking only when there is a huge south swell.

Alonzo Wiemers and Buzzy Trent took me to the North Shore on a day in 1955 when all of the outside reefs were breaking—or, rather, exploding. Infinite tons of whitewater crashed and blew up with the force of the bottom reefs, and trade winds scanned the broken wave faces. It was a sight I had seen only from afar, when I lived in San Francisco.

We drove to Sunset to find it completely closed out. No decision needed there except to turn around and drive to Makaha. Laniakea was

The power and grace of Fred Van Dyke, pioneer outer-reef surfer. PHOTO FROM VAN DYKE COLLECTION

breaking a mile out in the ocean, so we passed on to Haleiwa. Stopping there, we went into a little coffee shop fronting the sea. From the window we saw the outside break at Haleiwa. It was a snowy mountain avalanching, cascading forward, tons of soup filling the horizon. If it looked huge from three-quarters of a mile away, what would it be like up close?

We finished our coffee and headed back to the car. Buzzy took one more look and said, "Let's just paddle out and look at it, before we go to Makaha."

I looked at Alonzo. He had a pained expression on his face.

Buzzy asked again. Alonzo looked at the avalanching break. The vein on his neck reddened. "Yeah, sure. We'll just go out and give it a little check. What do you think, Fred?"

"Uh, sure, sounds good to me." It looked big, but from shore it looked just like any other break—except for its huge size.

We drove to the Alii Beach, where we could wax up and paddle out through a small channel on the edge of the boat harbor. Pat Curren was sitting on the beach, his board tucked under his arm.

"How does it look?" Buzzy asked.

"Good to me," answered Pat. Buzzy and Pat picked up their boards and headed to the shorebreak.

Alonzo looked at me and said, 'Well, you wanted to ride big waves."

"Yes," I answered, feeling my throat and tongue dry, my heart racing.

"Yes, let's hit it."

We paddled and paddled. I changed from knee paddling five times before I could really see the size of that outside reef break. It was an entirely different dimension.

Lining up, I backed off on the first wave. Buzzy and Pat caught it and disappeared. The set ended, a lull filling in with silence. I looked over at Alonzo drifting toward Kaena Point.

Relaxing for a moment out there was my first mistake. Mistake number two was not turning around fast enough. I looked seaward and saw, like a herd of galloping horses, a set of waves racing across the horizon, their manes waving wildly in the wind. They crossed the outside harbor channel and climbed skyward. They were moving mountains, and I was sitting directly in front of their forward momentum. I paddled frantically outside, barely making it over the first one, only to be confronted by a second, even larger, wave. It sucked out, vacuuming ever higher. I paddled and was suddenly sliding backward down the face. I bottomed out in the pit, pearled tail block first, and fired off, all 30 feet plus cascading down upon me with my board placed less than a foot away from my head.

The initial impact drove me deep into darkness. I told myself to relax, but whitewater wrenched at my arms and legs. I waited for the wave to abate—to let me go as other waves did. This one didn't.

When I had waited long past the time to fight for the surface and air, the soup dispersed into churning blackness. For a moment, time seemed suspended. I felt as if this might be it. What a fool to lose my life this way! In the utter darkness I stroked my last struggle for the surface and bumped my head full force into lava. The soup had driven me into a cave. I was trapped.

I threw up water and surrendered. It wasn't so bad after all. I had chosen to go out; it was my fault. That was all!

And then, just before dizziness prevailed completely, I saw sunlight down by my feet. I was upside down. I had lost all equilibrium and had swum down instead of up, bumping into the bottom.

Surfacing, I got a breath before the next wave broke upon me and repeated the same driving spin cycle. This time I was pushed in toward shore and surfaced to face a near-mile swim through breaking waves, rips, crosscurrents, and shallow reefs. A 20-foot soup carried me over an exposed reef still half a mile out in the ocean, but I made it to the beach. Dragging myself out of the water, I felt much the same sickness as the day when I had nearly drowned in the surf off San Francisco.

Flippy still tries to get me to go outside Haleiwa, to surf Avalanche on big days, when the North Shore regular spots are all closed out. I always say, "No, no way!"

His usual reply: "God, Van Dyke, Avalanche is an old man's dream for riding a truly big wave. It's a cinch. It's got the drop and it was made for guys like you and me."

I think to myself, "Not this old man, Flippy."

HELICOPTER SURFING
OUTSIDE PIPELINE
IN SEARCH OF THE BIGGEST WAVE!

Ace Cool

*I*n 1983, Alec Cooke, aka Ace Cool, declared his intention to take up the "Kaena Point Challenge" and ride 40-foot waves at what was then generally considered the largest ridable surf spot in the world. "I intended to show the world that I didn't want to be a member of the big wave riders club," said Cooke. "I wanted to be chairman of the board." Cooke got his first opportunity to surf Kaena on March 5, 1984, but the waves never reached titanic size. Seven months later, when Outside Pipeline started firing at 30 feet plus, Cooke immediately changed course. After riding waves miles offshore, Cooke had to paddle out through the fearsome break to return to the lineup. Longtime surf photographer Warren Bolster, who has witnessed countless big wave heroics in his years on the North Shore, calls Cooke's performance the "heaviest thing I've ever seen."

Thomas Fuller said (circa 1732) that "every ass loves to hear himself bray," and few surfers have ever brayed as loud as the outrageous Ace Cool. His judgment has been questioned; some consider Cooke more daredevil than calculated athlete. Yet few would deny that Cooke's effort, captured in the following account, helped shift focus to outer reefs, prefiguring the tow-in movement that would sweep the big wave surfing world a decade later.

‡   ‡   ‡

After waiting all through the winter of '83 to '84 for the 40-foot swell necessary to make Kaena Point serve up the biggest ridable waves (theoretically) on the planet, I drew several critical conclusions. Even if

Kaena Point's swell came this year, it might not have the right swell direction, and the wind direction might be wrong as well. Kaena is a particularly moody spot. I also realized that I wasn't obsessed so much with riding Kaena Point but rather by the concept of riding the biggest wave ever ridden (and hopefully getting a picture to prove it), wherever that wave might be found.

Whenever the North Shore swells get truly titanic, numerous huge "cloud" breaks peel on the outside reefs. "Wildman" Neece never rode Kaena Point, but he did catch a hellacious wave at Outside Pipeline (the photograph of which is still probably the most awesome shot in all of surfdom). Wildman, among others (including Greg Noll), had already proven that Outside Pipe was ridable—and survivable. There was little chance of hitting the bottom out there because it was so deep. In a sense, the outer reefs seemed safer than Kaena Point. Of course drowning was still a strong possibility, but it always is in waves over 25 feet. In any event I would have the modern convenience of a helicopter to pluck me out if things got really heavy.

I decided that in order to prepare for the challenge of riding a 40-foot wave at Kaena Point (or elsewhere), I would launch a personal assault against the various outer reefs, whenever the waves got over 20 feet plus and appeared clean enough to ride. I was especially fascinated by the huge right at Outside Pipeline.

I had watched Outside Pipeline during the Off Shore Masters in 1984 and noticed occasional sets that looked insanely clean—and ridable. At Outside Pipe, the right peak peels off as perfectly as the left, although maybe a bit faster. But the size! I flashed on the picture of an ant in a washing machine.

On the morning of January 5, 1985, surf photographer Warren Bolster came pounding at my door. "Alec, you're blowing it!" he screamed. "The waves are 20 feet high and getting bigger! Why'd you take your phone off the hook?" I ran to the beach to behold 20-foot-plus walls grinding on the outside reefs.

After some quick calls to the fire chief to allow for a helicopter landing at the Pupukea Fire Station, we met Royal Helicopter's Ron Thrash as he landed at exactly 2:00 P.M. My videographer, Berne Kuebitz (who was involved with the original project last March at Kaena Point), showed up right on time. We loaded my 12-foot Brewer board into the hold section of the helicopter, accomplished by removing the doors. The board stuck out 3 feet on each side. I jumped into my bright orange wet suit and we were ready to go. Just then Frankie Ramos motored up. A notorious big wave Jet Skier from the Flippy Hoffman/Brian Surrat school, he had his Jet Ski in tow, fueled and ready to roll. "Need some help out there?" he hinted. "Sure," I screamed. "You might be able to help me get back to the lineup or find my board if I lose it!" I told him I was headed for the giant right outside of Pipeline, the one that peels toward Log Cabins and Waimea Bay. We could all see it from the fire station. It looked perfect—majestically huge and awesome, even from 2 miles away.

Waimea Bay was packed with surfers on this, one of the biggest and best days of the winter. It was 20 to 25 feet and evidently still coming up. I didn't want to estimate how big the waves were at Outside Pipeline—we'd see when we got there!

We took off at 2:30 P.M. Berne and pilot Ron Thrash manned the cockpit, while Warren and I strapped ourselves into the hold, manhandling the 12-foot surfboard to keep it from buffeting about owing to forceful winds blowing off the copter's blades. In several minutes we gained Outside Pipeline, where we hovered for awhile, checking the sets and watching the lineup. A huge right broke about a mile and a half offshore from Inner Pipe and it looked pretty lined up, though with each oncoming set the peak would shift hundreds of yards in either direction. "Are you ready?" asked the pilot. "Let me watch another set," I replied anxiously. This time a bigger set came through, lining up more to the west, outside of Log Cabins. "Aha!" I shouted. "Let's fly west a little and you can drop me off out there so I can paddle in toward the peak from a distance. That way I won't get cleaned up!"

I threw the 12-foot Brewer gun out the door and down toward the water so it wouldn't get near the rotors. "Should I wear the oxygen tank?" I thought to myself. "I may have to do a lot of swimming out there." I decided against it (though I was soon to find out I'd made the wrong decision). Then I launched myself into the water, pushing down and away from the strut with my hands. I'd learned this trick doing helicopter jumps for a Japanese television commercial. I didn't want to get caught in those rotors.

I jumped on my board, and as I paddled around it appeared that I was way outside the lineup; but I soon found myself scratching for the horizon as massive swells loomed menacingly. "How big is it out here anyway?" I didn't want to think about it. Then, just as I was about to get hammered inside by a set roughly as high as the Rocky Mountains, Frankie Ramos blasted up on his Jet Ski. I hung onto his feet as he maxed the screaming engine and rapidly towed my surfboard and me beyond the approaching monsters. We barely made it through set after set, until finally I was in position. "Well, it's now or never," I thought, as another gnarly set swept toward us. Frankie roared away in the direction of the channel, leaving me like a Christian to face the lions.

I stroked into the first wave of the set, but I couldn't quite catch it. Maybe I hesitated looking down at that killer drop. I mean—who wouldn't?! Then another, even meaner looking wave bore down on me. It seemed I was committed. Whether I wanted that wave or not, it wanted me. I scratched like a dog, cranking up the sheer liquid wall. Halfway up the face I whipped around and started my downhill run. The wave lifted straight up and down underneath me. It was totally top to bottom and steep as the side of a high-rise building—so steep, in fact, that I couldn't angle down the face. The only way to go was straight down. I didn't look back; rather I set my sights on the infinite right-hand wall stretching before me. It felt like an ultimate Waimea Bay, but would I make the section? "No way!" I decided. The wave pitched all the way down the line! I straightened out and projected as far out into the flat as I could. Then I proned out, hanging on to the tail section of my board with all my might and keeping my weight back so I wouldn't pearl. The whitewater covered me up, but I popped out and bounced along in front of that wave like a kangaroo—and kept bounding all the way to Inside Pipeline, more than a mile distant.

This would have been a good time to quit, but no. I had to get tubed— and besides, we still had helicopter time left! A war was taking place inside my skull. Then, like an answer, along came Frankie on the Jet Ski. "You want to go for another run or retire to Waimea?" he joked. "You think we can get back outside again?" I asked. We did, but only by the skin of our teeth. We almost got caught inside as huge Outside Pipeline lefts ground through mercilessly.

After he got me outside, Frankie went in. He was running low on gas. So was the helicopter. I took off on another giant right, only to find that the wind had come up quite a bit. Halfway down the face, I caught complete air and then reconnected as a powerful gust momentarily turned my surfboard into a hang glider. "Too heavy," I gasped. I shot back up and over the top in the nick of time as the wave closed out.

The wind was really picking up now. I stroked into one more huge right, but as it peeled off toward Kaena Point I saw I couldn't make it and would have to go left. Quickly I realized that trying to go left was equally as impossible as trying to go right. I made like a deep-sea diver and dove, straight down, and pronto! I was glad that I wasn't wearing a leash.

When you're down about 20 or 30 feet, with a 30-foot wave passing overhead, it gets very dark and quiet. It's like your own little world down there.

I call it the Black Zone, an eerie and hostile place somewhere between a Black Hole and the Twilight Zone. Nasty! Yet somehow it's sort of peaceful and serene and warm—kind of like a cross between the womb and the grave.

On sheer willpower I finally made it to the surface and was amazed to spot my board floating nearby. I stroked over frantically, climbed on, and looked around. "Well . . . I'm still alive. Better call it a day!" I thought. But, no. Something inside me said I just had to catch one more wave. Besides, I might as well take advantage of the fact that I was the only one out.

Then came the cleanup set of the day! I must have stroked over 10 or 11 mammoth walls—each bigger than the last—when finally, Ms. Gargantua herself reared up from the deep. She had her nose about 40 feet in the air, and it looked like she was going to blow it right on me! So I made like the proverbial groundhog who has just seen his shadow and went looking for the submarine races. Maybe this time I would get lucky and make it to the bottom where I could hold onto the reef, although I wasn't sure what good that would do. Maybe there was a lava tube down there with an air pocket in which I could hole for a few days until the swell subsided. Damn, I hadn't even made out a will. That's okay. I was sure that the boys would divide up all my surfboards equally.

But this was no joke. I was beyond the Black Zone and into the Void itself. I could feel the pressure from the depth. That wave must have driven me down 50 feet. At least I didn't have to worry about hitting bottom out here. Too bad I didn't have that air tank—I was going to need it. Is there air in Heaven? Is there surf in Heaven? Was I even going to Heaven? It felt like I was headed in the opposite direction. I waited for the turbulence above to subside. I could feel it, like the ominous presence of dark clouds just before a heavy rain. I swam up and up and up and up and up—and it was still pitch black. I began to wonder if I was swimming down or sideways. Or was I just dreaming I was swimming? Maybe I was already unconscious. Then suddenly I saw the light! Instinct took over and somehow I broke the surface, coughing and gasping and seeing stars before my eyes. I was weak—I had just spend two solid minutes underwater at the very least. But who's counting?

The helicopter was hovering way inside, directing me to my board and trying to blow it back out to me with the wind from the rotors. It was a long swim! I finally made it to my board. The helicopter was almost out of gas and so was I. Since by this time I was close to shore, I sent the helicopter back to home base. They could have dropped me a rope, but I wanted to save that magic board. (Unfortunately, Owl Chapman broke it the next day at Waimea Bay.)

Alec Cooke's postcard commemorating his incredible feat is a bestseller in Hawaii. PHOTO BY WARREN BOLSTER

I paddled in through the 15-foot shorebreak at Log Cabins. As I came crawling up onto the beach, kissing the sand like Robinson Crusoe after he'd been lost at sea for months, a small crowd near the lifeguard tower broke into applause. I checked in with the lifeguards and they radioed to the fire station that I was all right. Mission Impossible was over and I was glad that I didn't self-destruct!

As the sun took a nosedive into Kaena Point, I sat and watched a few more awesome sets peeling through Outside Pipeline. It felt good to be back on the beach—real good! But I knew I was already addicted to the Outer Reef.

TODD CHESSER: NOT FADE AWAY

Ben Marcus

*H*ow ironic that someone's aquatic sanctuary could likewise be his grave. Some say that the essence of surfing is a soulful one, hinging on both a profound respect for and a deep connection with the sea. There's also the energy and grace of surfing—the ease of dropping into a whistling barrel and finding a piece of heaven. But for every piece of heaven found in big surf, there's also a piece of hell. Consider horrendous wipeouts, where the beast can drill you to the ocean floor and pin you there like a mounted bug. These are all elements of big wave surfing. On the morning of February 13, 1997, at Outside Alligators, Todd Chesser, Aaron Lambert, and Cody Graham paddled out to catch some user-friendly surf—nothing of epic proportions. But then came hell in liquid form, and it carried away one of Hawaii's most charismatic big wave champions. Here's the gut-wrenching story of what began as a calm day and ended in unforeseeable tragedy.

‡   ‡   ‡

The surf forecast for Thursday, February 13, called for a quick-rising swell along Hawaii's north-facing beaches. That morning, Cody Graham and Aaron Lambert checked Pipeline but didn't like what they saw. Lambert suggested driving back toward Waimea, to scope an outer reef in front of his house at Alligator Rock. Cody had never surfed Outside Alligators, but he was game. When they arrived, they ran into Todd Chesser, who also was checking the spot and seemed ready to go.

"Before we got there, a civil defense guy pulled over and warned Todd that the swell was going to rise fast through the day," Lambert said. "He had seen Todd standing there with his surfboard and suggested that he not go out."

Chesser's reaction to the troubled bureaucrat is easy to imagine—outwardly polite, inwardly sarcastic, and overly unconcerned. At age 28, Chesser had more than a decade of Hawaiian big wave experience, and he had earned the right to trust his own judgment. Originally from Florida, Chesser moved to Hawaii in the '70s with his mother, Jeannie, after his father was killed in an auto accident. He learned to surf in town but soon gravitated toward the North Shore. Chesser loved the power and the challenge of North Shore surf, the physical and spiritual pleasure of surfing there, and the close friendships he developed. But Chesser was also a stern critic of the surf and media scene. He despised pretenders and frauds, and he watched with growing concern as the places he loved to surf became overrun with newcomers, bodyboarders, and others.

In recent years, Chesser found it more and more difficult to stay ahead of the crowds, and he watched with growing despair as his happy hunting ground, the outer reefs, swarmed with serious big wave surfers and tow-in wannabes. In the past year, Chesser had even discussed the unthinkable: moving away from the North Shore for good. He was engaged to a California girl named Janet Rollins and looked forward to their August wedding—and beyond that a normal adult life on the mainland.

The morning of February 13, Outside Alligators was pristine. No Jet Skis, no surfers, just big, blue, empty peaks a half mile from shore. Around 9:00 A.M., Chesser stuck a swim fin into his wet suit and paddled out on a 10' 0", leading Lambert and Graham through the turmoil of the inner reef.

"It was a beautiful day," Graham said. "Dead calm, sunny. The surf was 12 to 15 feet—not giant by outer reef standards, but we were alert and kept clear of the impact zone. We were real careful in that first hour, and we didn't catch many waves. We'd learned from experience to be careful."

After a couple of hours, Chesser asked Lambert what time it was. "I remember looking at my watch and it was 11:00 A.M.," Lambert said. "Todd said that was when the civil defense guy predicted the swell was going to show. I said my watch was 10 minutes fast. We began paddling outside, and sure enough about 10 minutes later we saw a huge set coming right at us."

Graham and Chesser were in the lead and Lambert was just behind, but all three were caught. The trio dove through the face of the first one, but the second wave was bigger. "Cody and Chesser were side by side," Lambert recalled. "I saw Chesser stand up on his board and dive under, trying to go deep. That was the last time I saw him alive." Lambert took the brunt of the second wave and was pushed far inside, leaving Graham and Chesser in the impact zone for the third wave of the set. This one was even bigger.

"I don't know where that third wave came from or who made it or what," Graham said. "I couldn't comprehend how big it was. It was like a mountain, breaking top to bottom. Todd and I were paddling like crazy for the channel, but I knew we were in a serious position. I just bailed and started diving deep. I saw Todd stand up on his board and dive under."

The wave impacted almost directly on top of the two. "I thought to myself. 'Why am I even going under this wave? It's too big. Too powerful. We're never going to make it,'" Graham said. "After that, I don't remember anything. I went into the green room. Where I was—everything was green. And I must have hit bottom, because when I came up I had scratches all over me."

Graham doesn't know how long he was under, how many waves passed over, or how he came up. The next thing he knew, he was on the surface puking, crying, and looking for Todd. "I felt like Jell-O. I was dizzy, had no strength, and could barely paddle. I looked around and saw Todd's body, just floating there. I started screaming for help because I was so dizzy I could barely move."

Lambert also took the third wave hard, and when he came up he saw Todd floating face down. "I thought he was kidding around," said Lambert. "But then I heard Cody screaming and crying and I knew Todd was in trouble."

For Graham and Lambert, the next 45 minutes were a surfer's worst nightmare. They were exhausted and alone a half mile out to sea, trying to bring life into the unconscious body of their friend. "We tried CPR. I tried clearing his throat. We tried everything we could, but Todd was full of water and there was no sign of movement," Graham said. With the ocean now gone calm, the three drifted slowly shoreward. "I was praying someone had seen us and that the Jet Skis would arrive any minute," Lambert said. "But no one came."

As they approached the inner reef, Lambert gave up his board and began swimming to the beach, leaving Graham to help Chesser through the inside lineup. "I was dead beat," Graham said. "I was half drowned myself. I was tired and dizzy and I couldn't hold onto Todd. I tried to hold onto his wet suit, anything, but I couldn't. That was a terrible feeling—to lose hold of him."

Lambert began screaming for help as he got close to shore, and his cries attracted the attention of residents, who immediately called 911. By the time Lambert got to shore, North Shore lifeguards Terry Ahue and Abe Lerner were heading out on their Skis. They found Chesser at Marijuanas and brought him to shore.

Lambert rode with Chesser in the ambulance to Wahiawa General Hospital: "The whole time I was praying to God, asking him if there was anything I could do to help Todd. But I knew by then it was too late. Cody and I worked on him as hard as we could, but it wasn't enough."

Chesser was pronounced dead, of drowning, at Wahiawa Hospital.

News of the tragedy spread fast throughout Hawaii and the surfing world. In California, the Action Sports Retailer trade show was coming to a close that same afternoon as the tragic news entered the building. Many of Chesser's closest friends were at the show, and people were crying in the aisles and outside the Long Beach Convention Center as the grim fact sunk in. Chesser had drowned. Cheese was gone.

Brock Little was at LAX, about to fly home to Hawaii, and he got the bad news from his dad when he called home from the airport. "I couldn't believe it," Little said. "Todd Chesser? Drowned? How? Why? I felt like puking. I'd been friends with Todd since the 12-and-under menehunes contests."

Chesser was the third professional surfer to drown in big surf in three years. Mark Foo died at Maverick's in December 1995, and Donnie Solomon drowned a year later, to the day, at Waimea Bay. Chesser's drowning is likely to have a profound impact on the collective psyche of the big wave surfing world. Everybody knew Todd, everybody adored him, and everybody was shocked that a man of his experience and physical conditioning could drown in his own backyard.

A few days after his nightmare experience, Cody Graham had had enough: "I quit. I left my board at the beach that day and just walked away. Todd Chesser was solid as a rock. He was one of the fittest men on the North Shore. I don't know why he drowned and I didn't. I came that close to going with him. I quit."

TIDAL WAVE!

Derek Hynd (as told to him by Felipe Pomar)

*R*emember those classic old Japanese monster movies, budgeted at about
*50 bucks, where the dragon rears from the deep and tidal waves stream
off his back and course shoreward where they level many buildings as
though they were matchboxes—which they are. Well, this time, change locations
to Peru, replace the dragon with an earthquake—which produces the same
dreadful tidal waves as the Japanese production—and make it all for real. Then
stick a world-champion surfer and his partner out in the break, right in harm's
way. Preposterous? Read on.*

‡   ‡   ‡

Every grand achievement in Peruvian Felipe Pomar's 44 years—North
Shore veteran, 1965 World Surfing Champion, seven-time Duke Classic
finalist, religious big wave hunter, 007-like bachelor and whatever else—
fades into the background when compared to one of the most
catastrophically nightmarish surfing experiences imaginable. In fact, what
happened to Felipe and his old friend Pitts Block had such impact on their
lives that neither spoke of it for five years.

When Felipe told me this story, he spoke fluent English with a piquant
Latin twang and paused regularly to let the major points sink in. What
follows is his story:

‡   ‡   ‡

It was October 3, 1974, a time when Pitts Block and myself were the only
year-round surfers in Peru. The day was normal in every way. Not a big
swell by any means, perhaps 3 feet, and as we stood on the beach at La

Isla ready to go surfing. Righthand waves similar to Trestles or Malibu were breaking alongside an island just offshore. I'd known Pitts for many years, and he was a fearless big wave pioneer and car racer. Suddenly he started screaming over and over, pointing out to sea. I stared at him in amazement, too shocked by his actions to follow his eyes. I'd never seen Pitts show any sign of fear before.

He ran off into the village, and I still did not turn my eyes away from him. Then I heard the noise, and the *terremoto* [earthquake] hit. It sounded like the world was breaking apart—horses, houses, mountains, and the oceans—all roaring.

The island was moving everywhere . . . it was obvious the epicenter had been far out to sea. I looked around and thought, "No buildings to fall on me here." I held on to my board, to use it as a bridge in case the earth opened up. In the village I saw walls shaking, then shaking at 45-degree angles, then collapsing. There was nowhere to go. Thirty seconds passed, and still the world was shaking—dust, noise, vibration everywhere. One minute passed. I began believing this was more than *terremoto*—this was the end of the world. After an eternity, perhaps five minutes, it stopped. Then it started again, then stopped.

When the dust cleared I searched for Pitts in the village. I found him and we went back to the beach. We talked for a long time, deciding against making our way back to Lima because Pitts had seen the destruction of Lima in 1949, and he felt this quake was just as strong. The city would surely be devastated. After an hour I jokingly said, "Well, let's go surfing." Pitts said, "Okay."

We stroked out. The surf was small, and we thought we'd get good waves maybe with a little help from the terremoto. I wasn't worried—in Hawaii I'd listened to tidal-wave alerts since 1963, and I didn't believe in them.

Everything was normal. After perhaps 15 minutes Pitts paddled up to me and said, "Felipe, I want to go in." "Why?" I asked. "Is anything wrong?" He answered, "In all my years of surfing I just had the worst wipeout of my life—on a 3-foot wave!" So I said, "Okay, just one more wave."

But I waited too long.

A current hit us very suddenly, and as we pointed our boards toward shore and began to paddle, we were swept right out to sea. I started paddling like I had a 25-foot great white behind me and I didn't look up once. But the rip was 10 times as strong as anything I'd experienced at Sunset Beach, and when I was exhausted I finally brought my eyes up—and saw that we were racing backward! I told myself, "Relax, Felipe, don't fight it. Your life depends on it." Pitts yelled something at me, and I replied, "God, don't talk; I've got to make a decision." I'd been in the biggest Hawaiian surf but this was different, totally out of control! In minutes we were drawn over a mile out to sea, both on 7' 6" boards. The ocean had gigantic boils and whirlpools coming up out of the depths, and Hawaiian-style 10-foot wave-chops were upon us from 300-degree angles. Pitts said, "Let's find a slip." I cussed! The whole bay was being sucked out to sea—we along with it—and the only explanations I could think of were either the ocean was pouring into a massive hole somewhere or a tidal wave was forming up far out to sea. It was all I could do to hope for the latter. And if it came, it would be major. The *terremoto* had been too powerful for a small wave, and I'd seen the biggest waves in Peru before. I thought, "It will be bigger than 30. How big? 300 feet? No, 3,000 feet—and the continental shelf goes out so far it will be formed up and breaking by the time we ever see it."

At that point I saw some huge lefts breaking perhaps a mile across from us, tearing for shore. I cried out to Pitts. "I have a plan! Follow me and don't talk." So we tried to paddle across the current, hoping to connect with the breaking waves before being swept to oblivion or swallowed by a tsunami. We had a chance. We were making some ground. Still, the ocean was horribly turbulent. At the same time I was staring at the horizon, believing the 3,000-footer was closing in on us.

A long time passed. Eventually we made the lineup. All I said to Pitts was, "Catch a wave and don't lose your board!" The waves were solid—and big. I took off first and caught a nice lefthander, climbing and dropping on the face. Part of me was screaming, "I must be mad! If I lose my board I'll be swept away and lost at sea!" But the other part was saying, "Keep standing and turning. It's got good shape. Besides, if the tidal wave comes it will be my last wave, anyway."

The wave filled in, and I finally lost it, still a quarter mile from shore. As I paddled toward the beach, what I saw shocked me. The wave I'd been riding kept going, then jacked up a fishing boat and threw it above a retaining wall and into a building, smashing it to bits. But it didn't matter: even if a hundred hungry lions had been on the sand I still would have gone in. I paddled around the debris and made it to shore. Pitts came dragging in behind me a little later.

People came down from the hills, amazed that we were still alive. They had run for the high ground after the *terremoto*, only to see us paddle out for a surf, then disappear into the horizon as the entire bay was sucked dry. No doubt, the waves we rode back in were tidal waves. Fortunately, we did not lose our boards and the 3,000-footer never came. For the next several hours, the Pacific Ocean receded and returned with diminishing intensity.

TODOS SANTOS

The discovery of Mexico's Todos Santos (All Saints) marked the first time a venue—other than on Oahu's North Shore—was judged a world-class, big wave break. Soon thereafter, Maverick's, in Central California, received the same billing. "I remember when we first started surfing Todos Santos in 1986," Mike Parson wrote in 1998. "We just couldn't believe that there were waves like that on our coastline. After all the coverage came out, we pretty much thought we'd have the next couple swells, then it would be over: Everybody and their brother would be out there. As it happened, a few of the people who were drawn by the hype went out there and got worked. Now, almost 10 years later, you go out there on a big day and it's pretty much the same crew." This underscores the fact that big wave riding is sufficiently challenging that even specialists need time to dial a place in. And to be sure, when the big waves spool in at Todos Santos, even champions give them respect—or get worked.

*Mike Parson at
Todos Santos.*
PHOTO BY ROB GILLEY

TODOS SANTOS DIARY

JANUARY 1998

Mike Parson

*T*uesday, *January 13:* It was a nice warm-up swell to start off the season. I surfed Todos Santos with Alistair Craft, Shane Beschen, and Dino Andino. It was a little disappointing because it was not nearly as big as we had hoped, but still in the 10- to 12-foot range. However, one 15-foot set did pick us off. I guess you could say that this swell was the calm before the storm.

Tuesday, January 20: Well, this was one of those days you never forget. There were ominous black clouds, a nasty side shore wind, and an empty Killers lineup with sets easily 25 feet high on any macho scale. Any mistake on this day was life threatening. After watching a few sets, we decided "What the heck are we doing here? Let's give it a go." Alistair Craft and I paddled into the lineup. I caught a quick wave to get my confidence up. I was thinking, "Cool. The waves are ridable. Just play it smart." Within 10 minutes we were edging over the top of what Randy Laine was calling 50-foot face waves—and he wasn't exaggerating. Randy was out doing water patrol on his Jet Ski and riding a few of these beasts for kicks. Taylor Knox came out to join us and paddled straight into some huge waves. Not long after, the moment we had all feared came true. Taylor and I were caught in front of one of those waves you always have nightmares about. We were in the worst possible spot—no chance of getting through. I heard Taylor laugh as we paddled at this beast. It's hard to judge the size of waves when they are in that realm. All I know is this was as bad as it gets—and we both knew it. You just hold your breath and pray that God lets you live—that was all we could do. After being

110

held under to the brink of passing out, I popped up a few seconds before the next wave hit and instantly looked for Taylor—no sign of him. He did surface for a brief second before the next wave rolled over us though. Then we both surfaced, and I was a good 50 yards in from Taylor after getting rag-dolled underwater for the length of the lineup. Taylor's 9' 6" board was floating in three pieces. He was swimming toward me with that "deer in the headlights" look. He cracked a smile and we both began to laugh and wonder, "How the hell did we pull that off?" Taylor tried to reach the beach to find the remains of his board but was quickly swept into the rocks. Randy Laine came to the rescue on his Jet Ski and pulled Taylor back to the boat. We tried to ride a few more waves, but for the most part we were done for the day. All together we only rode nine waves between us, but many sets went by unridden. Overall, the place kicked our ass.

Tuesday, January 27: Joe Deskins and I went out with Rob Brown. Either nobody else could go this day or they were just a lot smarter than Joe and I. Once again, Killers was at least 20 feet. We were the only ones out there. It was sunny and the waves were beautiful. We each had a few unreal rides before the north wind came up. It was getting bigger and Rob Brown kept telling me, "Go Snips, that one's 50 grand!" and I kept saying, "Of course it is, but what good is 50 grand if you're not around to spend it?" [Rob, of course, was referring to K2's $50,000 Big Wave Challenge contest. Taylor won this contest in 1998 with a photograph (taken by Les Walker) of him surfing at Todos Santos.] Had Brock Little been there, the money surely would have been his. Sitting outside by myself, waiting for that last wave, I once again was caught inside by the biggest set of the day. This was again a very close call for me. I did the stand-up-and-dive thing to get as deep as I could, and the wave shook me to the core. I got up just in time for a quick breath before diving under the next wave for as long as I could possibly hold my breath. I proceeded to paddle back out and get sucked over the falls on the very next set. I was done. For the second day in a row the place kicked our ass.

Friday, January 30: It was the "Swell of All Swells." I couldn't sleep for three days with all the reports of the gigantic swell. Hawaii was maxing out and it was headed our direction. We had an awesome crew of guys this time: Taylor Knox, Mike Stewart, Keith Malloy, Allen Sarlo, Terrence McNulty, Alistair Craft, Marty Hoffman, Evan Slater, and Josh Loya. At first light, the surf was absolutely perfect—15 foot. Taylor, Alistair, Mike, and I surfed for the first two hours by ourselves. Taylor broke his second 9' 6" in two weeks after being stuck too deep on the most beautiful wave of the morning. Mike Stewart stole the show when he swung around late and got 20 feet of air on one of the meanest waves I've ever seen. But the real madman of the day by far was Terrence McNulty, who paddled out late when the wind was up out of the north and the surf was hitting that 20-foot-plus range. He paddled straight past all of us, swung around on the wave of the day, and made the drop no problem. He continued to paddle past every one of us and hooked three more set waves. We all looked at each other and said to ourselves, "This kid is sick." By noon the wind was blowing hard, so we all hit the boats and raced for Salsipuedes. We turned the corner to get our first look at the 8-foot perfect break point. It looked just like 8-foot Burleigh Heads out there. We surfed all afternoon and took turns getting barrel after barrel. I kept waiting for someone to pinch me and wake me up from this daydream because the waves do not get this good on this coast. Once again, Terrence stole the show by getting a stand-up barrel that you could fit two trucks in. In his own words: "I think that was the best wave of my life." We all drove home in a daze. This El Niño thing is for real. Why can't every winter be like this? It sure is sweet to live in California.

BIG TIME

Dave Parmenter

*H*ere, *Dave Parmenter gets philosophical on us, reflecting on mortality and advancing the now common notion that small surf is small time no matter how you gussy it up. Both themes neatly dovetail into an early Todos Santos experience worth reading.*

‡   ‡   ‡

There comes a time in every man's life when he faces his own mortality for the first time. The realization swamps him that, yes, horror of horrors, he is like everybody else—expendable and fragile. For many young men, this is the crossroads in their lives, when the boyhood aura of indestructibility evaporates. All too often the youthful dreams of heroics and achievement swirl down the drain soon after. Walking on the moon, flying a fighter plane, or running away to become a pirate suddenly become childish fantasies. The young man who wanted to be like Indiana Jones starts reading the *Wall Street Journal*. The waist thickens. The hair thins. A picket fence sprouts overnight. Some life-threatening incident had clearly defined the parameters of his existence, and that knowledge of mortality causes a strategic withdrawal from the front lines of life, to the safety of the Barca-Lounger and the beer-can pyramid.

Unlike most of humanity, surfers face their mortality not on the freeway, football field, or hospital ward but underwater. The ocean is a world unto itself, and the specters of death are many. Just paddling out, you are entering the food chain. There are poisonous snakes, jagged reefs, rip currents, and a million hidden dangers to contend with. At the fore of this gauntlet are Big Waves. No surfer can honestly say that riding huge surf is not the greatest challenge of the sport. The few men who pioneered the monstrous surf of Oahu's North Shore, and those who continue that effort today, can, in my opinion, take their place alongside the early arctic explorers, Himalayan mountaineers, and test pilots of the jet age as the baddest men that have ever lived. All of these men face their own puny mortality time and time again—and go back for more.

The surfing world is now taking a renewed interest in big waves. There seems to be a popular fervor for news of places like Waimea, Kaena Point, and Outside Log Cabins. Boards in the 9- to 10-foot range are fast becoming common tools, where once they were only ornamental talismans for all but the most committed surfers. Today's big wave riders are swelling in popularity. A few are becoming as renowned as the more mainstream ASP (Association of Surfing Professionals) deities, and in contrast, a few of the world-tour boys are becoming less popular as a result. A 20-foot Waimea wave has a way of separating the wheat from the chaff better than a 2-foot Burleigh Heads wave, a fact the general surfing public is beginning to realize. As their attention wanders from the insular, self-hyped, homogenized "me too" world of the ASP tour, they seem to be saying collectively, "Enough! Two-foot waves are boring!"

I believe surfing is entering a grassroots revival of *real* surfing—sort of an upbeat soul era, minus the drugs and localism of the late '60s and early '70s. The writing is on the wall for the last decade of competitive and commercial zeal. Pro surfing has become too listless and contrived to support itself permanently. The big wave revival is the cornerstone of this movement. The challenge of huge surf as a standard weeds out the phonies, the bikini contests, and the priority buoys. It's a timely catharsis for a lifestyle teetering dangerously on the brink of May Company Acceptance and Big Business.

While this renaissance is beginning in the monster surf of the North Shore, it could spread to other areas of the surfing realm. Huge, unridden surf frequently happens the world over, often just as challenging and exciting as the Hawaiian standard, if not as ideal. And besides, who knows? Who has really gone looking for 20-foot surf in such likely places as South Africa, Western Australia, Indonesia, or the Pacific Northwest? Perhaps the big wave revival, coupled with crowd pressure on the North Shore and a new surfing mood, may spur surfers to explore completely new frontiers of riding huge waves in all corners of the globe—to go, quite literally, where no man has gone before.

Islas Todos Santos, or All Saints Islands, are two tiny islets about 9 miles off the Baja seaport of Ensenada. Uninhabited and desolate, there are seven quality surf breaks in little over a mile of cumulative shoreline. Although the islets have been surfed for over 20 years and repeatedly photographed on smaller days, it is largely unknown that Todos Santos is home to one of the truly world-class big waves. During stronger winter groundswells, the northwest tip of the smaller northern islet regularly reaches the 10- to 12-foot range. These waves are largely unsurfed, as most visiting surfers don't bring the proper equipment, namely boards over 7 feet. For years there had been many reports and rumors of even bigger surf; about how it never closed out at any size, or how surfers felt the island quake with the fury of the largest surf they'd ever seen outside of Hawaii. Clean, offshore—and unridden.

At three in the morning, shivering in a cocoon of damp beach towels in a trailer in Baja California, it's hard to feel the energy it takes to be a surfer. Tom Curren, Chris Burke, and I had driven all night, racing a new swell down from Central California, to get there by dawn. In a few hours we would have to be at the dock in Ensenada for the boat ride across the channel to Islas Todos Santos. Sleep seemed impossible; we were chilled to the core and dazed from eight hours of driving. Outside, an erratic Santa Ana wind shook the trailer, and between gusts we could hear the telltale boom of rising surf. On a previous trip to the islets we had encountered 10- to 12-foot surf, and this time the swell was *much* bigger. The conditions promised to be flawless. We played the possibilities over and over in our minds, teeth chattering in the predawn chill. With only two hours of sleep and a quick Seven-Eleven breakfast, it seemed a daunting prospect that we would soon be waxing up to surf waves that would be, in all probability, well over 12 feet. Out in the bed of our pickup truck our 7' 6"s and 7' 10"s drummed against each other in the wind. And suddenly they seemed small.

Larry Moore, aka Flame, our photographer, was absolutely rabid with excitement. I watched him, jealous of his energy, as he loaded the boat with all the boards, camera gear, food, water, and duffels. He was raving about the light we would have when the sun came up. F-stops and ASA numbers spat from his mouth like a viper. He was still bubbling when, halfway out of the harbor, the speedboat's motor just quit. For good. Flame didn't even get upset.

While we were reloading our gear into a smaller, very unseaworthy-looking skiff, I asked Flame where the rest of the "crew" was. So far there were only the four of us.

"Normally even the rumor of a photo trip causes a frenzy like a gold rush," Flame said. Then he shook his head, "But this time I told 'em to bring big boards, that it could be huge. They thought I meant 6' 4"s or 6' 6"s. Ha! All of a sudden it became so very important for so-and-so to rearrange his sock drawer and what's-his-name to take his cat in for a flea dip."

This time we made it out of the harbor. The freshness of the open ocean revived us from our all-night driving stupor. There is nothing like going surfing by boat. Just being at sea, well-equipped and moving forward, is the very essence of optimism. Like my friend Jeff Chamberlain says, "If there's a parking lot in front of it, it ain't surf."

Chris and I snacked on Snickers bars washed down with Gatorade, while Tom struggled to warm a huge lump of wax under his armpit. Flame readied his waterhousing, polished the lensport, checked the seal of the O-rings. Ahead of our yawning skiff loomed the islets. The golden morning sun highlighted the lighthouse and clefts in the rock face. An eerie mist hung over the northern tip. Even from 8 miles away we could see waves breaking and white spray erupting into the winter sun like volcanic snow.

An hour later we were anchored in the channel, climbing over each other to wax our boards, suit up, and tie on our leashes. One hundred yards away, 10- to 12-foot peaks rammed into the teeth of the offshore breeze. There was not a soul out. We leashed our longest boards: Tommy a 7' 8" single-fin, Chris a 7' 6" thruster, and I a 7' 10" single-fin. I have never felt such anxiety to get into the lineup. Huge, perfect waves, completely empty! The three of us sprint-paddled toward the outside peak, hooting and screaming each time a thundering set folded over and barreled toward the inside point.

Reaching the lineup during a lull, we positioned ourselves relative to the boils from the last set. Flame was just getting into position in the channel when the entirety of the Pacific Ocean began rearing up in front of us. A set approached off the point, a huge Waimea-like wall that refracted and accelerated with the curve of the headland into a jacking Sunset Beach peak. The sheer mass of the waves was unlike anything I have ever seen outside of Hawaii.

I took the first wave, testing the fin placement with the longest bottom turn I could muster to evade a very frisky end-bowl. Kicking out, I watched Tom swing it around at the last second on an even bigger wave. A skipping drop, high-compression bottom turn, a 2-g top turn, and he was back in the channel next to me as we watched the rest of the set unload, giddy with excitement. Out the back Chris had the lineup to himself. A wave approached that seemed to possess the very soul of the devil.

Burke whipped it around—what else can you do when your friends are hooting in the channel? Now there are quite a few girls out there who believe, knowing Chris, that he can't even say the word "commitment" (the C-word!), but he bulldogged to his feet as this beast of a wave was already pitching and somehow hung on beneath the vaulting lip long enough to beat it to the trough. From there he fought a losing battle with 40 feet of churning soup. But what the hell, he went for it.

Tom dominated the session, recklessly asserting himself on waves no one else wanted any part of. He surfed with a freedom and flair befitting his notoriety in the surfing world. Often we paddled for the bigger waves together, one of us conceding to the better positioning of the other at the last possible second. Tommy seemed to always get the better of these exchanges.

The swell seemed to grow stronger as the tide came up. The sets were consistently 12 feet, with the odd rogue waves pushing that mark. Really huge sets broke on some strange reef pattern outside, which confounded us for hours. These superwaves would jack horrendously, then go bottomless. The entry point was hideously disfigured by a multilayered boil, making takeoff nearly impossible. After a few hours I got lucky. Having the biggest board in the lineup, I was able to catch one of these beasts early enough to drop in around the boil. The drop down the face seemed endless, and it was by far the largest wave I've ever ridden in North America.

A little later Tom and Chris were caught inside by a similar wave. I was paddling back out and saw it coming before they did. Flame and I tried to warn them, but it was too late. We could only watch helplessly as the meanest, thickest wave imaginable flared up in front of them. I have never personally witnessed anyone get caught inside so horribly. Nausea surged through me as I watched my friends scratch frantically to beat the cresting monster. Somehow Chris made it through unscathed by bailing out halfway up the face, but Tom copped the whole billion gallons right on the head. He popped up a good 75 yards inside the point of impact, leash broken, board God knows where. Tom then spent a miserable half hour scrabbling along the urchin-infested cliffs of the islet, searching for his board. Often he had to dive into oncoming soup from rocks or wedge behind boulders to avoid being smashed into the cliff face. Miraculously he found his board in one piece and eventually made his way through the shorebreak, headed toward the boat to get a new leash.

Toward noon the swell became even stronger and more consistent. After another hour or so of trading waves, I made a serious error and paid for it dearly. For some silly reason I had strayed over toward the point from Tom and Chris, trying to hunt down a wave that saddled and thus allowed a deeper takeoff. Missing a wave, I wheeled around to find my companions clawing for the horizon. I went over another, smaller wave, and then suddenly in front of me was a malevolent hillock of water surely sent from the bowels of hell. It was a no-win situation. I didn't know which way to paddle. Easily five times my height, the wave felt bottom, skidded, and vaulted out in the lethal slow motion of all deadly things. I felt like I was in the throes of a nightmare. I couldn't penetrate the water enough to avoid the lip and caught the full force of it on my head and shoulders while only a foot or two underwater. For a second I worried that my leash would tear my leg off, but the impact of the wave was so fierce that the urethane snapped immediately and I never even felt so much as a tug. That wave took me deep.

I opened my eyes to a dark, swirling world that man was never meant to see. After what seemed an eternity (but was actually only about 15 seconds), I clawed through the surface foam and cleared my eyes just in time to see another, meaner wave with a frothy white cement-lip halfway pitched. Apparently the first wave pounded me so deep that I didn't get dragged in far enough to avoid further punishment. A pitiful suck of aerated foam was all I got, and I could only sort of scrunch under the surface before the lip hit me square and consumed me in what felt like a tornado of grenades. The oxygen was pummeled out of me and there seemed no end in sight. It just wouldn't let me up, and I only remember a strange confusion of sorts, like "Is this how it ends, after all these years?" I was waiting to pile into a sea stack or boulder, as the current on the inside point was torrential, and I felt sure I'd been under long enough to reach the jagged part of the promontory. I finally popped up, a full 75 yards from the impact zone.

Swimming feebly toward the channel, I kept getting hit on the head by mountains of soup. By the time I reached the relatively calm water near shore, I was exhausted. The boat was a long swim away, and the shoreline was an even worse option—surging shorepound over craggy boulders and sea urchins. Blowing air into my wet suit, I drifted easily until I could spot a likely landfall.

Meanwhile, the surf was getting out of hand. Tom and Chris were dodging the monster sets in the boil and grabbing the cleaner waves for some all-time rides. It took me at least 45 minutes to spot where my board had washed ashore, climb over the cactus and scrub to reach it, make the hike back, paddle out through the bouldery shorebreak, stroke the 300 yards to the boat, tie on a new cord, speedload a pack of M&M's, and finally join my friends in the lineup again.

At about two in the afternoon, the offshore Santa Ana winds started roaring over the sand, growing increasingly stronger with each ensuing minute. Although the waves got much saner, our Mexican skipper was eager to leave the island. The passage back to Ensenada into the teeth of the wind would be no picnic—and downright hazardous if the wind continued to gain force. Chris and I caught our last few waves and headed in. The boatman had already pulled anchor and was gunning the outboard engine in no uncertain terms.

Tom was alone in the lineup. He wanted the proverbial "one more wave." The problem was, he wanted "one more wave" five times. On his last wave he free-fell to midface, reconnected, raced a hissing lip to the bottom, and skillfully squeezed past the meeting of crest and trough— just in time to be horribly blasted from behind. His board exploded so violently in the air we thought it had broken. It was the worst wipeout of the day, but Tom reeled his board back intact and paddled to meet us as the boat was drawing out of the channel. His eyes were bloodshot and tinged with salt rime from the dry wind, but I've never seen him so thrilled.

In the boat we sprawled in the litter of the day: mutilated surfboards, broken leashes, and candy-bar wrappers. We were completely exhausted. Flame was so excited he became seasick. The jarring two-hour passage back was hell. The McDonald's at the border seemed years away. But we were in a boat, we had surfboards, and we were surfers. Damn, it was great to be alive.

Epilogue

On the afternoon of February 5, 1987, the day on which the previous story took place, a 57-foot fishing boat was struck broadside by a 20-foot wave less than 150 miles south of Todos Santos. The chartered *Fish-n-Fool* was capsized by the freak wave while anchored off the sea stack near San Martín Island. The ship sank almost immediately to a depth of 170 feet. Of the 12 people aboard the vessel, only two survived.

MAVERICK'S

In the late '80s, big as Godzilla and just as unlikely, Maverick's emerged suddenly from the foggy, Northern California coastline. And like Godzilla, no one quite knew what to make of this monstrous break. The word spread. A small cadre of local regulars reported epic winter sessions: The waves were huge, dark, and mean, the water freezing, and, following wipeouts, avalanches of whitewater drove surfers, often underwater, hundreds of yards to a barnacled rock garden known as the "boneyard." The crowds grew. Yet the definitive word was still not out because Maverick's, like all innovations, was neither widely established nor completely understood. Only time, and the accumulation of many experiences in all conditions, could produce a bulletproof verdict. By the mid '90s, rumor was rounding into fact.

Old-timers balked at comparisons to time-proven Hawaiian breaks—until several illustrious North Shore hellmen actually surfed Maverick's, and one was killed in less-than-maximum conditions. Yet the surfing world still considered it blasphemous to mention Maverick's in the same breath as Waimea, or even Sunset. No more. A decade of stories, articles, magazine covers, photos, videos, web sites, and, most recently, competitions have proved that when Maverick's is firing, its treacherous, cold-water peak serves up paddle-in waves as challenging and serious as any on the planet. No question, big Maverick's is the real deal, a triple-X, red-flag break for experts only. At the recent (February 1999) Maverick's contest, organizers were so concerned about possible drownings that only people with experience at Maverick's were allowed to compete. "I don't care if you won the Quiksilver match (held at Waimea) and surf Outside Pipe at 50 feet," one organizer said. "If you're not familiar with Mav's— well, this place can kill you. That's our concern."

One of the first to consider Maverick's in global terms was *Surfer's Journal* publisher Steve Pezman, who in 1995 wrote, "The emergence of Maverick's and Todos Santos over the last seven years has required the world's surfing community to revise its conception of Hawaii being the only legitimate stage for big wave riding. In terms of the relatively small number of people who have surfed them to date, both Maverick's and Todos are at similar points in their evolution, as was Waimea (first ridden in 1957) during the early 1960s winter seasons. A fairly recent estimate suggests there are between 15 and 20 Maverick's regulars, perhaps another 15 part-time riders, and another 15 visitors who have surfed there in big conditions. That makes 50 to 60 in total who have ever ridden big Maverick's, out of a universe of perhaps 500,000 to 600,000 active surfers in California and Hawaii. By those standards we're still in the historical 'early years' of West Coast big wave riding."

The excitement Maverick's has generated in the past three years has resulted in a minor reverse migration of surfers from Hawaii to California. It's a natural transition in that Oahu's Waimea Bay has been the "sleeping giant" as of late. Waimea's potential is undeniable, yet until it comes out of its slumber, surfers who live to challenge the biggest ridable waves will make their seasonal pilgrimage to Baja's Todos Santos Island and Half Moon Bay's Maverick's.

No individuals to date have ridden all three spots at their biggest and best, and only a handful have ridden all three spots on equivalent swells (in the 15- to 18-foot range)—yet comparisons are inevitable. Evan Slater, 23, one of the few who has ridden all three breaks, draws the following comparisons: "Todos is similar to Waimea in the sense that it's more of a steep drop and one quick section. It's a smaller version of Waimea—more playful. Waimea is much heavier, though the length of the ride is half the length of Maverick's. Maverick's is the scariest because the peak is so intimidating—it's so open and top to bottom—more so than Todos and Waimea. Waimea is much warmer, and it seems more inviting. The water feels heavier at Maverick's because it's so much colder, though I don't know whether there is any scientific basis for this."

Josh Loya, 25, adds that "Maverick's easily compares to Waimea in the 15- to 18-foot range." But, according to Loya, the comparisons stop when Maverick's breaks the 20-foot barrier. "Maverick's is a lot scarier—with the cold water, the rocks, and the distance from shore. There's no helicopter that can pluck you out at Maverick's, no lifeguards on Jet Skis. When Waimea goes off big, all the emergency people are there and ready to go. That's a huge difference right there."

With barely a decade's heritage, Maverick's is quickly growing from a phenomenon into a legend. Perhaps the most telling fact is the profound respect Maverick's commands from anyone brave enough to paddle out in peak conditions. To be sure, Maverick's can be as unforgiving a break as

Jeff Clark stares down a monster at Maverick's. PHOTO BY LAWRENCE BECK

any on earth. When Maverick's goes off big, bad things can happen to anyone, regardless of their skills and conditioning.

There is much speculation as to how Maverick's will ultimately figure in the history of the ever expanding world of big wave surfing. Several times every winter the surf grows too big to be surfed by traditional methods. There is talk that on these "unridable" days, when the waves are pushing 40, even 50, feet, Maverick's will become the ultimate tow-in venue. Tow-in converts are already exploring this idea—in March of 1999, Ken Bradshaw towed Dan Moore into one of the biggest waves ever surfed at Maverick's.

The following stories highlight the short, amazing, and sometimes tragic history of what's rapidly growing into one of the world's premiere big wave venues: Maverick's!

COLD SWEAT

MAVERICK'S EMERGES FROM THE MIST

Ben Marcus

*T*he following article, published in the June 1992 issue of Surfer, helped hoist the curtain on a dormant surfing attraction that would soon have the whole world watching. In the months following publication of this article, Maverick's became a media hot spot for mind-blowing performances as well as nauseating wipeouts. Here, renowned surf journalist Ben Marcus tells us how it all began.

‡   ‡   ‡

Maverick Was a Dog

Maverick's is the perfect name for the place: a cold-water, 20-foot, hush-hush, voodoo big wave deal with a history of attracting, as *Webster's* defines the word, "an independent individual who refuses to conform with his group." Funny, then, that the name is a coincidence and has nothing to do with the character of the wave or the maniacs who ride it. Maverick's was named after a dog: a white German shepherd, to be precise.

The dog belonged to Alex Matienzo, a San Francisco native and pioneer among Northern California surfers. Maverick loved to surf on the nose of his owner's board, and he would tag along on Matienzo's surf trips up and down the coast. On a winter day in 1962, Matienzo and a couple of friends checked a reef they'd seen between Santa Cruz and San Francisco. On big days the reef broke a half mile from shore. The place didn't have a name, and no one surfed it: "I had Maverick with me,"

Matienzo, 66, remembers. "I didn't want him swimming out there because it was so far offshore. We paddled out, but Maverick kept following us so I had to turn around and tie him to the car. It wasn't too big a day, maybe a 6- to 8-foot swell. We didn't surf there too often after that, but we knew what to call the place: Maverick's Point."

Maverick's had a name but remained an enigma. Dick Keating, a surfer and commercial fisherman who's lived in the area since the '50s, understands why there weren't many takers during the '60s and early '70s: "As far as I know, nobody on a longboard ever went out there. We saw Maverick's, but it was just this giant wave, like Potato Patch or something. I don't know who was the first one to ride it, but I do know a local kid named Jeff Clark was the first to ride it consistently. As far as I'm concerned, the place should be called 'Jeff Clark's.'"

15 Years of Solitude

Maverick's has an aura like Edward Scissorhands' mansion: gray, gloomy, isolated, inherently evil. The reef is surrounded by deep water and lies naked to every nasty thing above and below the Pacific: Aleutian swells, northwest winds, southeast storms, frigid currents, aggro elephant seals and marauding great whites that snack on aggro elephant seals. The shoreline is craggy rocks backed by sheer cliffs. Paddle through the lefts and you skirt a twisted, tripled-up bowl that makes brave men nauseous. Paddle through the rights and you fight a current that sweeps through two big pinnacles, then turns out to sea across one of the worst navigational hazards on the California coast. Maverick's radiates danger. It takes a rarified sort of person to surf the place, alone, year after year.

Jeff Clark has lived all of his 34 years within 5 miles of Maverick's. He first saw the reef in junior high, but it wasn't until 1975, his senior year of high school, that he had the sack to paddle out: "I had a friend I surfed with, and I tried for hours to talk him into it. He said, 'No way, man. You leave me alone. I'll watch you go out there if you want to kill yourself. I'm not going out.' The first board I paddled out was a 7' 3" single-fin. I was a goofy foot, so I went left. It was about 15- to 18-foot faces, and I caught five waves. Going left out there was just incredible."

Clark stayed in the area after high school, earned his contractor's license, got married, learned to shape surfboards, took up sailboarding, and kept surfing Maverick's. "I rode it pretty much every winter from 1975 on, mostly alone. I'd have friends come out with me, but they'd sit in the channel."

By the winter of 1989 to '90 Clark had Maverick's wired. He was riding the rights switch foot, shaping 10-foot guns for himself, and had figured out the weather-buoy equation that signaled when Maverick's would be happening. Around Northern California he'd developed an underground reputation as a crazed guru charger who'd pioneered a spot that most considered suicidal. But Clark was doing most of this solo, and even hellmen get lonely.

Hogs to the Trough

Monday, January 22, 1990, was the day after the Quiksilver/Eddie Aikau contest at Waimea. The same swell that Brock Little and Mike Parson rode to fame at Todos Santos was mostly out of control in Northern California. That morning, Clark bumped into two Santa Cruz surfers, Tom Powers and Dave "Big Bird" Schmidt, in the parking lot at Ocean Beach, San Francisco. Ocean Beach was on the horizon and out of the question. Clark knew Maverick's had to be off the Richter, and he pulled Schmidt and Powers aside: "I said, 'You guys want to surf these sets in a perfect peak? Come with me.' We snuck off to Mav's and walked to the top of the lookout. Schmidt was looking off going, 'Where is it?' and just then a set came through. Big Bird started pacing back and forth, going, 'Oh my God!' Powers was going, 'What? What?' And Schmidt said, 'That's—Waimea!'"

Maverick's was huge under pristine conditions that day, one of the best in memory. Schmidt and Powers paddled out with Clark and went into shock. They were undergunned on 8' 4"s, staring into a stupendous pit that Jeff Clark charged with little regard. "Clark had always been one of the hottest guys from that area," Powers said. "But that day he blew us away. He was taking off super deep, charging into these big, black, hideous pits. We were worried about him. There was a wave he didn't make that gave me the heaviest gut wrench I've ever felt. The bottom dropped away as he was getting to his feet on like a 15-foot bomb. I swear I almost got sick. Schmidt and I paddled into the impact zone to look for him, but he was gone. He broke his leash and we didn't see him for another hour. He paddled out through the lefts and took a 15-foot set right on the head. All that, and he came back and didn't bat an eye. We were awestruck." Schmidt caught a half dozen waves, Powers rode two, and they made it to shore grateful, baptized—believers. The ribbon had been cut.

Through that spring and summer, Powers and Schmidt held their peace out of respect to Clark—and because they figured no one would believe them. One person they did tell was Vince Collier. Vince isn't what

*Richard Schmidt
taking no prisoners
at Maverick's.*
PHOTO BY LAWRENCE BECK

you'd call squeamish, but he wanted nothing to do with Maverick's—he didn't have the right boards and the place reeked of *Jaws*. In September 1990, Powers and Schmidt dragged Vince out to Maverick's on a big west swell. When Vince found the adrenaline bonus outweighed the fear, he became a disciple: "The place was off the scale. I'd traveled from Australia to Japan to Brazil to South Africa to Hawaii and driven from the tip of Baja to Canada in search of this place that was right under my nose."

From 1990 into 1991, it was Team Old Fart—Clark, Schmidt, Powers, and Collier—surfing Maverick's. The season ended on April 5, 1991, with a huge, clean day and the biggest crowd so far: a dozen guys, including Marcel Soros, Doc Renneker, Mark Coin, and David's brother, Richard Schmidt. The buzz got loud.

Todos Santos vs. Maverick's vs. Waimea Bay

It may be an overblown case of NorCal rhetoric, but the guys who have been surfing Maverick's regularly are convinced they have a world-class big wave spot in their backyard.

On the local scale, "The peak at Steamer Lane is probably the closest thing to Maverick's size-wise," Collier believes, "but there's no comparison. Not even close. Maverick's pitches out at 20 feet. Out and *up*. I've seen waves that could hold five lighthouses in the tube."

Ocean Beach patriot Mark Renneker has learned to love the drop at Maverick's, but he is more clinical and cautious in his evaluation. He compares it to Ocean Beach, San Francisco's big wave beachbreak: "Ocean Beach is more complex in every respect except for the takeoff. Maverick's can be a dry-hair paddle out, and it's not hard to line up, but it's like a big wave Shark Island."

On the international scale, Maverick's surfers rank their spot between Todos Santos and Waimea. "You could fit Todos Santos on the inside bowl at Maverick's," Marcel Soros offered. Peter Mel backed him up: "Todos is like a drop wall, but at Maverick's you're taking off in a pitching bowl. The wave looks like 8 feet when it's coming at you, which is probably good, because you might not go otherwise. You paddle for it and the wave hits the bowl and the bottom drops out and all of a sudden that 8-foot lump is a 15-foot wave. It's radical, man. It's *so* radical."

Richard Schmidt spends most of the winter in Hawaii, but he had that big day at Maverick's in April last year (1991), and caught three days in a row this January. He doesn't know Todos well enough to make a call, but his word is gold-plated credible when it comes to Waimea: "I never thought I'd hear myself say this about a California wave, but as far as the takeoff and the speed and everything, Maverick's is real comparable to Waimea. The peak comes out of deep water and hits a shallow shelf so it has the same kind of a ledge. Also, Maverick's doesn't back off into deep water, so it's more exciting after the drop. I surfed it last year and it was Hawaiian 20-foot solid, and I know it gets bigger than that. I think of all the huge days I've surfed in Santa Cruz and I can only wonder what Maverick's must have been doing. It's nice to come home from Hawaii and know there's a place that offers that kind of challenge."

Big January, 1992

Maverick's was destined to emerge from obscurity during the 1991 to '92 winter, and it cooperated with a bumper season. It began with a big west swell in September. Christmas Day was 15 feet and smooth, and it broke on New Year's Eve and New Year's Day. The rest of January was relentless, including a flawless five-day stretch from January 25 to 29. Prior to that stretch, Clark and Collier were the undisputed kings of the place. On Wednesday, January 29, they were joined and, some say, surpassed, by Richard Schmidt.

Schmidt had just returned home from a two-month pilgrimage in Hawaii. That morning he paddled out on a 10-foot Rawson Waimea gun and proceeded to raise everyone's consciousness. Although Clark downplayed the day, Collier built a verbal pedestal for his buddy. Doc Renneker was there, too, and gives witness: "Richard has perfected the big wave takeoff—-all his weight on his back foot, low and crouched with his front leg lightly stretched forward like a Paul Strauch cheater five. He has natural wave judgment and impeccable positioning. He was gliding into waves no one else wanted any part of and he was doing these insane S-turns, fading into the pit. It felt like we were just your average basketball players—and then Michael Jordan paddled out."

About halfway through the session, Schmidt took off on a bomb that raised the Maverick's performance bar several notches. The wave started breaking way outside, peeling a hundred yards and through three bowls before approaching the lineup. Vince Collier screamed at Richard not to go, but Schmidt took 10 big strokes, stood on the edge of the bowl, and sped. He dropped in on a running angle, got about two-thirds of the way to the bottom, then headed balls out for the channel. He outran the section for about 50 yards before another bowl began to break beyond, above, and behind him. The section threw about halfway down the face, spitting and exploding 50 feet laterally and 50 feet up. He turned down to get around the section, saw he couldn't make it, dove off, and got annihilated.

Maverick's holds you down and beats you as if you owed it money. Schmidt admitted the wave gave him "a good spanking" but shrugged it off and spoke of the next step: "The hollowest part of the wave is probably right at the peak, but with more west you get that inside bowl. There's potential for tube rides on the right wave, but it's not going to be easy."

The Future

The handful of people who have surfed Maverick's longest and best have been gracious about the threat of magazine exposure, but they stress that any story about Maverick's must be delivered with a caveat: It's no place for amateurs.

"I took Flea Virostko, Shawn Barron, and Zack Acker out at Maverick's on a Tuesday night in January and it was about as big as I'd ever surfed it," Collier said. "I was truly worried that they were going to get hurt, or worse. These kids had never ridden boards over 8 feet long, and they were out charging on these giant boards. Zack and Flea got caught inside a huge set and they were scared shitless. I felt like Uncle Al Bundy."

If Maverick's brings out the father figure in Vince, it amplifies both the purist and the public health official in Doc Renneker: "I hate to say it, but Maverick's is becoming the kind of place that people surf to try to prove something. I've seen a lot of foolhardy attempts at Maverick's, and I've witnessed some of the most shocking wipeouts imaginable. My prediction is there's going to be some major injuries, perhaps deaths. That's what worries me about the publicity."

Clark and Collier are confident that whatever hysteria sweeps through the lineup, it will be short-lived. Collier echoed what Clark said a few months ago in *Surfer:* Maverick's will take care of itself. "You guys at the magazines will do your thing, but it will eventually pass. Maverick's isn't going anywhere. There's only a certain amount of people who are going to want to ride it. Anybody can paddle out, pretty much, but to paddle out there time after time, year after year, they gotta either have something, or lack something. I can't put my finger on it yet."

MAVERICK'S AND THE
DEEP BLUE SEA

Ken "Skindog" Collins and Skip Snead

*B*y 1998, a subculture of California big wave riders had developed a common crusade: challenge Maverick's at its biggest and baddest. Maverick's helped create this group as sure as it helped fashion the inimitable stories of Ken "Skindog" Collins, who, along with Surfing editor Skip Snead, has concocted an adventure narrative style bold and direct as a 20-foot shorebreak. At once dire and hilarious, these stories give readers what great adventure writers always strive for but rarely achieve: a contact high replete with twitching and sweaty palms and yelling out loud and, of course, a craving for more. "A 60-foot Face" and "Freaky Friday" are two stories that exemplify this.

‡   ‡   ‡

A 60-foot Face

On the morning of November 14, 1997, there was the highest tide of the year, a full moon, the buoys were 20 feet at 20 seconds, and Maverick's was producing some of the biggest, baddest waves on the planet.

In the parking lot, Josh Loya and the Wormhoudt brothers were suited and walking down the trail, so I [Skindog] just threw on my suit and grabbed my board. When I got to the beach and saw the waves bashing over the jetty into the harbor, I knew Maverick's was going off big. On top of the cliff the high tide made it look deceiving. The sets were breaking on the inside. The wind was a crosshatch offshore with staircase set chops climbing up the face. I should have realized how heavy it was when Jay Moriarty and Richard Schmidt didn't go out. But I was already suited up and Mike Brummit needed a paddle partner.

On the way out, sets would close out on the inside, which never happens. Just reaching the lineup took careful timing and navigational skills. One guy spent 40 minutes paddling his arms like a bee's wings and he never got past the rocks. We were lucky, got a long lull, and got out quick. Loya was stoked he got out with dry hair.

There were about nine guys out, one boat, one WaveRunner, and a water photographer bobbing around the chop like a cork. No one had gotten a wave yet, when all of a sudden the biggest set of the day appeared on the horizon. Everybody scrambled for the shoulder. As the set steamed in, the first wave jacked up on the inside bowl as the wind tried to hold it back. The beast stood up—it easily had a 60-foot face. Jagged chops pushed up the face and a disturbing warble rose within the wave. What I saw next scared me more than anything I've ever seen.

When the warble got a little past halfway up, it started to crest and the monster doubled up. The thick lip just threw out with brutal force and the bottom dropped out like a trapdoor. For those few seconds the wind, the water, and everyone's screams went silent. I gaped down over my shoulders and could see the lip flying far out into space and the bottom inverting about 10 feet down. There were these ghastly boils sucking from the reef and warbling into darkness as the wave began to tube. The silence was broken with a thundering crash as the lip exploded on the water. Even though I was safe, I shuddered. At that moment, I realized how heavy it really was and that there are waves that are not meant for man. I looked into the huge black hole and my body started to shake. You could easily fit a telephone pole upright in the tube. Once over the top, I noticed the wave had hardly any back to it as it continued to suck over. I was amazed by this hideous and yet beautiful natural creation.

After the set roared passed, Loya said something like "On the count of three, let's all go in." We kind of took it as a joke, but I don't think he was joking. I knew one thing for sure: There was no way in hell I was paddling into that bowl!

After a couple of sets, Loya decided to have first go. He clawed into a wave early and stood up. It looked like he had it made, but from the inside I heard somebody scream, "Oh no!" Then, farther on the inside, I saw 2 feet of Josh's 10-foot board tombstoning through the water. With his cord being 15 feet and his board more than half submerged, he must have been drilled down better than 20 feet deep. This was not good. About 20 seconds passed before he popped up. Fortunately, there wasn't another wave or he would have been in the two-wave hold-down club. Josh's reputation of never blowing a drop at Mav's was history. He later said it was his new booties that wouldn't grip. Doug Acton snagged him with his WaveRunner and headed for the boat as Josh yelled, "My hair's still dry." Josh had wrenched his knee, lost his bootie, and the leg of his suit was pulled clear over his toes. He was done.

Zack Wormhoudt was the next volunteer. As he paddled into the bomb you could see this lump in front of him start to crest. He stood up and sailed off the lump like a snowboarder. Then his board totally submerged and Zack was off, sliding on his back for many yards before penetration. He was harshly dealt with but came out with only throbbing ribs. He was done.

Suddenly a colossal set spooled in and Brummit paddled right into the bowl. Mike went for the first one and it looked massive, a 50-foot face or so. I was astonished he was even paddling for it. He was a complete madman just scratching his ass off. It looked like he wanted to win the K2 contest. He stood up, fighting the wind to get down the face. As he came to the double up, he pushed forward on his front foot and went hurtling over this giant ledge. It was the craziest thing I'd ever witnessed, and once again I heard someone scream "Oh no!"

I looked in and saw the wave detonate. Luckily Mike popped right up, but he didn't feel too hot. He said he almost pulled the drop, but the board got wicked speed wobbles and he dove. When he hit, the drink felt like cement and he got compressed. Neck wrenched, tingling all over and his arms numb—he was pretty much done.

After seeing my bros go down, I knew there wouldn't be any success stories. And when the next set was capping way in front of me, I knew it wasn't safe. As I was paddling toward the mountain, I looked behind me and saw everybody just scrabbling like crazy. The boat and WaveRunner gunned it for the channel. Right in the impact zone the water photog dived under, and next to him some poor soul jumped off his board and dove. I paddled up the face and decided to get off my board and try to push it up and over the wind. I took a deep breath and swam through the face. I could feel my leash being pulled and for a second I thought about disconnecting from it as it stretched out beyond its 20-foot length. I popped out the back of the wave and immediately started being pulled back by my cord. I felt I was going over when my board finally popped up. I was stoked it was in one piece. Everyone was gone but three of us. The poor soul on the board got washed in, and the boat picked up the dizzy water photog and bailed. At this point we knew it was suicide so we went in,

Daryl Virostko (aka Flea) styling at Maverick's. Virostko won the 1999 Quiksilver contest at Mav's. PHOTO BY LAWRENCE BECK

too. I didn't even attempt to catch a wave in. I just paddled in with my tail between my legs as fast as I could. I was so stoked the moment I felt the earth under my feet.

It was hard to gauge the size of the waves since there wasn't much back to them, but one thing's for sure: That day was the biggest surf I've ever seen. The waves were as thick as they were tall.

Freaky Friday

I knew it was going to be big when buoy 59 gave the report of 28 feet at 20 seconds, but I didn't know it was going to be too big. Then I saw waves washing over West Cliff Drive in Santa Cruz—that hasn't happened since 1982. On the drive up, every time a huge set broke way out to sea, I'd get a blast of adrenaline just thinking how Mav's must be going off.

Once there, Pete and I watched from the bluff as Flea and the boys battled the inside close-outs trying to get out. The waves were massive, 25-foot-plus, big-O bowls just throwing out and spitting. I'd never seen it so hollow. As Flea and company battled out to the lineup, Pete and I suited up and did the same. Or tried to. It took me 40 minutes to make it out. Pete got beat back. As I worked to the bowl I saw seven boats, each trying to go deeper in the pit than the other. It was out of hand—like some kind of crazy fishing derby or something—with surfers screaming at them to get back. I think the photographers are more amped on the K2 contest than the surfers. Everyone sat a safe distance from the bowl, except Flea. He sat right in it. He'd already caught two waves and was ready for the next. Sets were heavy and most waves looked impossible. Some would cap and others would back off then double up and just unload. The double ups were not recommended. Today's goal was to surf the 20-footers. Flea was totally focused and grabbed another beast, so I followed his lead and got an easy one. Sometimes we'd paddle for waves and the things would jack up, bottom out, and chuck out all at the same time, and we'd have to back out or die. After the second set I realized that most of the waves were tubing death wishes. Flea got his fourth wave and I got my second, and I thought things were going good.

Then things took a turn for the worst.

As Flea went for his fifth wave, the lip mushed over him and he caught his rail. He didn't get that hammered but was sucked deep into the bowl. The next wave was a bomb, a grisly 25-footer. I barely scratched over it. When I got to the top I glanced back at Flea and wished I didn't because what I saw made me sick to my stomach.

Flea was marooned smack dab in the impact zone, the exact spot you never want to visit. He frantically swam toward me to get under the lip. Then he dove. As the wave broke over, Flea's hand punched through the back of the beast for a second, then he got dragged over the falls. I almost puked and everybody started flipping out. I kept looking for him on the inside, praying that he was alive. It's funny how you always ask favors of God in these situations. Flea finally popped up around 200 yards inside and we all thought he was safe. But he wasn't.

Doug Acton (WaveRunner photog/lifeguard) tried to reach Flea but was bashed back by torrential whitewash, only yards away from him. Acton remembers the situation: "It was the most ill feeling I've ever had. I couldn't get to him. I was thinking, 'Holy shit, he's gonna die . . . he's gonna die. . . .' Every time I tried to get to him I was denied, and then he'd disappear. Then he'd pop up and then he'd disappear again. Finally I raced to the rocks on my Ski.

"Later, Flea told me that he was thinking, 'Yes, I'm saved. . . . Hey, wait a minute. Where are you going? Get back over here. Oh, shit!'"

Doug has been doing everything in his power to save surfers out there, and I think he deserves a lot of credit.

Flea now had to face going through the rocks of doom. Naturally his leash snagged and he was pinned to the bottom. He said he couldn't get up. "It was like trying to do a sit-up with a fat chick on my face," he said, and after a few minutes he was getting really tired. He was thinking, "This is the way Mark Foo died!" and felt as if he was right next to him. Spooky.

Flea finally mustered the strength to unstrap his leash and get washed to the safety of Acton's WaveRunner. Whoever thought your leash—a life line—could turn against you and become a death trap?

"The first words out of Flea's mouth," Acton recalls, were "I almost died . . . I almost died."

At this point, nobody knew how bad a mugging Flea had taken, so we stayed out. Pete finally made it out and right off the bat grabbed a wave. Brummit jumped in on the program and bagged one biggy over in Latez Bowl. After a few more mountains steamed past, a couple of the boys sat up and said, "So long and good luck," then paddled in. This got me thinking, but Pete was charging and caught two more waves. So I kept trying. As the tide peaked at 6 feet high, it started to dawn on me that every wave was now a double up, 50- to 60-foot faces, spitting pits with 12-foot-thick lips and no backs. I felt like G.I. Joe at Stockton Avenue, and after my hundredth backout with my nuts in my guts, I told myself, "One more."

I got one more—and decided to get another.

On my way back out, a macking set came in and I started scrambling to get out of its path. My brain started twitching and I was thinking, "Dear Mr. Wizard, I don't want to be a surfer anymore." As I paddled up the face, I saw Neil Matthies turn around and start stroking in for it. He'd only been out for a minute and had no clue what he was going for. At this point, everything turned slow-mo and as I got to the top, I wanted to scream "Don't do it!" but I was silenced by the wave. It was probably for the better because Neil was already committed and I didn't want to hex him. I looked over at Pete and asked if he made it. Peter shook his head no! As the wave blew up and exploded, I got sick to my stomach again. There were two more bombs and we still hadn't seen Neil pop up. He was dragged under water the farthest I've ever seen. People on the cliff said they saw his board tombstoning all the way to the rocks (almost 300 yards!) and that he was down for over a minute. We were fully freaking now and I was praying, "Come on, God. Neil's a pretty decent guy. Don't let him die." My brain just kept repeating "Get out of here!" Finally Neil popped up, clearly alive. But I had lost my drive, so I paddled to one of the boats.

At first I felt like a quitter. But a few minutes later, when a 28-foot cleanup set came smashing through, I was pretty damned stoked to be kicking it on the boat. Don Curry paddled for the first wave, missed it, and had to deal with the rest of the set on his head. It was weird being so close, watching everyone get worked while I enjoyed a hot shower from the engine hose. Peter's board got sucked over the falls, and his leash and board splintered on impact, but Pete surfaced in one piece. Nacho's board got sucked over, and his leash dragged him along for the hell ride over the falls. He was pulled down deep. His board was tombstoning for 20 seconds until he pulled himself up on his leash. He came over to the boat looking like a ghost, claiming he was done for a while.

After that set, the show was pretty much over. But to my amazement, Don Curry came paddling back out looking like nothing happened. He is such a stud and a cool cat, totally down with the boys. Everyone left, but Don stayed for a couple more hours. He had to get his wave quota for the drive up (at least one wave per hour drive; the more waves he catches brings down the cost of gas per wave). The guy's a legend.

Once in the harbor, I couldn't believe how many people were watching. In the parking lot it was total chaos, total gridlock. A friend told me Perry White started doing tow-ins, and we heard he took some bombs and got perfectly and repeatedly mashed.

I went back to the beach to fetch my clothes, as well as Peter's, and found that the surf had washed them out to sea. I was a little edgy, and to make things worse some knucklehead ran over my board in the parking lot. I started to blow a gasket but took a few deep breaths, and it was all good.

All in all, it was a historic day and I was glad to witness it. No question, the best part of surfing Mav's is getting *back on the beach*.

MAN IMITATES ABALONE

Lawrence Beck (as told to him by Jeff Clark)

During a generous swell in the winter of 1992 to 1993, veteran photographer Lawrence Beck was setting up his gear on the cliffs overlooking Maverick's. "As I fastened my camera to the tripod, I watched Jeff Clark pitch down a mountainous face that suddenly started folding over like a giant hand. Clark dove off his board just before it closed out. What follows are Jeff's thoughts and words as to what has to be his closest ever brush with death."

‡   ‡   ‡

I dropped into one bowl, and then there was another bowl across the crease in the wave, so I pulled up into it. I could see the wave beginning to clam shell, so I dove off. I came up, pulled my board back, and began paddling left as I was still in front of the bowl and this was the beginning of a set.

The next double up snapped my board, and the turbulence was unreal. I was thinking, "I've got half a board and it's dragging me toward the rocks. This leash has got to come off!" I tried to get under the next wall of whitewater as it passed overhead, dredging everything in its path. The bottom was shallower with each passing second and the water seemed to accelerate as it hit the shallows. I remember seeing the rocks getting closer, and I tried to reach down and pull off the leash with my webs but couldn't find the strap! At that moment I was hit by another wave and I was upside down and fighting to stay on the surface in all this turbulence. I struggled to stay afloat while trying to get the leash out from under my wet suit, and I was burning air while being rolled wave

Pinned to a rock with colossal waves burying him every 15 to 20 seconds, Jeff Clark gets ready to hit the deck and hold on for dear life. PHOTO BY LAWRENCE BECK

after wave. The next thing I knew, I was 20 feet from the face of the big rock and there's lots of whitewater coming right behind me—I knew I had absolutely no control over this situation. I was at the mercy of Poseidon's washing machine and it was locked on spin cycle. A lot of things would have to happen right in order for me to survive, and I had no control over any of them. What scared me most was the possibility of my board hanging up on a rock and me being attached to it, with no possibility of escape.

The next wave pushed me into the rock wall and I could feel the back pressure of the water off the wall while underwater. I was swirling around and was shoved through a gap between two large rocks. As I swept through I was able to reach up and grab a handhold on the rock. The water level began to drop as it pulled and tried to rip me off the rock. My hands were 2 feet from the top of the rock, and my feet were out of the water as the current sucked out to sea.

Within seconds, the next wave hit, covering the rock with water as I hung by my fingers. The splintered board, still attached to my leash, pulled at my ankle as the wave swept over and exploded around the rock through the narrow channel. All I could think of was the rock climbers hanging by their fingers in the video *Blood, Sweat and Glory*—these crazy rock climbers totally suspended by their fingers. I didn't have a good handhold—I was suspended on the face of that rock solely by my fingertips. I was fortunate to have gloves on as the rock was encrusted with big mussels and barnacles.

The third wave covered me over, and as it started to recede, I pulled myself up the face and over the top of the rock and got rid of the leash. I was so relieved to be on the rock that I took a moment to reflect on the situation.

As I was standing on the rock—I'm thinking about what I had just gone through—a massive wall of whitewater came roaring in. I lay down and held on while the wave rolled over me. I realized that I was going to be there for a while—providing I could hang on and the surf didn't rip me off the rock. I could see off the jagged back side that the current was sucking all the water out from around these rocks during the sets, leaving no water behind for me to swim in to get out of there. The alternative—swimming back out through whitewater—was not good. So I jammed my right arm and knee into cracks across the top of the rock and just held on, wave after wave.

After 10 minutes of hanging on with all my strength, my arms were shaking and I was getting really cold. I had shut down circulation to my arms and legs while I played abalone, keeping a death grip on the rock. I knew I was finished if I got hypothermia or if my muscles became so fatigued that they were useless. In between blasts of whitewater I started shaking and moving my arms, trying to restore the circulation.

I kept looking in to see if anybody was going to come out to the rocks because by now I was totally pinned down. Then I heard this voice shouting, "What are you doing?" I looked up to see Jim, looking crazy, standing on a 15-foot-high rock not 25 feet away. He had scrambled to the top, barely escaping being swept off by a wave. He asked if I was all right and if I needed a helicopter. I lied and told him I was okay.

For the next half hour, Jim would yell at me when to brace for a big swell and when to get up and rest for a moment. The danger was not so much the big sets—their energy would dissipate as they crashed from the outside reef through the impact zone and finally through the inside section to the rocks. But the waves too small to break on the outside reef would gather energy as they roared into the shallows, eventually focusing their fury onto the rocks where I was stranded.

Matt Ambrose and Mike Mirnsey had paddled in to see if they could help. They could see Jim on one of the larger rocks just inside the one I was pinned down on. Just as they climbed up the face of another rock on the inside, Jim shouted, "Look out!" A huge inside wave had just broken. After burying me with several feet of water, it rushed over and around the inside rocks, sweeping Matt and Mike off into a narrow channel where they were dashed into the surrounding rocks. I couldn't see them from my vantage point, but I knew they were getting worked.

Within seconds, Jim shouted, "Jeff, jump now!" I didn't hesitate. I trusted Jim's judgment because I knew he'd be conservative in a situation like this. I swam the 30 or so yards of swirling, boiling whitewater to the edge of the tidal flat just as another set started to roll in. Jim, Matt, and Mike appeared as I staggered onto the flat. Matt looked to be in a great deal of pain, limping on one leg while Mike helped him to shore. Blood poured from the top of Mike's head, and a knee injury had him limping as well.

As we approached each other, Mike started laughing. "Boy—some kind of rescue team we turned out to be!"

Jeff smiled and with characteristic calm replied, "Another day at the office."

THE APPRENTICESHIP OF JAY MORIARTY
BEHIND THE SCENES OF JAY'S CELEBRATED FALL INTO THE BIG WATER CLUB

Jason Smith

*A*t the remarkable age of 16, Jay Moriarty paddled in on a doubled-up Maverick's monster and suffered a wipeout for the millennium, one of the most horrific ever recorded on film. The picture and the boy, immortalized on the cover of Surfer magazine, briefly became the talk of the surfing world—and the national media as well. Who was this kid, and how did he survive such a flogging? On that hangs this story.

To the vast majority of surfers—those who will never challenge big Maverick's or anything like it—a prodigy like Jay Moriarty seems to arrive on the scene ready made. He survived and thrived by dint of a special mental steel that the rest of us lack—or so the thinking goes. The following story sets the record straight. Yes, indeed, Jay Moriarty has special qualities. But his success followed the path of most every big wave ace and most every difficult task: It's all in the preparation.

‡   ‡   ‡

It never occurred to him that he was going to die. There were still too many cards he could play before Jay Moriarty would fold to Maverick's 25-foot version of a royal flush—the now famous wave that called his bluff on his big wave ambitions and placed him on the cover of *Surfer* magazine in what has been described as a "wipeout for the millennium."

It was the morning of December 21, 1994—a day that would later be referred to as Big Monday—and Maverick's was stretching her arms in dramatic fashion. Jay's first wave was a joker, a well-timed burnt rotten draw, and by the time he regretted his play, it was too late for him to discard.

Of the incident, Jay says, "I stood up, looked down, and saw nothing but air below me for 35 feet. I had a split second to think 'Oh, shit!' as spray flew up in my face. The board flew up and over me, and I got impacted in the top of the lip as it curled. The impact was really bad. Then I was drilled to the bottom and bounced off the reef. The turbulence was incredible. I tried to concentrate on staying relaxed. I was tossed and rolled and was lucky to get my feet under me to push off. The swim up to the surface took a long time. I had my eyes open and everything was black. I knew if I didn't get up soon, the next wave would be on top of me, so I swam as hard as I could and caught a breath just before the next wave hit me. The second wave wasn't as bad as the first, but it rolled me pretty good."

Somewhere along the way the glow of sunlight disappeared and the water turned icy. He felt forsaken. Fortunately Jay was prepared to rely on himself for escape. He exercised practiced patience and, when the time came, used trained muscle power to propel himself back to the surface, back to light, back to play again another day.

It was the winter of 1994 to '95, and Maverick's had become surfing's premier dramatic author. When all was said and done, the big wave's own brand of pulp fiction swept surfing's Oscars: the death of famous Hawaiian big wave champion Mark Foo, the Collier tow-in incident, and the emergence of 16-year-old Jay Moriarty. Adaptations of the Moriarty story appeared in everything from local papers to the *New York Times* to NBC's nightly news. He was called a wunderkind and prodigy. He was painted a magician, a sort of surfing David Copperfield who arrives in a flash of smoke, unloads his death-defying artifice, and retreats again to shadowy origins. But Moriarty's feats were hardly the result of magic, more the fruits of a labor of love. An intense, two-year preparation—facilitated by elder Maverick's surfer Rick "Frosty" Hesson—was the source of his success as well as insurance that he would survive the realization of his dreams.

By age 13, James Michael Moriarty was discovering a passion for big waves hidden among his classic longboarding repertoire. He found himself attacking overhead days at Pleasure Point with a zeal that was born of pure, unadulterated enjoyment. "I could do it, too. I was good at it," he recalls. Rumors of Maverick's were widespread around Santa Cruz in

1991, and Jay first caught wind of the new discovery while eavesdropping on a conversation between Frosty and another surfer. The waves they were describing sounded like a dream, a veritable theme park for those with Jay's special fancy for big waves located just beyond his back doorstep.

In the beginning, Jay was afraid of the 45-year-old Frosty. Most Santa Cruz grommets agree with Jay when he says Frosty was "mean," a sleeping giant reputed to ride huge waves. But Frosty was Jay's ticket to Maverick's, and soon the diminutive gremmie was tugging at his surf trunks, beseeching the towering local figure to take him there. To spare the boy's pride, Frosty laughed silently. But the gesture was an early example of something the mentor later came to admire: that Jay possessed maturity and insight beyond his years. Frosty explains, "Most people in surfing hang out with their peers—I mean, who less apt to teach you than your peers? They only know as much as you do!" Jay's departure from adolescent wisdom earned Frosty's consent but not without a condition: First, Jay had to get his mother's permission. Permission slip in hand, Jay was a kid with a Mickey fetish in anticipation of his first trip to Disneyland. But it would be two years before he walked through the fabled gates to get his first view of the Matterhorn.

"When I work with someone," Frosty says, "what I am interested in, number one, is are they going to do the work." Frosty teaches college construction classes at San Jose State and coaches the Soquel High School surf team in addition to individual surfers like Jay. Ten years spent coaching surfers has led Frosty to develop his own, unorthodox slant on the job. "Wingnut" and Kim Hall (currently ranked eighteenth on the ASP Women's World Tour) both attest to his unusual methods. Discussion is the chief medium, the aim of which, says Jay, is analysis. "Frosty explained things to me very thoroughly, usually going into extreme detail. He helped me with my analytical viewpoint by really trying to get me focused on breaking things down to find the nature of them." Frosty's impromptu classroom—the front seat of his van—was the site of so many marathon discussions between them that Jay began to confuse the Ford van with home.

Frosty's approach with Jay was a comprehensive study of surfing. The goal was for Jay "to understand surfing, what surfing is," Frosty says. Signs of the unorthodox approach came early. In order to develop sensitivity while riding immense waves, the two sought to ride the smallest surf they could find. Then, with Jay already feeling like the Karate Kid, Mr. Miyagi assigned him an essay and told him to start writing. "Most

Jay Moriarty screaming down a steep beast at Maverick's. PHOTO BY LAWRENCE BECK

people don't understand that the shortcut to improvement in your surfing is understanding and thinking," says Frosty. "The best way to understand your thinking process about anything is to write it down." Jay complied unblinkingly with his teacher's demands, finishing the paper in an enthusiastic fury. Appearing at Frosty's van the next day, beaming, masterpiece in hand, he was dismayed to find Frosty's board gone and a note attached to the driver's side window. It was a list of 15 essay topics, all to be completed before Jay could surf Maverick's.

To date, Jay has written 55 essays on the subject of surfing, mostly reflective post analyses of technique, training, and contest performances. Each paper was required to be two pages minimum. And Jay recounts flatly that Frosty had him revise each one of them a daunting three times. Healthy, two-hour discussions between drafts made sure Jay burned out any chaff left in his thinking. Altogether, Jay put in roughly 500 hours discussing and writing about surfing, resulting in 330 pages of composition and the replacement of half a dozen dome lightbulbs in Frosty's van.

Visualization, sort of an au naturel version of virtual reality, augmented Jay's mental preparation. Frosty helped him to imagine riding Maverick's, including even minute details like sun, wind, and surface conditions and occasionally the image of the coach from behind as he snaked the rookie. There have been cases where prisoners of war have returned home from Vietnam to find their golf games improved by having visualized swinging the clubs in captivity. Frosty designed Jay's imaging to "emphasize positive outcomes, but with a scenario where bad things can happen." The specific goal was to preclude panic, the broker of survival. "Panic is 'I've exhausted whatever plan A was, whatever I thought I could do,'" says Frosty. "'Now, I don't have a plan B or plan C.' But Jay has been to plan E!"

"Jay, what motivates you to do the work—desire or fear?" I ask.

"Desire."

"It was a drug," Frosty says. "He had a love affair and he was learning everything he could about his mistress." Frosty doesn't hesitate to use metaphors of love to describe Jay's motivation. Bob Pearson of Pearson Arrow surfboards says Jay is "entirely self-motivated"—which is good, because his coach is notorious for his disinterest in helping surfers who won't help themselves.

"All I am is a facilitator," reiterates Frosty. "I don't have time to babysit somebody. In all of Jay's training, I didn't do anything to encourage him, other than to say 'Do this.' I didn't make him do anything." Jay proved he was doing everything Frosty asked of him one day during a swim around the Capitols Wharf with Frosty and Wingnut. Swimming along with them were a few other Santa Cruz surfers who were also under Frosty's supervision. Frosty (a former collegiate swimmer) took his accustomed lead when developments in the rear forced him to double back (Matt Tanner, local longboard talent, lost his shorts due to a freak occurrence and Frosty, obligated as the coach, went to his assistance). Having rectified Tanner's situation, Frosty turned to find Jay out of reach, leading Wingnut by a length on the second leg of the swim. The performance forced the stoic veteran to lift an eyebrow, albeit with his head turned. "I was impressed," Frosty says. "I didn't tell him I was impressed. It's not my job to tell him I am impressed."

"The basis of surfing, of all sports, is conditioning," asserts Frosty. Jay was assigned run, swim, and bike workouts concurrent with the first essay in '91. Frosty further promoted his eccentricity by encouraging Jay to play beach volleyball in preparation for Maverick's. Expecting him to quit early, like an overeager adolescent dropping out of flute lessons, Frosty refused to work out with him for the first six months. "I didn't go for bike rides with him in the beginning," says Frosty. "I didn't go swimming with him." But by the summer of 1992, Jay had more than proved he was serious. He had built himself into a well-conditioned athlete and had prepared himself mentally for any nasty eventuality Maverick's might throw at him. "Anyone can go through one wave. If they don't panic, they can handle one wave," says Frosty. "Jay was in shape. He could handle five waves, piece of cake."

In the winter of 1992 to '93, Frosty announced that Jay was ready. They were goin' to Disneyland. There was a problem, though: Jay's idea of the happiest place on earth was closed for repairs that winter. Desirable conditions for his introduction to Maverick's didn't materialize the entire winter season, leaving the anxious young argonaut more eager than ever.

Nevertheless, the two visited Maverick's that winter, if only to continue Jay's education. They drove up from Santa Cruz at minus tide to examine the reef and correlate lineups. They drew diagrams. They paddled around. They discussed. Frosty imparted to Jay knowledge garnered over six years of surfing Maverick's, the more vital and esoteric of which he was reluctant to reveal for this article, fearing surfers with aspirations for Maverick's would use it in lieu of true preparation.

Frosty's instruction of Jay wasn't as much about the stockpiling of information as it was an extrapolation of what was already there. "Jay already has so much water knowledge at his age," says Frosty. "He isn't even aware of the extent to which it benefits him." Frosty predicted that

Jay would laugh when asked if he considered himself a waterman. "Because," he says, "it is a function of Jay's personality to laugh when things hit close to home."

By the summer of 1993, Jay was entering the final phase of his training. He spent most of his time in the water surfing, sailing, fishing, and paddling, and it was another beneficial tutelage for him. The ocean taught him the subtle intricacies of her way, administering her lessons about nobility and integrity through his genes, changing the way he lived, not just the way he surfed. The school of watermen has taught generations of the surfing family, too many people to name. But the common denominator among graduates seems to be respect—namely, respect for life. Jay received the Duke Kahanamoku Award for sportsmanship at the 1994 Big Stick Surf-o-Rama. "The essence of this kid is that he cares," says Frosty. "That is part of being a waterman. He has this deep-seated caring, not only for himself, and not only for other people, but for his surroundings. And his surroundings are the water."

By 1992 to '93, the winter of Jay's discontent, he and Frosty had nurtured a strong mutual respect. Sometime after the first year, the structured teacher/pupil contract began to recede in light of a growing camaraderie, a companionship built around their shared passion. "This is not a reflection of anything I have taught him," says Frosty, "but maybe this is one of the reasons that we have the relationship we have, that we have this respect." Frosty and Jay are the sponsor and pledge of an exclusive fraternity, and their experience relegates all nonbrothers to the periphery when the conversation turns to related subjects, like plane crash survivors who can only find consolation in other survivors. The object of their passion, the evidence of which Frosty calls "the glow," began waking Frosty up in the middle of the night a few years ago, when midnight swells were peaking and Maverick's was calling out for playmates from her mountaintop. "That's another thing we share," says Frosty. Starting two years ago, whenever Maverick's tumbles in the night and wrestles Frosty from slumber, Jay wakes up, too.

The winter of 1993 to '94 almost came and went without the fulfillment of Jay's rabid desire for Maverick's. But finally two late-blooming days in April delivered what he had been craving. His first paddle out into 15- to 18-foot Maverick's was a coming of age, a graduation of the apprentice from reliance on his master. Jay remembers the turning point: "When we first paddled out, Frosty was directly beside me. But by the halfway point I ended up being about two minutes ahead of him. Then my thoughts began to pound. 'Should I go right out into the lineup and try to get a wave, or should I sit and wait for Frosty?' I pondered for a couple of minutes, realizing eventually that even if Frosty were there, he couldn't answer that question for me. Only I could. That was when I decided to go and sit in the lineup."

Jay's metaphorical leap out of the nest parlayed him into his first wave at Maverick's, and the result was nothing short of his long-endured expectations. "The feeling after my first wave was incredible. I felt like I had just conquered Mount Everest or won a gold medal in the Olympics. I really felt on top of the world." Frosty was there, sitting in the channel, watching the fledgling's first flight. He confirms Jay's excitement with an unexpected metaphor for a 15-year-old surfer riding 18-foot surf. "He was having a great time. He was laughin' and gigglin', just like a kid in a candy store!" The first day was Jay's commencement ceremony and later he took credit for it with characteristic deferment. "I couldn't have done it without Frosty," he said. For the coach, it was an unveiling of the sculpted creation he had wrought in Jay. What was revealed, as Frosty had expected all along, was the image of a waterman in the classic mold.

At a party celebrating Jay's banner week at Maverick's in December, Frosty kept hidden a small, gold-plated wheelbarrow. This wheelbarrow was a joke that had been passed down through generations of his students, a friendly jibe about coach Frosty, whose myriad idiosyncrasies make him an easy target for caricature. It was said by one of his early students that Frosty, by virtue of his seemingly elephantine ancestry, would need a wheelbarrow to carry just one of his balls. When it came time for Jay's congratulatory roast that evening, Frosty handed down the gold-plated symbol of respect with utmost pride.

A tender moment followed the day of the wave that eventually landed Jay on the cover of *Surfer*. Frosty was relaxing at home with his wife, Brenda, and two children, Lake and Rogue, when the phone rang. It was Jay. He was calling with something to say, a burden to unload, but before he came to it, the two fell into a chatty conversation about the day. Frosty was on the injured reserve list and was not present to see Jay's horrific plunge. He listened intently as Jay elaborated on what tales had already trickled down the coast with surfers returning from Maverick's. He related the wipeout, his worst yet, and the first real road test for all his preparation. Frosty remained characteristically aloof, showing little surprise or emotion at the harrowing tale. Jay recounted how, half swimming, half paddling his broken board, he proceeded directly back to the boat and retrieved the board Frosty had lent him as an alternate. He then paddled back into the lineup and within an hour was into another beast. Jay surfed eight waves that day, all with the courage and concentration of a veteran.

The events of the day having been accounted for, Jay cleared his throat to say what he really called to say. There was a silent but not awkward pause, finally broken by Jay's voice. His tone was lower, signifying a swing to a more significant topic. "What you taught me saved my life," he said. "If you hadn't helped me train and practice all those things, I would have died. And I just wanted to thank you."

Death of a Legend

Matt Warshaw

*I*n the end, no one could question Mark Foo's big wave credentials or
his status as a self-made media darling. The sad irony is that it took
Foo's bewildering drowning at Maverick's, on December 23, 1994,
to thrust big wave surfing onto international headlines. Virtually every
network sports show, all manner of print media from Time to Sports
Illustrated to Rolling Stone, as well as various foreign media—they all
covered the death of Mark Foo. The effect was profound. For decades,
mainstream media painted big wave surfers as daredevils and lunatics, a
view often promoted by the insular surfing world itself. Then Foo died
and suddenly the sport was talked about in the same breath as football
and boxing. Unquestionably, big business greatly increased surfing's
exposure, but ultimately it took a personality—namely, Mark Foo, a big
wave surfer who had always reached out to the public—to shift public
perception. In embracing the late champion, the public finally embraced
big wave surfing as a "legitimate" sport.

All true adventure sports contain the great opposites of joy and terror, known
and unknown, tragedy and triumph. Risk-taking adventurers step over the
threshold of life and death and are not always guaranteed a floor beneath their
feet, though they can usually delight in the exhilaration of finding one. Mark
Foo lived his life this way—and made sure you knew all about it. On that day at
Maverick's, Mark Foo willingly stepped across the threshold and fell into the void,
a tragic event by popular reckoning.

That notion is both embraced and challenged in the following story by Matt
Warshaw, noted surfing journalist and a personal friend of Mark Foo. Warshaw
tries to make sense of the fact that within every tragedy there is triumph and
within every triumph there is tragedy. The mind balks at the merging of these

seeming opposites, but the great waves roll on and the Mark Foos of the world
live to take the big drop.

‡ ‡ ‡

Mark Foo died surfing Maverick's on Friday, December 23, 1994, and that's as fixed as it gets. Almost everything else about the day, the many beliefs and opinions, remain in some state of flux and conjecture.

How did Foo die? Drowning followed by head wound, or the other way around? Why did Foo die? Random occurrence or destiny? Did it have anything to do with all the cameras on the scene, his lack of sleep, not knowing the lineup and taking off too far back, too thick a wet suit, too long a surfboard, rushing out without carefully looking the place over—or was it that the North Shore had been so small in December that Foo was out of practice?

Foo fell off at the peak, in the middle of the action, with a dozen surfers outside (including big wave notables Brock Little, Mike Parson, Ken Bradshaw, Mark Renneker, Evan Slater, and Jeff Clark), three boats in the channel, eight to ten cameras and camcorders, and about a hundred spectators on the beach and the bluff, plus a helicopter circling overhead—so how is it that nobody saw him drift away to the south?

Is Maverick's really as heavy as everyone says? Parsons escaped death—with Little just a few yards away, in a struggle of his own—even as Foo was dying. Can we still say big wave surfing isn't really all that dangerous?

Mark Sheldon Foo was born in Singapore in 1958. His father was a photojournalist for the U.S. Information Agency, a branch of the Foreign Service. Mark had a brother who was twelve years older and a sister who was three years older. The family moved to Honolulu when Mark was four. He was raised as a culturally assimilated middle-class American but remained mindful of his Chinese roots. He didn't learn to swim until age ten and began surfing when he was eleven. However, the following year, his family moved again, this time to Rockville, Maryland, just north of Washington, D.C. Mark was twelve, and after two years of nurturing on the south shore of Oahu, his love for surfing had already developed into what he recognized as a true calling. Life in Rockville, however, was the heaviest situation he'd faced yet, possibly the heaviest situation he'd *ever* face—East Coast suburbia. Almost 150 miles to the nearest surf. Four years to go before he was old enough to get a driver's license.

"He was miserable," says Sharlyn Foo-Wagner, Foo's older sister. "He'd have tantrums and fits; he'd lie on the floor and kick and scream. You know how intense Mark was—well, he was intense back then, too."

Mark had died just a week earlier, and Sharlyn seemed to welcome the distraction of talking about her brother's childhood. She wouldn't have picked up on how grateful I was to hear about Mark's reaction to Maryland. The image of a twelve-year-old freaking out in the middle of the family room was, to me, an anodyne to the inevitable posthumous cliches: Mark Foo as the "fallen warrior" or "big wave hero," or, as the *New York Times* put it, the "Joe Montana of Big Waves." For starters, a sixth-grade fit was something Foo himself would laugh about, and that reminded me of how he could be pretty funny. (His comparative read on tennis, golf, and surfing, for example: "Young guys running around, hitting a fuzzy ball over a net. Old guys walking across the grass and hitting a little white ball into a hole in the ground. Surfing *shits* on what these other guys are doing.")

And it probably isn't stretching too far to say that a well-thrown tantrum demonstrates a profound feeling for the sport, a point that had been diluted—not so much over the past couple of years as throughout the 1980s—by Foo's insatiable self-promotion. Foo, probably more than any surfer I can name, wanted to be famous, and toward that end he could be boorish, maybe even deluded. In his most recent resume, he called himself "surfing's preeminent big wave rider." Perhaps thinking he hadn't quite put his finger on it, he repositioned himself later in the same resume as "surfing's consummate living legend."

But on a level that predated and superseded his commercial ambition, Foo signed up for a life of surfing motivated by nothing more than the pleasure of being in the ocean. And that pleasure hadn't faded much, as far as I could tell, from the lost years in Rockville to his last day at Maverick's on December 23, 1994.

"Everyone wants answers, and wants 'em fast," said Ken Bradshaw on December 29, one week after Foo died. "I think Mark's death was a fluke. An accident. But people's thinking on the whole thing is still evolving. Mine is for sure. I'm still thinking about it all the time."

The 1980s big wave rivalry between Foo and Bradshaw had fizzled out three or four years earlier. They began to surf the North Shore's outer reefs together. They called each other on the phone. They were going to buy a Jet Ski together and become tow-in partners.

Throughout mid-December 1994, as the North Shore winter refused to kick in, Foo and Bradshaw were well aware that Maverick's was consistently going off big, and both were in contact with Renneker time and again for the latest update. "It was the swell of a lifetime," Renneker said later. "Maybe the greatest Northern California swell ever. For eleven days it stayed up between 10 and 20 feet, even bigger, and for almost all that time it was smooth and clean."

Bradshaw flew to San Francisco on December 16 and caught a midrange Maverick's session, then turned around and flew back to Hawaii. Foo hadn't yet surfed Maverick's but was already expert at flying to the mainland for big surf—to Todos Santos in Mexico, specifically.

On Thursday evening, December 22, Bradshaw and Foo had to make a decision on whether or not to leave Hawaii. According to reports, Monday and Wednesday had been huge at Maverick's. The waves had tapered off Thursday, but forecasters predicted another increase on Friday. The situation couldn't have been better—except both surfers wanted to be back home in Hawaii before Christmas morning. Foo called the airlines and discovered they could catch a return flight to Oahu on Christmas Eve. Foo then called Bradshaw. Green light.

The two met at Foo's house that evening, and an overnight flight put them at the San Francisco airport at 5:30 A.M. the following morning. Bradshaw arranged for a rental car while Foo slept by the boards. Foo continued sleeping on the drive to Renneker's house at Ocean Beach and stayed in the car while Bradshaw went inside. All three then drove twenty-five minutes south to Maverick's.

Tactical ingenuity was shown early on in Foo's life when, at age fourteen, he enlisted Sharlyn's help in convincing their parents that he should be allowed to move to Pensacola, Florida, and live with the family of a friend.

"He wasn't a regular fourteen-year-old, because of surfing," Sharlyn remembers, "and I told my parents that they had to give him permission to go, or he was just going to run away." Mark's parents were certain their younger son was going through a phase. Letting him move south seemed incredibly indulgent, but they relented. It was a long time before they came to understand surfing as a legitimate career choice. "Nothing would make them happier," Foo said in 1989, "than if I quit surfing and went back to school. Even now."

He spent two years in Gulf Coast Florida. *Surfer* did its one and only feature on Pensacola in early 1974, and sixteen-year-old Foo—in what he would undoubtedly construe, in years to come, as early proof of a special destiny—scored a nice half-page color shot.

Later that year the Foo family moved back to Honolulu. In 1975, Mark graduated from high school, one year ahead of his class. In the mid-seventies he had fair-to-good results in the Hawaiian Surfing Association's junior circuit, competing against the likes of Dane Kealoha, Buttons Kaluhiokalani, and Mark Liddell. He joined the IPS world tour in 1977.

Foo would later say he quit the IPS because the money was poor, the waves were often small, and, more importantly, because it was keeping him from making a full contribution to the sport. But the ratings must have factored into his thinking as well. He was unranked in 1977, unranked in 1978, 66th in 1979, 68th in 1980, unranked in 1981, and 67th in 1982. At this point he was twenty-four years old and had gained an implicit understanding of what surfers such as Tom Carroll, Tom Curren, Martin Potter, and the rest of the post "Free Ride" generation were going to do to the ratings over the next decade. Consequently he began looking for an alternative surf-career passage.

He discovered it the following year. In 1983 Mark surfed Waimea Bay for the first time and began an accelerated, self-directed big wave apprenticeship.

His dramatic and controversial entry into the top ranks of big wave surfers came two years later and was based on a single afternoon's surfing. On January 18, 1985, Mark, James Jones, J. P. Patterson, and Alec Cooke all dove under a baroque Waimea close-out (Jones, through a calculus method known only to himself, pegged the wave height at 48 feet), breaking left across the middle of the Bay. When they all surfaced, Mark was the only one who still had a board. The others swam in and were picked up one at a time by the rescue helicopter. Mark paddled back toward the point, caught a 30-footer, and got to his feet just as the wall went concave. He kissed off the edge, floated momentarily in space, then fell into the void. A long and horrendous deep-water wipeout followed. The helicopter moved in. Mark surfaced, reached for the basket, climbed in, and was ferried to the beach.

A harrowing story. Mark wasted no time getting it down on paper and sending it out to the magazines. Ken Bradshaw, that same day at Waimea, had one of the defining sessions of his career and rode at least a dozen huge waves before Foo paddled out. As Ken noted later, Foo didn't even make a wave that afternoon. But it was Foo's account that went into circulation and Foo, in the weeks and months to follow, who was lauded as the big wave hero. He'd hit the ground running. Ken was disgusted.

A rivalry was born. Ken, although just in his early thirties, was positioned as defender of the old guard. Foo, more or less, spoke for a party of one. (Darrick Doerner was the only other surfer Foo's age making a serious study of Waimea, and his approach was more traditional.)

Foo saw that he was onto something progressive. Bradshaw and the Waimea regulars ("the bearded crew," as Foo called them) saw him as insolent, brash, and garish. Both were right. Certainly the old guard was put off by his corporate attire in the mid-eighties, after Anheuser-Busch signed him and he turned up with a metal-flake gold board, framing a huge red-and-white Michelob logo. (The metal-flake silver Michelob Light model was, of course, for smaller waves.)

But Foo was doing a lot more than acting as company advance man at Waimea. He rode smaller, narrower, more performance-oriented boards. He wore a leash. He was one of the first—possibly *the* first—to ride Waimea on a tri-fin. All standard procedure today.

He probably stepped over the line in 1987, as we taped an interview for *Surfer*, when he said, "I don't think anyone surfs 20 foot Waimea better than I do, in terms of performance." Part of me liked the audacity; part of me was a little put off. I didn't necessarily believe in the Waimea brotherhood, but Foo's qualitative remark seemed untoward and disrespectful.

On the other hand, as I sat on the point at Waimea on the afternoon of December 6, 1988, during the Eddie Aikau Expression Session, it occurred to me that Mark Foo, at that point in time, could very well have been the best at Waimea. It was below maximum size, with just a few sets topping out at 20 feet, but Mark began by nailing the biggest wave of the day, and finished by pulling into—and very nearly coming out of—a gigantic, snaggle toothed barrel. The Expression Session was an exhibition, so no results were announced. But nearly all the heavyweights were on hand and Mark was plainly the standout surfer of the day.

I flew to Hawaii in the summer of 1987 to do a piece on Bradshaw and Foo for *Outside* magazine and very much enjoyed listening to their barbed—but never really vicious—comments about each other.

Foo: "To me, good surfing is making it look easy. Kenny's approach has always been a make-it-look-hard approach."

Bradshaw: "Just the way he [Foo] warms up . . . this big public display, like, 'Here I go, everyone. I'm getting warmed up now.'"

In the early 1990s, the North Shore's outer reefs—not to mention the duo's looming middle age—created a middle ground where Bradshaw and Foo could become friends. No surprise. A few years ago Foo told me a story about how, in 1977, he'd broken both his surfboards one morning at Sunset and Bradshaw had lent him one of his. Bradshaw, too, in 1987, had a moment of near-gentle reflection. "I guess if you really stop and look at it, [in 1977] I was sort of a toned-down version of Mark."

Bruce Jenkins, in his book *North Shore Chronicles*, wrote that Foo almost always went surfing by himself: "He's a self-described loner who neither seeks nor desires friendships with other surfers ('I guess I don't have many friends,' [Foo] says, not at all bothered by the admission.)" But later, at Foo's wake at Maverick's on December 30, Jenkins also noted that on the last day of his life, Mark Foo walked down to the beach side by side with Mark Renneker and Ken Bradshaw.

Foo, Bradshaw, and Renneker arrived on the beach around 9:30 A.M. The water was a cold 52 degrees Fahrenheit, but the weather was unseasonably warm, and the morning offshore waves—primary cause for dozens of mind-blowing wipeouts earlier in the week—stayed bottled up in the canyons. But the surf hadn't developed as expected: It was 12 to 15 feet, with an 18-footer every hour or so. The swell direction had gone west-northwest, a change from earlier in the week, when it had rolled straight north.

The surf wasn't booming, but there was nonetheless a definite sense of "event" to the morning. More cameras and spectators than ever before. More famous surfers.

Mike Parson, like Foo and Brock Little, had never surfed Maverick's. Parsons had flown up by himself from Orange County the night before and checked into a Half Moon Bay hotel. By chance, he met Evan Slater in the Maverick's parking lot. The two went out by boat and were in the water by 7:15 A.M. Jay Moriarty, Peter Mel, Josh Loya, Matt Ambrose, Shawn Rhodes, and a few others arrived later. Jeff Clark was in the water around 9:00 A.M. Little paddled into the lineup shortly before Clark, broke his leash on his second wave, then swam into deep water to the south, all the way to the harbor jetty, where he climbed out, looked for his board, and saw it drifting out to sea. He swam, retrieved, and paddled to the beach—a thirty-minute tour all together. There was mild rock damage across the bottom of Little's board, and he'd just switched to his second board and paddled back out when Foo, Bradshaw, and Renneker arrived.

The visiting surfers were all somewhat disappointed by the size of the waves. "But it was a nice consolation prize," says Little. "Beautiful day. Pretty easy, for the most part. A good size to check the place out, learn how to line up, all that." Foo was overgunned on a 10' 6" and briefly considered running back to the car—about 1.5 miles round-trip—for his smaller board.

Slater, who had put in career-making performances earlier in the week, was the only pro not feeling a little bit let down by the size. "I really don't know if I was ready for another huge day. That morning, Friday . . . well, compared to the other days that week, it wasn't even close. I was relieved, actually. But even so, now and then a beast would steam in and there would be a moment or two when you'd feel what the place is really like."

Three boats were in the channel, just a few yards from the breaking waves, and at least two photographers were on each boat. Contributors to *Surfer*, *Surfing*, and *Surfer's Journal* were either up on the cliff, in the water, or on the boats. At 10:30 A.M., a *Surfer* photographer went up in a helicopter. The weather had gotten so warm that a few people watching from the cliff were going shirtless. The swell seemed to be dropping. The amount of time between sets increased, and there were fewer in-between waves. A three-wave set moved in just before 11:00 A.M., and the biggest wave caught all the pros out of position, too far to the north. Renneker, lined up to the south, scored a long, beautiful, smooth wall—probably the best wave of the morning.

I had always thought Foo's reputation as a loner was a little over-played. He only made as much small talk as he had to and was content with his own company, so he often seemed to be quiet or aloof. But if he felt comfortable with the person he was talking to, and the conversation took a turn that interested him, Foo's reserve would vanish, his staccato delivery would be cranked up, and he'd become almost garrulous. Storm tracking; love, romance, and the single man; the outer reef visible from the window of his well-appointed house just west of Waimea—all were topics that could start him talking. He had greater depths than his "mul-tifaceted professional profile" (his words) might suggest. The world outside of surfing interested him. He was able to connect with a wide range of people. I always thought it spoke well of Foo that the quiet and gracious Bobby Owens counted him as a lifelong friend.

It's hard to say for sure if Foo was the first to create a sustainable professional niche outside of the world tour, but he was definitely in there with the advance guard, and I'd argue that he and Gerry Lopez were the first real masters of the art. The party line was that Foo did what he did in order to "create more public awareness and apprecia-tion" for surfing, but that was always a little hard to swallow. It's difficult to put his career in such a purely altruistic context. Mark Foo's contri-bution to surfing was great, but rarely, if ever, was it disconnected from the sport's contribution to Mark Foo. One hand washed the other. But he worked hard and was never dissembling about his ambition and was right on the money when he said, "I'm trying to set a precedent for surfers to make a living within the spotlight, but outside of the Tour." Brock Little's whole career, in fact, is loosely based on a pattern Foo had worked out long ago.

Two reasons for Foo's success are obvious. First, he was a great all-around surfer. Until Brock Little came along, Foo was the only top big wave surfer who could shine in waves of any size. Second, he surfed well for the camera. His driving, high-speed crouch never went out of fashion in big surf (as the December 1992 cover of *Surfer* beautifully proves), and his surf media longevity—always as a contemporary act, never an oldie-but-goodie—was virtually unprecedented: He and Dane Kealoha were the only people to have *Surfer* cover shots in three different decades: the 1970s, 1980s, and 1990s.

Maverick's doesn't need to be full strength to be terrifying, as local surfer Shawn Rhodes discovered midmorning on December 23. Rhodes took off on an inside wave, rode for a while, then fell. The whitewater pushed him deep and his feet brushed the bottom. He surfaced and ducked under two more waves. The next wave, not too big, "but more of a wedge than the first two," broke directly in front of him and drove him straight to the bottom, where his leg wedged into what he thinks was a crack in an overhang. His kneecap was caught, while his foot and lower leg remained clear. He thinks it was probably three or four seconds before he was able to work his leg free and swim up. He then paddled in.

Twenty minutes later the next set arrived, this one with more waves. It was somewhere around 11:20 A.M. Bradshaw and Foo paddled for the second wave, with Bradshaw on the inside. The wave wasn't particularly big, about 15 feet, but drawing hard off the bottom. Bradshaw was too deep and backed out. Foo stood, made it halfway down the face, and pitched forward. He disappeared with a splash. Everybody's attention went almost immediately to Little and Parsons, taking off on the following wave, which was slightly bigger than Foo's. Parsons was in front. He was held up momentarily at the top, regained some forward drive, then caught his outside edge. He fell on his back between his surfboard and Little and was run through by a thick, boxy lip. Little carried on for a few yards and then he, too, was snowed under by whitewater.

The fourth wave in the set was equal to the one Little and Parsons rode, but it went unridden. Two small waves followed. Bradshaw rode the seventh wave all the way across and pulled out near Mushroom Rock.

He paddled back out, and photographer Bob Barbour, on one of the boats, yelled at Bradshaw, telling him he was lucky he hadn't caught the wave that Foo had caught. Barbour said Foo had eaten it and broken his board. Bradshaw kept paddling, sure that Foo would return as soon as possible on his backup board.

At that point, people up on the bluff began to notice that Little and Parsons were in trouble near Sail Rock.

Sail Rock, about the size of a small moving van, is at the northern end of a 150-yard chain of rocks, mostly submerged, separating the Pillar Point lagoon from the surf break. Mushroom Rock is at the opposite end, closest to the channel. Just to the south of Sail Rock sits a big, tightly clustered group of rocks, all of which are closer to the wave energy than the rocks just a few dozen yards to the south. Whitewater— particularly from waves that miss the outside reef and break farther inside—roars up, over, and around these rocks, then spills into the lagoon. Some people think this area is the most dangerous place at Maverick's. Jeff Clark was memorably stranded just to the south of Sail Rock in April 1993. Now, Little and Parsons, after wiping out together, were quickly being rushed into the same pocket of rocks.

About eight waves rolled through, including the one Parsons and Little had ridden, before the two surfers moved into the rock zone. Little's leash snagged almost immediately. The surge was so powerful that he couldn't reach the Velcro strap on his ankle. Two or three waves went by, and the normally unfazed Hawaiian began to worry. Then his leash broke, and he was rolled into the lagoon. "I think I just willed it to break," Little said a few days later. "Maybe I moved my leg up and down and rubbed it against the rocks, but it just seems like I knew it was going to break, and it did. It was weird."

Parsons's leash had also caught on a rock, and, like Little, he wasn't able to reach down to his ankle. Unlike Little, his leash didn't break, and he was held underwater for two waves in a row, surfaced for a quick breath, then held under for two more. "Right then, I was absolutely, totally convinced I was drowning and I was going to die. Getting held down for a long time in Hawaii, or at Todos Santos—this was something totally different. Once I was in the rocks, I gave up trying to relax. Instead, I fought the whole time for a breath. I got two, and they saved my life." Parsons was stuck for six to eight waves all together. Then the Velcro on his leash came undone and he pushed away from the rock he'd been stuck on, grabbed his board, and was flushed into the lagoon. "I didn't even try to get to my leash. I don't know how it came undone. Brock and I talked about that last night, and, like Brock said, it is really weird how that worked—for both of us."

Little had a scrape across the back of one hand. Parsons had scrapes across his back, feet, and hands, and he'd hit his Achilles tendon. Neither was hurt seriously.

Parsons, shaky and pale, decided to paddle back out to the boat and change into his clothes, rather than wait on the beach. Before leaving he asked Little if the two of them had bumped into one another underwater. Little said he didn't remember. Parsons paddled to the boat; Little again went to the beach, attached his third leash of the day, and paddled back to the lineup.

Perhaps ninety minutes went by. Bradshaw at one point wondered to himself where Foo was, then added up the long swim in, the jog to and from the car, and a conversation or two with people on the beach, and Foo's absence seemed accounted for.

A light west wind came up around 1:00 P.M. and the water began to clear.

Evan Slater joined Parsons on one of the boats, along with photographers Steve Spaulding and Doug Acton and the boat driver. They began the short trip back to the small Half Moon Bay harbor, located just to the southeast. When the boat was almost to the harbor entrance, somebody noticed the purple-and-yellow tail section of Foo's board floating about 20 yards away, between the boat and the harbor jetty.

It was Slater who noticed Foo's body, floating face down next to the board. He yelled to the boat driver to turn around. Slater, still in his wet suit, then jumped in, swam over, and, to the horror of all, grabbed Foo and passed him up to the others. None of them knew CPR, but pressure was applied to Foo's chest and water poured from his mouth. Meanwhile, the boat driver called the harbor master and went full speed through the entrance; the harbor master called the two harbor paramedics; the paramedics met the incoming boat, jumped aboard, and began CPR. Foo had a shallow cut over his right eye and an abrasion across the left side of his forehead.

Once docked, Foo was turned over to an ambulance crew who worked on him for nearly an hour. But he'd been down for nearly two hours and there was no chance for revival.

Jeff Clark was on the dock at the time and brought the news first to the parking lot, then the beach. His eyes were red-rimmed, and he couldn't quite sequence his words properly as he approached Little.

"They picked Foo up . . . they tried for an hour . . . he didn't make it."

Gone but not forgotten: Friends of Mark Foo join together for a floating wake at Maverick's. PHOTO BY LAWRENCE BECK

Little, stunned, turned away, looked up, and shouted something unintelligible. Foo was still lying on the dock about forty-five minutes later when Bradshaw pulled back the blanket that covered Foo's face, saw his friend, and began to cry. A south wind began to blow by late afternoon, and the long December run of good surf was over.

Foo's death earned feature-length coverage in *Sports Illustrated*, the *New York Times*, the *Los Angeles Times*, *Paris Match*, and *Outside* magazine, among countless other newspapers and magazines. The story also received television coverage. A number of people, family included, commented on how Foo would've dug the publicity.

"Dennis Pang and I sat under a tree at Waimea the other day," Bradshaw said, about a week after Mark's death, "and Dennis said to me, 'Foo's just laughing. He couldn't have done it any better.'" And he was right. Mark Foo rode a ton of big waves, he surfed all over the world, he got to be famous, and he went out in a big way. Now he gets to be remembered forever. And, man, he'd just love that.

In the hours and days that followed, before people saw the videotape and photographs, nobody seemed to remember Foo's wipeout as particularly rough—by Maverick's standards, at least. The film and pictures, however, tell the real story. Foo gets to his feet and assumes his usual low-centered crouch. The nose of his board lifts slightly and Foo straightens up, presses the nose back down, and tries to reset his inside edge. No luck. He falls forward and skips down the face. He doesn't penetrate. The lip throws out and Foo disappears. A second goes by and then, suddenly, Foo's board pops through the curtain as it gets pulled over the falls. Foo, harder to see, shows up as an indistinct shadow, a few feet to the right of his board, just before the explosion. The wave was more concentrated than big, and Foo was driven down at the power centerpoint. His surfboard eventually turned up in three pieces.

There was almost no variation in the three different videotapes that turned up over the next few days. In all three, the camera swings out to Parsons and Little on the following wave. After they fall, four or five heads (depending on the videotape) can be seen in the aftermath: Little and Parsons, plus John Raymond and Jake Wormhoudt—who had ridden a smaller wave together just before Foo and were caught inside—and Greg Head, also caught inside. Nobody on the cliff or in the water remembers seeing Foo come up—but it was a fast-moving field, too distant for those on the cliff to be able to recognize one surfer from the other and critical enough for the five surfers inside that they were thinking only about each approaching wave. Raymond, who ended up on the rocks to the south of Little and Parsons, remembers a piece of broken surfboard rushing by overhead in the whitewater.

Most people's attention, in the minutes that followed, was on Little and Parsons as they struggled on the rocks. Still, the question that wouldn't go away, later in the afternoon and over the next few days, was how Foo could have possibly drifted off unnoticed.

Bradshaw, tentatively, has put a few other questions to rest. He says Foo was ready to surf the day he died. He'd done the late-night, last-minute hustle plenty of times over the past few years to get to where the waves were big; he'd surfed cold water and was comfortable in a full wet suit; and he'd surfed big waves on two separate occasions the week before he flew to Maverick's. He was in excellent shape. He wasn't surfing recklessly. He wasn't scared or even tense. "No, Foo was stoked," Little says. "He was being sociable, in fact, which is unusual for him. He was having a good time."

"And that whole thing about all of us sitting too far over," says Bradshaw, "you know, that's just the way it goes when you have those kinds of surfers in the water. Is it smart? Well, no. But it's always been like that, and it always will be like that. Plus the thing is—and this is important—Foo was playing it really well that day. He was sitting a little inside and farther over, more where we all should've been sitting. That's why he got so many waves. He probably rode twelve waves, and that's a lot."

And his last wave? "It was pretty heavy, but no way was it stupid. He had a good shot at making it. A really good shot."

The mainstream media coverage of Foo's death was, for the most part, shallow, inaccurate, and shamelessly exaggerated. The *New York Times* provided some unexpected comic relief with a December 29 article that described Foo as "the Joe Montana of Big Waves," and Maverick's itself was transformed into a general term for big waves ("It was these same Maverick's that attracted Foo"). Two exceptions were the *Los Angeles Times*'s well-researched front-page article on December 31 and surfer/sportswriter Bruce Jenkins's fine piece for the *San Francisco Chronicle* on December 26.

In virtually all of the other articles, Maverick's was pegged as the villain. But how culpable was it, really? The answer might depend on how Foo died. A blow to the head, followed by drowning, could happen almost anywhere, even in medium-small surf. If that was the case, Foo's death would be less site specific and due more to terrible luck.

However, Bud Moorman, San Mateo coroner, looked at the results from Foo's December 24 autopsy and said that Foo drowned first and was struck on the head *afterward*. Suddenly the weight of blame seemed to shift back to Maverick's. "The cut on his head wasn't enough to knock him out," Moorman said. Foo likely died from a "conscious drowning." Peter Benson, the pathologist who did the autopsy, says there was no skull fracture and no clinical contusion on the brain.

Because Foo didn't turn up in the aftermath of his last wave, or the one following, it may be that he was held down for three or more consecutive waves. Because the coroner says Foo wasn't pushed into the rocks (no barnacle scraps; no algae)—as was Raymond, who rode the wave before Foo, and Parsons and Little, who rode the wave after—it may be that Foo's leash caught around a rock somewhere in the impact zone and held Foo in place. (Little is now certain that he didn't bump into Parsons underwater; but Parsons is certain he bumped into *somebody*; both now think it was Foo.) Because the tail block of Foo's board was so damaged (missing side fin, swallowtail and one rail crushed in), it may be, as Jeff Clark surmises, that the board, or at least the tail, was wedged into a cave or crevasse.

The exact circumstances of Foo's death are probably unknowable, but a "conscious drowning" scenario at Maverick's—especially in moderately sized waves—implicates the place to the hilt and should draw a heavier, more discerning line between those who surf and those who watch. Foo is dead, Parsons came close, and Little had what he called a "heavy experience," all as the result of a single set of waves. Add to this the fact that Rhodes got his leg caught on the bottom, Clark had a near-fatal encounter on the rocks two years ago, and there exist at least a dozen "worst-ever" testimonials from people with enough big wave experience to make the claim indisputably authentic. The obvious conclusion would be that the risks involved in surfing Maverick's, if anything, are higher than previously thought. Maverick's, along with Pipeline, should properly be seen as one of the most deadly big wave spots in the world.

Different people have different thoughts as to how Foo came to die when and where he did. Evan Slater said it was a "freak accident." Mark Renneker, in a turn toward the mythical, sought to put it in context with the ten preceding days of good, clean, big surf and said Foo's death may be something the modern western mind can't quite grasp. Foo himself—for promotional reasons, spiritual reasons, or both—certainly would have cited a special destiny and acknowledged the work of an unseen hand.

Finally, what do surfers think now about big wave danger in general?

The shock of Foo's death, at least in part, comes from the fact that never before had a famous big wave surfer died while surfing big waves. Dickie Cross died under horrific circumstances at Waimea Bay in 1943, but he wasn't especially known as a big wave rider, and it was just terrible misfortune that he was caught out by a fast-rising swell. Bob Simmons rode big surf but certainly not with the same focus as big wave surfers of the past thirty-five years, and he died in late-summer conditions at Windansea, in 1954, with the surf running perhaps 6 to 8 feet, hardly in the realm of really big waves.

Foo's death was the first of its kind. The case could be made that death-by-surfing is extremely rare—consider the annual festival of wipeouts at the Pipeline Masters or the fact that people are now surfing Waimea shorebreak, or even the steady and inexplicably unpunished series of wipeouts at Maverick's earlier in the week, before Foo died. All this seems to indicate that big wave surfing perhaps isn't as dangerous as people make it out to be. When people think of dangerous sports, they think of bullfighting, auto racing, motorcycle racing, rock climbing, hang gliding, cave diving—but big wave surfing doesn't make the list. The numbers don't portray it as a truly dangerous sport.

Foo himself probably wouldn't have bought into that notion. He loved what he did and was enlightened and defined by big wave experiences. But he was also sensitive—to a degree well beyond that of any of his peers—to the danger. He understood the extremes. He'd issued the "ultimate thrill, ultimate price" comment on big waves so often that it had nearly become cliché. But that doesn't mean he didn't take it to heart.

He went deeper into the subject during a December 1986 interview, and his thoughts on big waves and mortality didn't change over the next eight years. "The only way you can really prepare for big waves is to ride big waves. And we'll go out there and do it . . . maybe we'll die trying, but we'll go out and give it a shot. I'm not afraid of dying like that. To me it's not tragic to die doing something you love."

NEW DIMENSIONS: THE
TOW-IN MOVEMENT

All adventure sports are driven by an inner dynamic that insists the sport build upon itself. Successive generations keep the venture alive by their drive to contribute something all their own. But if athletes of a new generation feel they lack the opportunity for fresh expression, it is only a matter of time before a fresh movement bursts onto the scene with original ideas, budding egos, outrageous beliefs about what is possible, and the anxious energy to conquer the never-before-thought-of. Such were the circumstances that spawned "power surfing," also known as JATO (Jet-assisted takeoff) or, simply, "tow-in" surfing.

Through the early 1980s, the new hellmen raised the bar not so much by riding bigger waves but rather through wave performance. By the late 1980s, however, surfers had performed everything imaginable on the biggest Waimea mackers. Those busting into the 1990s big wave scene were looking at more of the same, with little chance of expanding the art and developing their own identity. Moreover, gridlock at the big venues was starting to drive people crazy. There were no longer enough big waves to go around. How was an aspiring hellman to hone his chops if every wave was as clogged as 2-foot Malibu? People were getting antsy and a revolution was brewing. Something had to give, and tow-in surfing was the next natural step.

The following selections highlight this spectacular new approach to big wave surfing and review the life of one its cardinal players, Laird Hamilton. Some of the old guard has been reluctant to consider tow-in surfing as anything but a quirky, high-tech novelty. Though privately marveling, many so-called purists called the tow-in movement a swindle. After all, with a slingshot entry, one bypasses a most critical and challenging aspect of riding huge waves: the takeoff and initial drop. But the *size* of the waves these guys were riding! And the *speed!* For sheer magnitude and drama, no one could doubt that the tow-in boys had laid claim to Mark Foo's much publicized "Destination X: The Unridden Realm." Big Waimea was one thing, and a remarkable thing at that. But this tow-in stuff was in a different league altogether. It was also, by all accounts, the only possible way to ride a 30-foot-plus wave. The few people who ever paddled into such a wave were, according to Bruce Jenkins, "blown into oblivion."

It only took a few seasons before true big wave addicts could no longer bear the crowds at the classic paddle-in spots, nor stomach seeing the tow-in boys ripping up the greatest waves all by themselves. One by one, many of the old boys joined the action. For several years Kenny Bradshaw cursed the crowded conditions at his old hunting grounds; then he cursed the $10,000 it touched him and tow-in partner Dan Moore to outfit a tow-in rig and fabricate the special boards. (In 1999, Moore towed into one of the biggest waves ever ridden at Maverick's.) Most of the other premier hellmen also teamed up, got the scratch together to buy the required Jet Ski and custom boards, then started refining the rudiments to towing-in on less than mythic-size waves.

Several years passed. There were many memorable sessions, mostly unreported. Then came January 28, 1998, the "Ultimate Big Wednesday," as the media called it. The entire North Shore went off, and the outer reefs were firing waves upward of 35 feet. And the new tow-in boys made history, as chronicled in Jenkins's piece, "Rediscovering the Old Stoke." Soon after this legendary tow-in session, a photo in Surfer showed Kenny Bradshaw cranking the bottom turn on a wave at Outside Log Cabins, a wave that on the face of it looked about 80 feet tall. At the age of 45, Kenny Bradshaw had, remarkably, once again jumped to the forefront of big wave surfing.

To be sure, we've only seen the first returns of this dramatic innovation. As more outer reefs are explored and surfed by tow-in crews and other frontiers such as Maverick's are explored, the stories can only get bigger. The new generation will settle for nothing less. The following articles start at the beginning and take it from there.

Dave Kalama towing in at Jaws, New Year's Day, 1999. PHOTO BY CLAY ROGERS

POWER SURFING

Ben Marcus

*I*n this short piece from Surfer, *Ben Marcus describes the basics of the tow-in movement.*

‡   ‡   ‡

There are two kinds of surfing on the planet now: paddle surfing and power surfing. Paddle surfing is what you and I do. We lie down on surfboards and use our arms to paddle us out to where the waves are breaking, then use experience and skill to find the peak of the wave, paddle into it, stand up, and ride.

Power surfing is different. Power surfers don't have to paddle out and worry about rips or currents or stroking into waves. They get towed into giant waves behind boats and Jet Skis, feet wedged into foot straps on small, spear-shaped boards, and do the most remarkable things. Imagine driving into a 30-foot peak at 30 miles an hour, fading deeper into the pit than you ever thought possible, coming around the corner, up the face, and doing a tail-slide turn on a 40-foot wall. That's power surfing.

This past winter (1993) a handful of bold surfers invested a great deal of time, money, and physical energy to explore this new epoch in big wave surfing. They experimented with foot straps and surfboards and jet-powered watercraft and discovered they could ride very small boards in very large waves, that the difference between surfing with foot straps and without foot straps is like the difference between riding a snowboard with bindings and without. It makes all the difference in the world.

They did most of their experimenting at a heavy, deep-water outer reef in Maui that up to then had been ridden by very few surfers, mainly because it's almost impossible to paddle into.

One wave this winter summed up all the potential for good and bad. Pete Cabrinha got the wave of his life, pulling backside into a barrel as big as a gymnasium. On the same wave Laird Hamilton was forced to straighten out and got nailed by a 40-foot wall of whitewater. It was, he said, "like getting hit by a gravel truck."

WaveRunners and foot straps and 14-inch-wide surfboards may never catch on with the general surfing public. Then again, these guys simply could be 20 years ahead of their time.

THE NEXT REALM

Bruce Jenkins

*M*any first thought that tow-in surfing somehow made things "easy," overlooking the fact that bigger waves meant bigger consequences, to say nothing of the tricky technical aspects of the tow-in procedure itself. Here, Bruce Jenkins takes a close look at how the original tow-in movement took shape.

‡   ‡   ‡

Bill Sickler had the binoculars out one day last winter, checking a huge north swell from a hillside spot above Sunset Beach. He was watching Laird Hamilton carve out a slice of the future, and he couldn't believe his eyes.

It takes a lot to impress Sickler. He was Jeff Hakman's roommate in the mid-'70s, and he's one of maybe a half-dozen guys to consistently surf Waimea, Sunset, and Pipeline at maximum size over the last 15 years. Bill's idea of a leisurely afternoon is to bodysurf Pipe in wild, jagged conditions with nobody else in the water.

But this was a vision for Sickler, something entirely new. Hamilton was more than a mile out at sea with Darrick Doerner, Buzzy Kerbox, a Zodiac boat, and a WaveRunner. They were towing each other into Hawaiian-style 35-foot waves, picking them up outside Backyards, S-turning their way across the unbroken face, then jamming at full speed as the wave began to crest. The rides were almost surreal, lasting a minute or more, all the way through the inside section at Sunset. These rides, Sickler knew, defined a bold new direction in big wave surfing.

"What Laird was doing just blew my mind," said Sickler. "He had built up so much speed, he was just flying at the point where you usually start your takeoff. He was getting around sections that were simply impossible to make. It was a windsurfer's capacity being executed on a surfboard. I found out he was riding a 7' 2" board with foot straps. He was cranking bottom turns where he was leaning so far over, the only thing in the water was the tip of that inside fin. Just flying, all the way into the channel. I talked to a couple other guys who saw it, and it was like we shouldn't even be out there with that kind of surfing going on."

Which is exactly the point. When it comes to tow-in surfing, you can appreciate it, study it, fantasize about it. But you won't be out there. Not unless you can match the knowledge and ability of Hamilton, Doerner, or Kerbox, who are risking their lives and equipment to find empty waves at spots you can't even see from the beach.

"If you want to try this," says Doerner, "you'd better be able to swim 5 miles, hold your breath for more than two minutes in churning water, and ride the biggest waves of your life in the open ocean. You kids: Don't try this at home."

What Sickler saw last winter, as it turns out, was only a warm-up. Tow-in surfing doesn't even begin until 12 to 15 feet, and for the guys at the forefront, that's just the start. "We're preparing to ride some of the biggest waves of our time," says Doerner. "We're just building up, getting our timing down on the rope, figuring the whole thing out, because one day a 30-plus set's gonna come in, and we're gonna be ready for it."

It is a common belief in the big wave community that waves in the 30-foot range cannot be successfully ridden. Greg Noll discovered that at Makaha in 1969, and while the equipment has changed radically since then, the physics remain the same. Whether it's Mark Foo at closed-out Waimea, Alec Cooke at Outside Log Cabins, or Brock Little at the Eddie Aikau contest, nobody has reached the bottom of a wave that big. "The unridden realm," they call it. Even if you manage to catch a wave that size and get to your feet, there's simply too much water. As the wave builds and goes vertical, water draws up the face faster than a surfer can descend. (Imagine trying to jog on a treadmill spinning at 40 miles an hour, and you have a general idea of the problem.) The few people who have tried to paddle into such a wave have been blown into oblivion.

But now picture a three-man crew with a little help from the modern age: One man in a Yamaha WaveRunner III 650, towing in a surfer with about 30 feet of water-ski rope. The third man in a 60-horsepower Zodiac, charting the sets and landmarks, ready to move in if the WaveRunner goes down.

Buzzy Kerbox showing his stuff at Jaws. PHOTO BY CLAY ROGERS

Three rotating assignments, like friends trading waves at a secret spot. And most importantly, that slingshot head start—something you could never accomplish with conventional paddling.

Is this cheating? Some people think so. "Either paddle into the waves on your own power or get the hell out of the water," they say. Ken Bradshaw, always the hard-core traditionalist, said that for years. But even Bradshaw has seen the light now. "We all know it's a whole new world at 30 feet, and this is the only way we'll be able to ride that," he says. "If you paddle out on a totally glassy day, maybe you could pick off a few on your own. But that's not the way it is out there. The winds are severe on the outer reefs, the lineups are constantly changing. This is the only clear-cut way to reach that next level. You lose two important disciplines: locating the peak and dropping in. But the experience is just as satisfying."

Hamilton never argued with Bradshaw's purist approach: "I can understand Ken's change of heart. You'd need a 20-foot paddleboard to catch a 30-foot groundswell in the open ocean. And even if you did catch it, you wouldn't want to be riding that thing. . . . Hey, I'm sick of paddling. I've paddled from Molokai to Oahu, I've paddled the English Channel. How much can you paddle? I want to change, make surfing evolve, so we're not stepping back and watching skateboarders and snowboarders do all the progressive stuff."

The choice of equipment is wide open. Doerner ripped the outside reefs last winter on a pair of Brewer boards, a 9' 6" and a 10' 6". Hamilton was given a new 10' 1" balsa board shaped by his famous father, Billy, "and that may be the longest we need to ride," says Laird. "It's a very modern 10' 1", and the weight (28 pounds) gives you the stability to absorb shocks out there. I've also got a mini version, a Brewer 8' 1". It's 17 inches wide and 2 inches thick."

Then there's the 7' 2" Hamilton used at Backyards/Sunset, with the foot straps that have become his trademark. "As we look forward, it's gonna be essential to stay on your board," he says. "When the big day comes, if I have a proper strap, yeah, I'll use it. Without a doubt. I've learned too much from my windsurfing. I feel naked without one now."

The history of tow-ins dates back to the mid-1970s, when Jeff Johnson took his 24-foot skiff with outboard motors to Avalanche with a regular crew, including Flippy Hoffman, Roger Erickson, and David Kahanamoku. The trend lay dormant for a decade, until Herbie Fletcher made an occasional foray to the outer Pipeline reefs on a Jet Ski. In 1987, on a dark, drizzly day that saw the Pipeline Masters called off, Herbie Fletcher astonished beach onlookers by towing Tom Carroll and Martin Potter into swells thundering in from the distant horizon. Potter, after S-turning for what seemed like an eternity, got one tube ride through the inside section that people still remember.

"That was phenomenal," says Pipeline lifeguard Mark Cunningham. "I felt we were seeing the future that day, and I was almost afraid to see who'd be out there the following winter. But it never caught on."

Which isn't surprising. For one thing, state laws prevent the use of Jet Skis or WaveRunners at mainstream Hawaiian surf breaks. As a result, this is strictly an outer-reef deal. This is the province of water safety experts like Terry Ahue, Brian Keaulana, Mel Pu'u, and Dennis Gouveia, who handle WaveRunners with sublime elegance in harrowing conditions.

The list of hazards is long and intimidating. The short list starts with power failure on the Jet Ski; getting torqued sideways with the tow rope and getting buried by a 50-foot face; and the ever-present danger of the long swim in to shore if all systems fail. Doerner always carries a pair of fins in case he has to swim to shore—rather small consolation if you're miles at sea. Ahue once took Foo, Bradshaw, and Clyde Aikau to Outside Leftovers in what would be an all-time session: clean, perfect, tubing 25-foot waves. They hitched a ride out but surfed the waves on their own. "Maybe the greatest session I've ever had," said Foo. But Bradshaw lost his board that day and Ahue, even on the WaveRunner, couldn't find him.

"I finally gave up," Ahue recalls. "Clyde says, 'No worry, he can make it,' but I was starting to freak out. Finally we go back to the Bay, and guess who's sitting out in the goddamn lineup?!"

Bradshaw. He got to the beach somehow and hitchhiked back. But think about it: How many surfers could pull that off?

A solid, 50-horsepower WaveRunner can outrun any wave, but it can't help a surfer if he's caught in the impact zone. "There's so much wind out there, the amount coming up the face is double or triple what you'd have on the beach," says Kerbox. "It can blow you right out the top. So let's say you don't actually catch the wave. Now there's three more coming, and the boat's not gonna be there. You're simply gonna get mowed."

While people like Ahue make the driving look easy, it's actually the challenge of a lifetime in big surf. "You see all these guys wanting to buy Skis, but nobody wants to drive 'em," says Ahue. "They all want to surf. It takes a lot of experience to pilot the Ski—when to run, knowing your exit zones, keeping a cool head, timing your run through 10-foot shorebreak."

As is the case with Himalayan climbers, there's always the "invisible." Kerbox and Hamilton were out once in a huge swell that closed out Sunset, but with Doerner in the tower, they felt they were being watched. They picked off a few waves, came in, and asked Doerner what he thought. "About what?" he said. "Were you guys out?"

As Doerner says, "Nobody's gonna be watching. Something goes wrong out there, you don't come home."

Hamilton's act at maxed-out Backdoor raises even the most jaded eyebrows around the North Shore, and yet it's probably Doerner, in his quiet way, who holds the whole thing together. That will be his North Shore legacy: the man who found inner peace in the worst possible situations, saving lives (Ross Clarke-Jones among them), soothing minds, and riding some of the biggest, baddest waves of all time.

Doerner wouldn't mind hanging around the conventional spots, waiting for a half-dozen Waimea days a winter. He could handle that. But the North Shore hasn't seen real Waimea since the historic 1990 Aikau contest. "The last time I rode Waimea was three years ago," says Doerner. "Thank God this (tow-in surfing) came along. We get a lot of days when it's too big for Sunset but not quite enough for Waimea. That's perfect for us. You've got 60 peaks between Kaena Point and Turtle Bay that are just firing, and no one's on 'em. I caught more big waves last winter than probably the last 10 years."

Last February 1 an epic northeast swell hit Hawaii, a swell so wild that everyone from Jeff Johnson to Peter Cole agreed it was the biggest of its kind they'd ever seen. The direction was so radical, it came sideways to Waimea, almost bypassing it altogether. By 7:00 A.M. Hamilton had arrived in Honolulu from his home on Maui. An hour later they were launching the Zodiac off Haleiwa.

"We must have been 2 miles offshore cruising," said Hamilton, "and suddenly Darrick goes, 'Stop.' I go, 'Stop for what?' And he goes, 'We're here.'"

If Darrick says stop, you stop. They waited about 15 minutes. "I'm all young and impatient, thinking we're too far out," said Hamilton. "Suddenly we turn around, and here comes a set. We were right on the peak. I said, 'I guess we are here. I'll shut up, you just tell me where to go.'"

Kerbox picked up the story from there:

"I towed Laird into the first wave, on his 10' 1". I just got out of there as it was jacking. How big? You almost can't tell out there. Start at 20 feet, that's for sure. We watched from the boat as this wave just reeled 200,

300 yards from behind, and we saw Laird pop out of the channel. We're going, 'How was it?' And he goes, 'That was heavy.'

"We towed Laird into another one—just peeling away, and all of a sudden this bowl just doubled in size and came over. Darrick looked at me and said, 'I don't think Laird made that one.' He got pounded real hard. Went to straighten out but the lip caught him. But he still had his board, ready to go to war.

"Now it was mine or Darrick's turn. I said, 'Aw, Darrick, I'm not in a big rush. You go ahead (laughs).' He was ready. He wanted one of the really deep ones, and he got one so perfect, lined up all the way, and he kicked out with a huge smile on his face. We got him into another one but the wave died out, and he got caught paddling back out and had to dive under a 20-footer."

"Now it was my turn," said Kerbox. "Laird pulled me into a big one, I let go, just streaking, did a couple of turns, and all of a sudden the bowl popped up at the end. I went to straighten out and the whitewater just engulfed me. Got completely annihilated. The most ferocious wipeout I've ever experienced. I came fighting up to the surface, got a breath, and these guys are in the boat with a smirk, going, 'Well . . . how was it?'

"The great thing about that day is that I got another chance, another big set. I didn't really know if I wanted to go. I was still kind of freaked out. But I figured, 'I'm on this.' Just descended into the nether world, dropped all the way to the bottom, turned, went up into the hook, and it lined up perfect. Amazing. The most memorable ride I've ever had in surfing."

Exactly where was that spot, anyway?

"Out of Bounds," said Hamilton.

The coming winter brings both promise and fear, perhaps the chance of new limits to be challenged. Dreading the worst—bad drivers, mediocre surfers—Ahue fears that things could get out of hand. And while drawing inspiration from the likes of Hamilton, Doerner, and Kerbox, we should heed the words of Roger Erickson, whose 26 years of big wave surfing have earned him the highest possible respect in Hawaii.

At a party near Pipeline last winter, Erickson was asked about the tow-in phenomenon. His look took on a fierce intensity, as only Erickson can. "Well, everything's okay until it isn't," he said. "I mean, I can come in through the rocks at Waimea with a broken arm if I have to. I'll do that, and somebody will be around with a tourniquet, and we'll pull through it. Out there, you just disappear."

QUANTUM LEAP
JATO (JET-ASSISTED TAKEOFF)

Gerry Lopez

P   *ipeline master Gerry Lopez saw firsthand the gradual development of tow-in surfing. The main players were his friends and the practice grounds were close to his home on Maui. He also helped develop some of the prototype boards. In short, Lopez was involved in the movement from the beginning, through the refinement stages and ultimately through the first successful venture in truly huge surf at a made-for-tow-in outer reef break named Jaws. Within a few short years following the publication of this article, Jaws was world famous.* National Geographic *even ran a cover story on Jaws and tow-in surfing in its November 1998 issue. In the following piece—originally published in* Surfer's Journal—*Gerry Lopez covers the early history of the tow-in movement. At the time he wrote it, Lopez was basically an observer. Several years later he became a participant.*

‡   ‡   ‡

While Maui does not enjoy the big wave reputation of the North Shore, a small group has been pushing the limits of big wave windsurfing like never before. The first effective assisted takeoff came from windsurfing. Sailboarders have actually had the ability to ride bigger surf than surfers because sailing into a big wave is much more efficient than paddling. For this core group, Maui's Hookipa Beach, one of the best wave-sailing locations in the world, was an ideal testing ground for developing equipment and courage. From there, it was a short, although not easy, step to a big wave spot appropriately named Jaws.

Located on Maui's north shore, this break doesn't even begin to show unless the swell is in the 10- to 15-foot range, and at that size, it's only just starting to break. Usually a spot needs to be surfed before it gets a name, but not this place. Before Jaws we called it "Domes" because you turned left at the dome house to get there. Before Domes, we called it the "Atom Blaster" because it broke like an atomic bomb.

Over the past 25 years, we made many long drives down the pineapple road when the surf was up, just to marvel at this wave. It works best on a northwest swell in the 15- to 20-foot range, ideal conditions being Kona winds. It's a big peak that has a pretty good left when it's smaller, but when it's big the right is better. The peak forms way outside and moves in onto an underwater shelf where it doubles up like the Pipeline and tubes over. The tube defies description. Simply put, it's big, thick, and terrifying. It doesn't spit, it vomits! After the wave has passed, the impact area boils and gurgles and froths so badly you get sick just thinking what survival might be like if you were out there. For years we watched this break, trying to figure a way to ride it, dragging our boards down the precarious cliff trail to the rock beach where the true size of the surf was revealed, and the ground shaking underfoot from the impact sent us dashing back up the trail. We never surfed it—as far as we know no one did, at least not when it was big.

Then one day Mike Waltze, Mark and Josh Angulo, Rush Randall, and Dave Kalama said, "Screw it." They sailed up there and windsurfed the spot like there was no tomorrow. Somebody took a picture of Josh and his 15-foot sail appearing very small on a huge wave, looking like he was in the jaws of a gigantic monster. They've called the place Jaws ever since.

At the same time, another group on the North Shore started using a motorized Zodiac raft to tow themselves into huge waves at various outside breaks. These waves sometimes formed up 2 miles offshore. They were difficult to line up from a surfboard and virtually impossible to paddle into unless you happened into precisely the right spot. The North Shore, on just about any swell direction with an easterly trade wind, is as clean a surface condition for surfing as you can get. The team of Laird Hamilton, Darrick Doerner, and Buzzy Kerbox made full use of the great conditions. They towed around at Outside Backyards, Outside Velzyland—anyplace outside they could find where they could operate the Zodiac with at least some measure of safety.

One glassy, clean day they tapped into a large north swell at Outside Laniakea that instantly validated all their hopes. Here was a wave in the 15- to 20-foot range that was almost impossible to line up, even with a boat blasting along at 30 miles per hour. That alone made the lineup very dangerous. But towing in was the only sane option, because in spite of the pristine conditions you would be gambling with your life trying to paddle around to get into position for such a wave. This group rode dozens of waves that day at Outside Laniakea, waves they knew they never would have caught on their own. They also gained significant insight about their equipment. Because of the size of the surf, they elected to ride a 10' balsa-wood full gun that Billy Hamilton had built for Laird. Under normal circumstances this seemed the ideal board for the day—plenty of horsepower, good paddling, a good solid board for big surf. On some of the other smaller days they had used Laird's 7' 2" hotdog board fitted with foot straps, but on the big day at Laniakea they knew the 7' 2" would be too short. Afterward they agreed that the big gun did exactly what it was designed to do—it felt solid and got them through the day safely. Laird thought his 7' 2" might have worked, but the fear of riding such a small board in big waves was still too entrenched in his mind, even though all his instincts were telling him to go for it. Two thoughts persisted that would eventually push Laird past the obstacle of the firmly established "big guns for big waves" belief system: The small board felt a lot faster, and with the foot straps, it didn't matter if the board was bouncing around. You were glued on, chop hopping, leaping in and out of the water—like wave sailing on a windsurfer but without the sail in the way.

Another somewhat fluky incident that would affect the equipment evolution was that Bruce Brown was filming *The Endless Summer II* and wanted to do a sequence on the outer reef exploits of Laird and crew. Hollywood studio dollars readily provided the boys with a much-improved tow-in vehicle: a rocket-fast Yamaha WaveRunner, a rig already used to great effect by the Hawaiian lifeguards as a rescue craft in big winter surf. Of all the watercraft available, the Yamaha had the best hull shape for working in the waves. Much faster and considerably more maneuverable than the Zodiac, the Yamaha was likewise a lot safer with the water jet propulsion system instead of the deadly spinning prop of the outboard motor. With the Yamaha they could work a tighter line into the waves, especially when someone got into a dire situation and needed a quick pickup. Being on standby for the movie, the whole operation began to take on a more serious demeanor.

Two final pieces needed to fall into place to complete the package: new specialized surfboards and a new surf spot.

Laird and Buzzy had recently bought some property together on Maui. Being avid windsurfers, they'd spent months sailing and hanging with the

Laird Hamilton outruns a mountain of whitewater while towing in at Jaws.

Photo by Erik Aeder

hard-core windsurf crew of Mark Angulo, Dave Kalama, Rush Randall, and the spark plug of the group, the multitalented Mike Waltze. When they reviewed the tow-in surfing on the North Shore and the windsurf expedition at Jaws, they concluded that Jaws was the ideal venue for tow-ins for two reasons: the waves were great, and there was a cliff overlooking the spot that provided perfect vantage points for filming.

The next step was to design and build the special surfboards. Dick Brewer shaped a board based on Laird's input and the result was, from a contemporary standpoint, a peculiar piece of work: very narrow with a wide, squared-off tail. It didn't paddle well but it didn't need to. While it turned poorly, it went like blazes behind the Jet Ski and kept going even after the tow rope was dropped, all the way until they ran out of wave. They attained astonishing speeds. Not even Laird had gone that fast on a surfboard before. They were stoked about the new possibilities unfolding before them and began to practice in earnest for the next big swell.

There is nothing easy about towing behind a Jet Ski, as anyone who water skis can attest to. Water starting in the surf makes it even harder, but the thought of getting caught inside at Jaws was ample motivation to hone their craft. The fact that the winter was slow in providing big waves for them did little to deter their enthusiasm. They purchased another WaveRunner and started two different businesses in their spare time: a small film production company to film their endeavors and another called Strapped, Inc., to sell the foot straps they had developed for strap surfing. Mike, Mark, Dave, Rush, and new recruit Pete Cabrinha got totally into surfing with the foot straps on their boards whether they were towing or not. The moves they were doing on their sailboards became standard operating procedure in their surfing: a dazzling array of aerial off-the-lips, loops, forward rolls, 360s, and other never-seen-before-on-a-surfboard stuff. They wanted to be ready when that first big swell rolled in.

Meanwhile Laird and Buzzy were not completely satisfied with the boards, and they came to see me about shaping some different ones. Both had their own ideas about what they wanted. Buzzy got a more conventional shape, about 17 inches wide, that resembled a pipeline gun for someone small like Darrick Ho, while Laird, ever the extremist, got something that was a cross between a snowboard, water ski, and surfboard at less than 16 inches wide. Considering that Laird stands 6' 2" and goes at 210 pounds, and Buzzy is only slightly less, it was noteworthy that both boards were 7' 10" long. Both guys were dead serious about riding them in 20-foot-plus surf. With that in mind, I got nervous just shaping the boards. The fiberglass jobs were extreme as well, by today's standards anyway: three layers of 6-ounce glass on the bottoms and six layers on the decks. More weight was actually considered an asset, as it gave the board more momentum at high speeds, providing more glide and a smoother ride. A conventionally shaped board with a light glass job not only bounced wildly in the inevitable big surf chop but actually slowed down when the tow rope was dropped. The foot straps were positioned for each surfer's individual stance and generally were set a little wider for stability. Laird's long legs made for a stance so wide anyone else would be doing the splits to get into his foot straps. With the boards, Jet Skis, minds, and bodies ready, the only thing left was to wait for the waves.

The boys were restless as they scrutinized each new weather picture, tracking every low-pressure area as it moved across the Pacific, listening to the hourly buoy reports whenever something promising moved into range. Surf is like that, when you really want it—it teases you, testing your patience, weeding out the posers and nonbelievers. And just when you approach total exasperation, a little depression that doesn't look like much of a storm in the satellite photos will turn its fetch in the right direction and the wave intervals on the buoy reports will begin to get longer. When they grow to 17 or 18 seconds, you know for sure some surf is on the way. When the intervals reach 20 seconds or more, it means something serious is happening.

And just like that it finally happened. The report came in late that night—the green light was on. The phone calls went out, mobilizing the troops. The plan was to head out at first light. Sometimes the surf will come up during the night and already be gone by dawn, so with these thoughts going through Laird's mind, sleep kept eluding him. Finally, at about 4:00 A.M., he couldn't take it any longer, jumped in his truck, and drove down the pineapple road to the overlook spot. It was pitch black—impossible to see anything—but as he got out of the truck he felt the wind was still, a good sign, and he could taste the salty air. Suddenly he heard it—the deep, low booming, like a battery of 175-millimeter field artillery on a fire mission. "Yes!" he screamed in answer to the cannonade. "Yes . . . finally!" There was no doubt. He could feel the ground beneath him rumbling ever so slightly. The surf was definitely up. He took a couple of deep breaths to calm himself, then jumped back in the truck. All the planning and preparation were over. Time for action.

Back at his house the others were just arriving as Laird ripped the cover off and loaded the 400-pound machine practically single-handedly into the back of his pickup. Racing down to the beach, he went over the pre-flight checklist: gas tank full, oil topped off, tow rope and tow board, that was it. They launched in the darkness, heading out the bay under the light-ening sky for the short trip up the coast. Everyone was shivering, not from predawn coldness but in anticipation of what was coming as each boat in their flotilla climbed up, over, and back down into the troughs of the strong groundswell rolling into Maliko Bay. It was a day of reckoning and each member of the crew was silent, lost in his own thoughts, the only sounds the beat of the two-stroke engines and the distant booming of the surf.

As they approached the edge of the lineup, the channel was unnatu-rally still—one of those long lulls that are an ironic part of any huge swell, as if to give sanctuary between the killer sets. The boats drifted together as the lull continued for so long that it elicited a somewhat meek com-ment from one of the crew, "Maybe there's no surf," almost as though the speaker wanted it to be flat. And at precisely that moment, the sharper eyes picked up movement on the horizon, prompting another response: "I don't think so."

In the dawn's first light they saw it—a set marching in, darkening the far horizon, impossibly far out to sea and big. "Oh shit," someone said as the drivers nervously moved their boats, spreading out farther into the channel. "There it is, no shit," said Laird, and the silence was broken by yells, shrieks, and groans from the boats and the deafening explosion as the first wave crashed over. "Well, this is what we came for," Laird said, as he began to unlimber his board. "Let's go!"

Dave Kalama threw him the tow rope as he sat on the side of the Zo-diac, his board in the water, his feet in the straps. Idling out to the full length of the rope, their eyes met. Laird nodded with a devil-may-care grin and Dave gassed it, pulling Laird to his feet. Away they went.

Outside they circled a few times, waiting as the next set moved in. Laird indicated to Dave that he wanted the third wave. Dave got into po-sition heading in and slightly down the line from behind the peak and at least 100 yards outside the whitewater line from the previous wave. The timing of the driver relative to the wave is absolutely critical. Too early could leave the rider in a position where he can't get into the wave—a bad situation if there's a bigger wave behind. Too late might put him be-hind the peak, too far back to make the wave, not a happy thought in big surf.

But Dave was right on this time, grinding along at about 30 miles per hour. As the end of the rope came even with the peak, he turned the Ski out to sea, giving Laird a whip action off the rope. This was the moment Laird was waiting for. He yanked hard on the rope, accelerating even more before letting go and gliding in at high speed, fading left on the big hump, maintaining his speed but maneuvering into the right spot as the wave began to steepen. Seeing a little ripple on the face, he ollied-up into a 20-foot chop-hop down the face, then dove farther down into the pit at breakneck speed as the wave stood up and pitched. After carving a big turn, he was back up in the hook again, whistling along as the wave barreled behind him, the spit shooting out of the tube trying vainly to catch him—but he was going too fast. Then it was over, he was coasting out into the channel with Dave right there with the rope, so all he had to do was lean over to pick it up as Dave accelerated back out to do it all over again. Laird hadn't even gotten wet yet.

The guys in the channel cheered. The ice was broken, it looked like fun, and they scrambled to get in on it. Soon they were all out there taking turns. In an hour Laird had caught about 20 waves, all in the 15-foot-plus category. He estimated that if he was paddle surfing he would have been lucky to catch two or three waves.

Afterward they were elated. It had gone like clockwork—just like they planned. There had been a few wipeouts, but the Jet Skis had come right in and pulled the guys out before the next wave. Laird's board had worked like a dream. It was super fast, but at 7' 10" it was small enough to pull some tight turns at the bottom and off the top. And the whole episode was on film—Bruce Brown would be stoked! They couldn't wait until the next swell.

And so it went. Then one day in late January, the swell of swells rolled in and they were there. The waves were in the 20- to 25-foot range, bigger on some sets, and, as before, everything went according to plan. In my opinion this day's surf was as big as the biggest waves surfed by anyone, ever. Most certainly they were the biggest waves ever ridden on 7' 10"s. Not that it matters, because there will be more days to come and these guys are seriously training to challenge whatever the ocean serves up. And not for glory or recognition because they already have that, but, as climbers say about mountains, "Because it's there."

Dough for Donuts

Buzzy Kerbox

*C*harging *down a lurching, carnivorous Jaws monster is frightening enough. Intentionally jumping off your gun at the most critical position, to enact a legendary wipeout, is, well, somewhat insane. Then again, not for Hollywood!*

✝   ✝   ✝

I was still a little bitter about being passed over for work on the movie in progress, *In God's Hands*. So when I first heard they were in need of some-one to wipe out at Jaws, I had to laugh. But when the producer called me to fill in as stunt double for the movie's star, Matt George, it started me thinking. I went down to the set to lay out my demands. To begin with, nobody was going to shave my head. Second, what were they willing to pay for such a feat? They agreed on a skullcap, then we hammered out a day rate, plus a per wipeout stunt adjustment that I hoped I could live with.

I'd be lying if I told you I wasn't having second thoughts as we headed out. Brian Keaulana was stunt coordinator and head of water safety, which was good and bad. Brian is the finest water safety guy you could ask for but also the most demanding stunt coordinator because he himself trains like a maniac for the heaviest stuff Mother Nature can throw at you. I chose the worst of three red boards, hoping to add realism to my endeavor. I also wore a flotation vest under my wet suit so if everything went south, at least my body would surface. Then, with safety crew in position, Brian began towing me in search of disaster.

The swell was on the way up and my heart was racing. Wave selec-

Totally insane: Buzzy Kerbox wipes out on purpose for the 1998 movie In God's Hands.

tion was tricky because I didn't want the first waves of a set and the last ones were too frothy. The first couple didn't provide the exact setup I was looking for, so I rode them out. Then came a clean, midrange wave that didn't seem big until it hit the inside, then doubled up to a 40-foot face. I stalled up to the top, then started down the wall. Trying to make it look real, I went off the back and skipped down the face as the board flew away. The impact felt like a Mike Tyson body punch. The force was frightening, but I was able to surface quickly out the back of the beast; then it started pulling on me, trying to suck me back down. Instantly swimming with all my might, I just escaped its grasp. Then the Jet Skis quickly swarmed in and pulled me from the path of the next one. Over Brian's radio I could hear the director say the wipeout was good, but we needed more height. I was still shaking as Brian started towing me in search of another. Finally, after one more smaller wave, a long lull made them decide to move on to their next shot. Thank God!

LAIRD HAMILTON

Bruce Jenkins

"*E*xtreme*" would be an understatement when describing Laird Hamilton, the Moses of the tow-in movement. His mind-blowing performances raised even the most jaded eyebrows at a time when big wave surfing was going nowhere. When Laird and friends showed up with techniques strikingly bold and new, they helped revitalize surfing in a BIG way.*

From early on, Hamilton was an amphibious phenomenon who seemingly possessed the instincts of the surf itself. His rugged growing-up years shaped the man much as a master shaper works a blank of foam into a big wave gun. From his rocky youth, the ocean quickly became his training ground for some of the most dynamic and daunting surfing ever seen. Some say the epitome of big wave surfing is going for broke, yet Hamilton took this one step further, matching the energy of big waves with that of his own—as though two beasts were locked arm and arm, going head to head, neither one yielding nor backing down but rather charging with their last atom of force and conviction. In the following story, Bruce Jenkins trowels back the topsoil and goes to the roots of the 1990s' most innovative and controversial big wave surfer.

‡   ‡   ‡

The story begins 30 years ago, on the beach at Pipeline, when a two-year-old boy chose Billy Hamilton to be his father.

The kid didn't have a proper name, just Laird something. Laird Nobody. His biological father had bailed early, leaving the mother to go it alone, but Laird changed all that. What happened that day in 1967 was almost mythical in its purity, a stroke of raw intuition and the genesis of a legend. The fatherless kid became Laird Hamilton on the strength of his will.

195

"As I look back now, I realize it was my destiny," Billy recalls. "I hadn't even met his mom yet. I was bodysurfing down by Pupukea and I saw this little blonde-haired kid rolling around in the shorebreak. I came up to him, and there was an immediate connection. We're bodysurfing around, he's got his arms wrapped around my neck, we just locked into each other."

When they got up to the sand, Laird looked Billy in the eye. "I want you to be my daddy," he said. "So you have to meet my mommy. Come meet her."

The story continues with a love affair between Billy and JoAnn, who were married not long thereafter. It finds young Laird in the company of Jose Angel, Butch Van Artsdalen, his newfound dad and the rest of the North Shore hardcore in the late 1960s. It takes him to Kauai, where his striking Caucasian looks worked against him, every single day. It covers a thousand surf sessions around the world, a growing study of power and innovation, leaving friends and onlookers in awe. And it finds him today, at 33, the most respected big wave surfer in the world—viewing life from a perspective others couldn't possibly understand.

By now you've seen the videos of Laird and the Strapped crew at Peahi, a stark and remote spot along Maui's north coast. You remember how you felt during that first viewing, how your jaw dropped, how words failed you and there was no reasonable response but to scream out loud, like the old surf-film days at the Santa Monica Civic or Roosevelt High School.

Except the sensation was different this time. There have been signature moments of high-impact film footage—the first glimpses of Waimea, the casual Gerry Lopez at Pipeline, the peeling rights of Cape St. Francis—but nothing like the tow-in surfing from Maui and Laird Hamilton's performance in particular. Nobody ever faded for 50 yards on the takeoff of a 50-foot face. Nobody came off the bottom quite that hard. Nobody worked a terrifying lip with such courage or precision, or executed such a slashing cutback in the face of disaster. Nobody handled a wall of chop like some carefree windsurfer, or finished a ride by throwing—and landing—a 360-degree spin through the air.

You can say it's not real surfing. You can scoff at the Jet Skis, lament the noise and the foot straps, argue feverishly for the classic paddle-in takeoff. But you won't look away. You might miss something. Laird Hamilton changed surfing, with the expert help of Dave Kalama, Darrick Doerner, Buzzy Kerbox, and the rest of an elite contingent. And in doing so, he found the ultimate outlet for his boundless supply of energy.

There was a time, many years ago, when just about every surfer revered Billy Hamilton. As much as we admired the rich variety of talent, we didn't really want to be Corky Carroll, Mickey Dora, or David Nuuhiwa. But we would have killed to be Billy Hamilton. He had the looks and the ability, he rode Hawaiian surf as if blessed by the Ali'i, and more than anything, he had style. You can't teach that kind of style; it simply is. James Dean had it, merely standing on a street corner with a cigarette in his hand. Billy had it with every cutback and bottom turn, every time he waxed up or turned his gaze to the sea.

Growing up in Laguna Beach, Billy always hung around the older guys—divers, lifeguards, firemen, and established surfers like Mike Hynson, Skip Frye, and Joey Cabell. He took to driving his '56 Chevy down to La Jolla, where he became a fixture in the Windansea surf club. He made his first trip to Hawaii in 1964, at the age of 16, claiming one of the beds in Van Artsdalen's house at Arma Hut. As he once wrote so eloquently, "It was a period in surfing history that was raw, adventurous, and untamed. The North Shore was the hunting ground, and the hunters laughed at everything below 8 feet."

JoAnn Zyirek (Zeer-ick), the future Mrs. Hamilton, was also a Southern California surfer. She knew Linda Benson and Rusty Miller and surfed Cardiff by the Sea at every chance. That's where she met L. G. Zerfas, and they found each other to be kindred spirits at San Dieguito High School. "Couple of Zs," she said with a laugh. "We were both in the back row. Last names in the phone book."

That was his legal name: L. G. Zerfas. Mostly Greek, with a touch of Italian, he was strong, attractive, rebellious, and one of Cardiff's best surfers of the day. Bound by a love of the ocean, L. G. and JoAnn got married. When she became pregnant, they made a deal: If the child was a girl, she could pick the name. It turned out to be a boy, so L. G. made the call: Laird John Zerfas.

"Laird is Scottish for lord," JoAnn said. "That was L. G.'s thing. It's another word for king—like a land baron, or lord of the land."

As JoAnn recalled, "L. G. was very intelligent, but also very intense and *very* angry. He was way ahead of his time, one of the first people who ever got loaded around the North County area. He was physically attractive—not as big or tall as Laird, but with the same body structure and

In a class all his own:
Laird Hamilton at
Jaws.
PHOTO BY ERIK AEDER

coordination. He has Laird's smile exactly. When Laird laughs, it's like looking at his father."

As it turned out, "L. G. was also an alcoholic," she said. "It's something that runs through his family history. He was drinking heavily after Laird was born, and out of the blue, he decided he was gonna join the Merchant Marines and sail around the world. He left us when Laird was four or five months old, and I mean left for good. I never saw him again. Talked to him on the phone a couple times but never saw him. To this day."

In the meantime, JoAnn had become friends with Greg MacGillivray and Jim Freeman, the fabled team of surf filmmakers, and noted surfer Ryan Dotson. "Ryan became my boyfriend after a while, and we decided to move to Lahaina," she said. "That's how I first came to the Islands. I wound up on the North Shore after I broke up with Ryan. MacGillivray and Freeman were over there, and they helped set me up."

JoAnn was seeing a surfer named Greg Tucker (later killed in an auto accident in Mexico) until the 2½-year-old Laird made Billy Hamilton his choice. So much for Greg Tucker. JoAnn and Billy fell in love, returned to California for about three months to gather some money, then moved back to the North Shore in a little house at Pipeline, right behind the lot now owned by Gerry Lopez. Their marriage lasted 11 years.

Even the kids on today's North Shore would have a hard time relating to Laird Hamilton's youth at Pipeline. "Sometimes I feel like I'm from the lost generation," he says. "There were just a few of us North Shore kids, Ronnie Burns and David Cantrell and a few others, who got to experience the last of the original big wave riders. The real men. All the big names who came after—and I mean, Shaun Tomson, whoever you'd like to name—were just boys. There was nobody like Greg Noll or my neighbor Warren Harlow, the kind of guy who'd wake up in the morning, have a bowl of bran, then swim up to Sunset and back in huge surf. 'Goin' for a swim, see ya later.'

"Butch—I loved him. He and Jose Angel were my guys. I remember Jose at Pipeline when the whole thing was just exploding, totally closing out, paddling straight into it like this (bear hugging the board with arms and legs). Leash? What leash? This was the experience I had, and the next generation was totally different. It was like the guys who had been to war and the guys who hadn't."

There's an incredible energy to Laird's conversation, full of hand gestures, facial expressions, and body movement. He's got it pretty well channeled now. It's a magnetic, pulsating kind of energy, impossible to ignore. "Laird's grown up into this real polite, impressive guy," marvels Gerry Lopez, who first met Laird when JoAnn was still with Ryan Dotson. "You should have seen him when he was a little kid. You just wanted to strangle him."

For one thing, Laird wanted to be exactly like Billy. Here was a man who had mastered Sunset, earning no less than seven invitations to the prestigious Duke contest. He'd go surf 12-foot Pipeline with Jock Sutherland and no one else in the water. He'd bodysurf Pipe during the full moon, and one night, with 4-foot peelers snapping perfectly across the sandbar, he surfed it naked on an 11-foot tanker. Billy wasn't as fond of Waimea, but on one 20-foot afternoon, all hideous and blown out, "I surfed the place alone," he recalled recently. "Just to prove to myself that I could do it."

Laird wasn't content to merely be Billy's son. He demanded that the entire world be informed. "He was obnoxiously aggressive," Billy says. "He'd come up to the guys sitting on the beach at Pipeline, throw tin cans at their heads, and go (defiantly), 'You know who my dad is?'"

Billy always felt the kid was tapped into an unknown source, something no one else could understand. "Like when he slept, he'd rock in the bed continuously, really fast, actually shaking the wall. And the first time we took him to the dentist, the guy tells us, 'Your boy has executive teeth.' Just from grinding 'em all night long. He had this motor inside him that was running constantly."

On big days, Inside Pipeline is like a raging river, churning furiously from left to right. It's no place for a little kid, even a charger like Laird. "But he figured out a way to get there," says Billy, "and this is the real uniqueness of Laird. The Laird Curve, I call it. When he was about four or five years old, he found a big slab of building tile, filled it up with sand, attached a rope to it, buried it, then threw the rope around his waist. Made sure there was enough slack to get him some real distance, and went right out into the water, where it's goin' sideways about 20 knots. And he's bodysurfin', man. He's hangin' onto this rope. Come to think of it, that was his first real tow-in (laughter)."

Laird did a lot of other amazing things, like leaping off the famous Waimea dive rock—a 60-foot fall—at the age of eight. But as JoAnn remembered with bittersweet pleasure, "Laird was a brat. An absolute holy terror. I guess there was no way for him to express the things that were inside of him, but he was a terror to bring up."

A few stories from the locals:

Gerry Lopez: "The Pipeline area used to be pretty lush, with a grove of coconut trees and other stuff growing around. It was kind of shady, a good place to hide. And this was Laird's backyard. If you lost your board, he'd run down to the beach, bury it in the sand, then laugh while you tried to find it. He had Rory Russell way down at Rockpiles, looking for the goddamn thing. And the kooks, they'd just totally panic. While Laird's up there laughing. What a little punk!"

Jeff Johnson: "One Fourth of July, we had Peter and Sally Cole and a few other people out on the deck, really relaxing and having a nice time. Laird snuck around underneath and lit off this whole stack of firecrackers. Just scared the heck out of everybody, and one of 'em popped right next to Peter's ear. He wanted to kill Laird. Chased him all the way down the beach (hearty laughter). I've never seen Peter so mad."

Jeff's oldest son, Trent: "I went to Kahuku School with Laird and we always got along well. But Laird really played rough. He had an ongoing feud with Michael Holton, the kid who lived across the fence next door. They'd throw rocks at each other, beat each other up. . . . One time Laird had some kind of BB gun and broke it over Michael's head. And I remember this one time, in the second grade, we had this big Hawaiian teacher named Mrs. Kalama. Laird wanted to cut into the front of the line for lunch, and when she told him to go back to the end, Laird socked her in the stomach. Just let her have it. He was pretty unruly."

David Cantrell: "When he was about four or five, Laird used to run down the beach and rip off the tops of the women sunbathing on the beach. Then he'd bring the tops home. And his dad says, 'Right on' (laughs)."

In his own twisted way, Laird owned the old Pipeline neighborhood. But things weren't going too well at home, where Billy and JoAnn had borne a son of their own, Lyon. Despite these erupting problems, the magical bond between Billy Hamilton and Laird persisted. Something happened between them, something that defies nature and common sense. While the biological son, Lyon, bears a slight resemblance to his father, Laird is a dead ringer. "Not so much now," says Billy. "But if you look at photos of both of us when we were young, it's scary. Girlfriend Gabrielle (Reece) was looking at an old photo album and she said to Laird, 'Wow, honey, you're really buffed here.' She couldn't believe it was actually me. He's like my natural blood. If people say he surfs like me (it's uncanny at times, especially the way both display their arms on a cutback), well, he learned his lessons well. He's proud of his daddy. He was down at the beach throwing cans at people's heads."

As Laird says, "You have to understand that I chose Billy. He was

Superman to me. Superman's my father, and I'm gonna do everything just like him. After a while I wanted to do everything better, and it got real competitive. I'd say, 'I'm gonna do more in surfing than you ever did.' And he'd say, 'Impossible. You'll never be half of what I was.' That was our big ego thing. But we have great respect for each other. We started as friends, and that's what we are, above all."

In the last week of her life, JoAnn marveled at a father-and-son relationship that transcended genetics. "It's like there was some kind of osmosis," she said. "Laird just became Billy's son, in every sense. He absorbed him. I look at Laird today, this amazing person, and I feel like he's outside myself. I was just the provider. I realize that the only reason L. G. and I got together was to have Laird. And as much as Billy and I respected each other, the main reason we got together was his attachment to Laird. He was Laird's choice. I understand that so clearly now."

Laird Hamilton is not a particularly well liked man. He draws the highest praise from surfing's most influential figures, but there is sniping in the trenches.

"Just between you and me, he's an egomaniac," said one North Shore surfer.

"He doesn't even say hello to me anymore," said another. "Guess I'm out of his league."

"He's a jerk," said another. "Gone Hollywood."

There were other opinions, from amateur psychologists, on Laird's broken marriage. All off the record, of course. It seems that nobody's too keen on criticizing Laird in public.

"Listen, Laird had a very well-defined ego at a really young age," says Billy. "He can be mean, arrogant, and gnarly. To the point where you want to slap him upside the head." Billy paused. "Except you don't, because he'd beat the shit out of you (laughter)."

I would argue that Laird has joined a select group of controversial public figures whose talent borders on genius. Go strictly by the headlines, and they're all a bunch of jerks. Get inside their lives, and there's a wealth of charm, generosity, humor, and loyalty. I saw all of those qualities in Laird, as well as a moody intensity and an intolerance for fools. And I knew that I would never understand him completely, because few of us have the slightest idea what it meant to be Laird Hamilton on Kauai.

"You have to realize that out here, nothing had really changed," the 48-year-old Billy said from his home on the Hanalei River. "There wasn't this big influx of people like you have today. We were one of the very few haole families living here, and we were dealing with people who basically had never forgiven Captain Cook for coming here. So when we came here as a family, it was like a couple of black kids pullin' into Tennessee."

Laird adds, "Every day I was tested. Yeah, fights, scrapes, always gettin' messed with. Slapped in the back of the head. You're readin' your book in math class and a guy comes up from behind and rams your face into the desk. Then you gotta get up and brawl with him, then you both get suspended. That was the rule, yeah, some kind of fight or hassle daily. You know when to run, when to fight, or you got some pal who's bigger that'll take care of 'em. But there's also the mental thing of being on guard. Always. Maybe you don't fight for a week or two, but you're always ready to fight. At any second, you'll do whatever it takes. I mean, at the time I was at Kapaa High School, it was ranked third in the nation for crime and violence. It's like the Bronx, then East L.A., then Kapaa! The amount of stabbings, fighting, drugs—all right there dueling for the top spot.

"It was almost like an out-of-body experience for me. Even today, I feel I'm a little bit separated from myself. This body, the vehicle that I'm in, is separate from my mind and my spirit. In other places, my body would have carried me. In California, you know, I would have had the Galleria, some babe, great car, the whole shot. On Kauai my body was a negative thing, and really, it's one of the best things that ever happened to me. Being a minority, you're forced to become a man. You're forced to become strong and courageous, develop the spiritual. You learn how to talk to people, read people, know who's gonna snap at any second, who's coming from the right place.

"I saw so much injustice. Just people gettin' their melon cracked for no reason. Stuff that made me—like, I don't really know what racism is, because I don't truly understand it. I don't understand what it's like to hate someone for their color, because I've been hated for my color. I talk to black guys and I tell 'em they have no idea what racism is. They really don't. In most cases with minorities, it's just that; they're a minority. It means there's a few more of 'em. They're together in a little group. I wasn't in a group. I was my own group. My dad was his own group. And we were two different worlds.

"You know what? Kids are way worse than adults. More brutal and more merciless. Adults might beat each other up and hurt each other bad, but they're not as consistently ruthless and manipulative. That's part of the reason why the ocean means so much to me. Because that's the one place I could find true equality. The wave comes, and it lands on you, me, and the next guy. It's bigger than human relations. We're all goin' under. I loved that aspect. I gravitated toward it. I wanted to be out there more than on land. The ocean was the only place I wanted to be.

"It's out of body. I might be haole, but the only thing haole about me is my hair and my skin, and that I can talk good English. And that's because my mother forced me to, because she said there's nothing worse than a boy who looks like me who can only talk pidgin. Can I talk pidgin? Oh, I can bust it out. Just sick stuff. I can go farther than most local people, because I was raised with the gnarly guys. But being Hawaiian is a heart thing, a spiritual thing, it's what your intentions are. Just recently they tried to get a tow-in contest going at Peahi, and a bunch of us (the Strapped crew) boycotted it. Somehow, a racial thing was brought up—like, these haoles are taking away our Hawaiian spot. That really blew my mind. Dave Kalama's half Hawaiian. I took it personally, too. For me, haole means someone who is conniving and weasely, someone who'll con you into taking your house and your land. That's haole."

The words may sound bitter, but they were delivered with sensitivity and a good-natured spirit, free of obscenities (on the rare occasion that he swore, he quickly apologized). Let's face it: If anyone on this earth has a godlike presence in the late 1990s, it's Laird Hamilton. He lives easily within his body now. It's his greatest asset. But there's a prowling beast behind the "Most Beautiful People" facade, always on guard, ready to break out.

"First day of the eleventh grade. That's as far as I got in school," he went on. "And proud of it, too. I was goin' backward at that point. Fighting every day. After the tenth grade I figured, okay, I'm older now, this is gonna be different. Well, first day of the eleventh grade, I got in a fight. I pretty much just flipped everyone the bird. I'm gone. I'm cured. It's funny. I always wondered what it would have been like to go to a school that was all white. You know, playing sports, got the killer girlfriend, the good grades, actually having fun. But no. Man, I had 10 years of torture. I'm done now."

Laird's surfing had already been honed to an extremist's level. He first surfed 12-foot Hanalei when he was 13 years old, right alongside his dad, and he grew into one of the biggest, gnarliest, and best surfers the Hanalei-to-Haena area has ever seen. He went to work after his sudden exit from high school, honing the skills he'd developed in electrical work, masonry, carpentry, and plumbing (with a little help, Laird can build a house from scratch). It was only by chance that he went to California at the age of 17, triggering the kind of exposure that launched his brief but successful modeling career, and as he says now, "You should have seen me. Boy, what a shock. Girls everywhere, white people—and it's okay."

There were drugs around, too, but in the wake of his upbringing, Laird just shrugged it off. "I grew up on Kauai, man. I got cured from watching. I grew up living next door to Bunker Spreckels (Clark Gable's stepson and heir to the Spreckles family fortune), and I watched him overdose. He had heroin, reds, acid, peyote, you name it, he did it. Eventually it killed him. I watched the transformation. First he got the money, then he got the drugs, then he died."

I hadn't fully grasped Laird's reputation on Kauai until Billy Hamilton invited me on a tour of the island's north shore last winter. This was about old haunts, longtime friends, paths well-traveled, the essential themes of Laird's childhood, and how the tormented little kid became a man.

We started on the Kalalau Trail, at the end of the road in Haena, hiking a half mile up to the first lookout point. Laird's beloved dog, Ridge, half-Doberman, half-Rhodesian ridgeback, came along (Laird figured Ridge was better off there than on Maui, where he could be lost in the divorce settlement). As the dog bounded up the trail, Billy pointed to the moss-covered rocks and sheer cliffside and said, "You should have seen Laird run these trails. He'd come flying down. Just banking. Bare feet. Top speed. It was a training ground for me, too, when I was surfing the Dukes. It became a sport. Rock leaping."

Billy pointed out old hiking, camping, fishing, and bodysurfing spots on the gorgeous, rugged coastline. Back on the main road, he pulled into the Haena beachside lot once owned by Spreckels, the Hamiltons' neighbor when they first moved to Kauai. He drove up Powerhouse Road, entryway to the lush Wainiha Valley, and pointed out the house (now owned by Graham Nash) where he lived for seven years.

"We're driving through the soul of this story," he said. "It was just bushes and jungle back then. This big valley was Laird's playground."

We passed the old Wainiha General Store, where longtime owner Mike Olanolan was sitting outside. Billy stopped to say hello. "Laird, he crazy from when he was born," said the smiling, dark-skinned man. "Run away from school and go surf. He got crazy from fahdda (laughs). Best I've seen, though. And lots of respect for the old folks down here."

It was just by chance that we encountered Bobo Ham Young, one of north Kauai's heavy locals. There's a surf spot named Bobo's, and a long history of ill-mannered folks who messed with Bobo and wished they hadn't. "He and his brother Warren were heavy fighters, real warriors out here," said Billy as he spotted Bobo driving past on a tractor. "The

Ham Youngs are a Chinese-Hawaiian family with a long history on Kauai and big, big heart. They really smoothed the way for us here."

Welcoming Billy like a brother, Bobo spoke in a soft, quiet tone, a voice that exuded strength and flowed like honey. "Laird was always interested in our way of life," he said. "He was practically raised up by my granddad. I remember he got his first pocket knife. He wanted to come kill pig with us. He was always over there, helping us when we butcher pig. He always wanted to cut. To be part of us. And we used to let 'im."

"He was a survivor, yeah? Just like all of us over here," said Bobo. "So he know all that, from young age. Always in the water, playing with us, thanks to the fahdda Billy. Such good happening times. Laird was tough kid, all the time I remember."

Billy was smiling broadly. "He's like a Hawaiian haole, that boy," he offered.

"He's like a Hawaiian," Bobo said with emphasis. "I wouldn't say haole, because in diapers he raised out here. He might be white, but inside, I think he all like us. And he always gives the aloha, the respect for the elders. He stop his car right on the road, come over there and shake their hand. He always talk about the old, too. I don't think the boy will ever forget those things."

Back in the car, Billy needed a few moments to get back in the present. "I always admired Laird for the way he earned his respect out here," he said. "This guy he went to school with told me, 'You know what? If more haoles was like Laird, we wouldn't bodda dem (laughter).' But man, you gotta get down and dirty first."

"Laird Hamilton . . . is he still alive?"
—North Shore massage therapist Brenda McKinnon

The man's body is a festival of pain. Just take the left leg for starters: gouged, punctured, battered, sliced and mended, everywhere you look. Just a great big series of patch jobs. "It's super stiff, I've broken it so many times," he says. "I'm like an old surfboard with all these ding repairs. Just knives and reefs and boards and bikes. I stopped counting stitches around a thousand."

Down around the top of each foot, bones shift grotesquely from side to side at the slightest movement. "Broke my arches, both of 'em," he says. "They look funny, but they're strong. Maybe stronger than they were before."

The 6' 3", 220-pound Hamilton seems delighted as he surveys the chaos. Four or five lifetimes worth of injuries, and he's still charging at top speed. "He's got the pain threshold of a shark," says Billy. When it comes to courage under stress, it's hard to find a comparison at all.

Laird appears on a TV show called "The Extremists." Every week he ventures into a strange world full of hardened eccentrics dedicated to sports largely unknown. And every week, he blows minds. The first time he ever went bungee jumping, he took a 700-foot leap off a bridge near Sacramento. In the sport of street luging, where people hit 60 miles per hour on compact boards with tiny wheels, most of the veterans go feet first. They figure it's too scary and dangerous to get your face that close to raw cement. Laird, first time out, went headfirst. Thrown into a play-fight situation with a full-grown tiger, Laird summoned the animal within, made some intense eye contact, then let the cat take him down. As they rolled around the dirt, Laird offered his right arm to a jawful of teeth. Perfect execution.

Only months after he began snowboarding, Laird was one of the fastest and most radical in the world. He's paddled everything from the Molokai Channel to the English Channel. His windsurfing is legendary, particularly on a rough-water speed track. At the age of 22, without much training or experience, he entered a speed-sailing competition in Port-Saint-Louis, France, and set a European record of 36 knots. You don't want to be anywhere near Laird and his Maui crew—Kalama, Waltze, Cabrinha, Mark Angulo, Brett Lickle, Rush Randle—unless you're willing to test the limits of sanity. They'll go bombing down Haleakala (the dormant volcano) on landboards, strapped onto a vehicle resembling a snowboard with tires. Or they'll jam around the rocky Maui coastline on Jet Skis, practicing rescue and driving techniques for the inevitable crisis, waiting for surges of water so they can travel directly over exposed rock.

"Unfortunately, with the group I'm traveling in," says Kalama, "you have to put yourself on the line in order to have fun."

An unforgettable moment from the video *Radical Attitude* shows a jeans-clad Laird at his most extreme: diving some 125 feet off a remote cliff, windmilling his body into the feet-first position, and landing in a pool of water. "I hurt myself pretty bad on that one," he says. "Somebody said it would look great if I took off like a sky diver, and that's the kind of height where if you land wrong, you can die. I bruised a lung, popped a rib off my spine. I was coughing blood for 15 minutes."

The experience didn't stop Laird from taking that jump again, a few weeks later. "That's fun," he says. "That's summertime activity. How to vent. I love the whole idea of going up there with a few other guys, and

Dave Kalama and Laird Hamilton styling in sync, Jaws. PHOTO BY ERIK AEDER

we'll see who will jump the highest. The challenge is super clear. Perfectly defined. Not like, 'Well, I could have. . . .' No. Did you do it or not?"

Some have wondered if there's a death-wish mentality behind Laird's passion for risk, but this is a man who cannot sit still, who thrives on a rush, who does these things because he can. "Laird's so skillful, he kind of gets bored with things," says his old friend Buzzy Kerbox. "So he'll just invent something. He'll do the fastest windsurfing run you ever saw, then he's like, 'Okay, let's do something else.'"

"Deep down," says Kerbox, "Laird is the world's greatest showboat. He doesn't like to enter contests, but he'll show up on competition day and put on a show for everybody. I've seen him at Hookipa, sneaking out upwind during a break and getting more photographs than anyone in the contest. He loves that. There was a longboarding contest in Biarritz about six or seven years ago, and he went down early in some pretty small waves. Later on it got bigger, and he started surfing down the beach, just going off. The guy on the loudspeaker said, 'Laird, you're in the contest area, could you move?' He kept surfing. Then, 'Laird, if you catch one more wave, we'll have to fine you.' Kept surfing. Then, 'Okay, Laird, that's a $200 fine.' But he just kept on surfing. Who's gonna go collect from him?"

Hamilton says he's been anti-contest since he was a kid, when he watched his dad go down in some controversially scored heats. "I hated watching him get burned," he said. "I hate that gray area. I hate that it's a young-kids' thing, full of guys who are being promoted and thus can be manipulated. That's why I've always respected a guy like Darrick Doerner. He's one of the greatest big wave riders of modern times, and he gets no respect. Not in my mind. You hear about it, yeah, but hey— pay him the cash. Give him the support the industry is capable of. Darrick's the kind of guy you won't see for months, and all of a sudden one morning it's just enormous, biggest waves in five years, and there he is. But who gets the money? Children. Because they can control 'em."

Over the 20-odd years of big-time professional surfing, only a few men have gained an unassailable reputation outside the contest arena. Names like Peter McCabe, Jim Banks, Charlie Walker, and Jeff Clark come to mind, and now Laird Hamilton, right there with Kelly Slater and Joel Tudor as masters of their craft. Even before the videos from Peahi, Laird's was a word-of-mouth legend. They speak of him reverentially at Honolua Bay, in Fiji and Indonesia. Malibu regulars watched him show up during the epic swell of summer '96 and leave the place in tatters. In any setting, his performances are too incredible to ignore.

"He's tremendously innovative in the water," says Lopez. "He made a trip to G-Land a few years back, and Herbie Fletcher happened to be there with his kids. Christian was doing aerials—the first guy we'd ever seen really pop his board in the air—and McCabe and I were really teasing Laird about it. Peter goes, 'I haven't seen you do any of those things.'

"So the next day we're paddling out, looking down the line, and here comes Laird on a really nice wave a couple hundred yards off. I'm like, 'Shit, I think he sees us. Get ready.' He gets maybe 50 feet away, going as fast as I've ever seen anyone on a surfboard, and just launches that thing in the air. He sailed almost the entire distance. Peter had to dive off his board to get out of the way. I saw that and did the same thing. Of course, Laird landed the thing perfectly and just stared at us as he flew by.

"And McCabe goes, 'I guess that about says everything there is to say about aerials.'"

Hamilton spent a few seasons on the North Shore in the late '80s and early '90s, and the Pipeline-Backdoor area is still trembling in his wake. For anyone who caught Laird's act, riding those trademark T open boards with the orange-and-black tiger stripes, the memory is clear for life.

"I've never seen anything like it," says Jim Soutar, the North Shore's head lifeguard at that time. "Billy Hamilton had kind of a subtle, sophisticated style. Laird was just full-on attack. I'm serious. I feared for the guy's life out there. That's how hard he was charging it. He pulled into one horrendous wave after another."

As Lopez remembers it, "That's when Laird really made his move on the North Shore. He came to surf the tube and did it as well as anyone. A lot of guys were grabbing the rail backside and getting deep, but Laird had a move where he never grabbed the rail. He'd do a layback to pull himself into position, get way back there, then lean forward right off the layback. Somehow he'd start planing with his left hand and be able to hold a high line in the tube, backside, without having to touch the board. For a guy already 200 pounds, that's a hell of a goddamn move."

Laird was living at Lopez's house at the time, walking the sacred ground where he first met Billy. He went there with a mission and an attitude to match. If you intend to get the nastiest waves, in that arena, there is no other way.

"Tube riding was my thing," he says. "I really learned how to do it at Kalihiwai and Tunnels and all the places on Kauai. When I came back to Pipe, I was laughing. I'd laugh because everybody was making such a big deal about all these guys. Everybody's all, 'Kelly Slater's in the lineup! And Martin Potter!' And I'm like, 'So what? They're the pros. Excuse me, but I'm gonna pull into the tube now.'

"I don't like contests or competition and never have, but at that point of my life, I needed to find out if I could surf at that level. I needed to surf Pipe just like everyone else did. And I had local guys giving me shit. So I had to go through the lineup, each guy, and have a confrontation. Fortunately for me—and them—I didn't have to go to brawls. Because I knew a lot of people and because they understood how serious I was about it. Every guy I went face to face and said, 'You wanna go or not go?' Whether it was Sunny Garcia, Dane Kealoha, Johnny Boy Gomes—just go down the list. I had to go meet all those boys. Otherwise, you're just like the other 50 guys who sit out there and don't get shit all day.

"Most people aren't willing to face that sort of thing, but that's my whole upbringing. That's like another day at the office. My dad was a great influence for that. He was a skinny white surfer kid, but my dad was gnarly. If he got pissed off, you wouldn't even recognize him. He'd scare everybody. I had situations where I got in fights at school, and then their dad wanted to fight mine. So my dad would drive straight to the guy's work. Just show up there, and the guy's working with like 50 other giant moko guys. Dad goes, 'I heard you wanted to see me.' People respect that. He always told me, 'If you're wrong, put your head down and take your punishment like a man. But if you're right, go all the way.'"

For Laird, stroking into the Pipeline lineup was a little like school. "If a kid gets into a scrape and runs away, pretty soon he's the kid everybody slaps. 'Everybody walking down the hallway, make sure you slap that kid. (Gesturing wildly) Bap! Bap! Bap! Slap him on the head. Bap!' Every day. But if you turn around and punch somebody in the head, the next day the guy goes, 'Oh shit, that's the guy who went off on me.' Those are the influences that I grew up with. When I got to Pipeline, that was my zone. I gave respect, and I demanded it back."

Brock Little calls Hamilton "The Human Muscle," a compliment he doesn't throw around lightly. "I know a whole bunch of tough guys," says Little. "But Laird is just a specimen. He radiates power. He's not the biggest or strongest guy I've ever met, and probably not the baddest, but he's definitely the most powerful."

And in that whole crowd of bad-boy characters, nobody wanted to mess with Laird at Pipeline. "I remember he got into Johnny Boy's face one time," says Kerbox, "and they were like two big dogs checking each other out. But nothing really happened. It's funny, as long as I've known Laird, I've never seen him fight. He can handle himself, but it never really comes to that. He puffs up like he does, and guys don't want any part of him."

When asked to sum up Laird Hamilton, Brian Keaulana stated, "Laird is like every single element known to man. Raw power that the ocean has. Strong foundation of Mother Earth. He can be as calm as the sea, as strong and swift as the wind."

The big swell will come one day, holding within it the biggest wave. There will be plenty of notice, but funny things will happen. Dentist appointments. Gotta go pick up the kids. Absences unexplained.

Laird Hamilton will be up before dawn, preparing for the day he's awaited all his life. He will bring together all the elements, from Butch and Jose to his mother's memory to the legacy of the Hamilton name. And then he will surf—as strong and swift as the wind.

Rediscovering the Old Stoke
Kenny Bradshaw at 45

Bruce Jenkins

*L*aird Hamilton, Darrick Doerner, Buzzy Kerbox, and others started a *good thing—so good that when other North Shore hellmen feasted their eyes on the fruits of tow-in surfing, all were dying to sink their teeth into it. Having little but videos, magazine articles, and hearsay to work from, aspiring tow-in chargers spent the first several years just getting the gear and procedures down on less-than-legendary waves. Then the "Ultimate Big Wednesday" hit the North Shore, and the art of tow-in surfing was pushed to the stratosphere.*

‡   ‡   ‡

I'd taken a shuttle from Maui over to Oahu the night before and was staying with longtime Pipeline lifeguard Mark Cunningham. Around midnight, a call came in from George Mason, the veteran Hawaii surf forecaster. I'd never heard him so excited. "It's just now hitting. This is the one," he said. "It's gonna be 35 feet with great conditions." After hearing that, it was difficult getting to sleep, and no problem getting up before daybreak.

We were parked at Waimea Bay when the first light graced the North Shore. Even in the still and gentle warmth of a perfect morning, the place was unrecognizable. You couldn't even find the break. At times it looked like an enormous left, throwing death waves into the corner. Then the middle of the Bay would close out. Then some hideous set would loom far to the north, peeling in the distance, looking like it might have some potential until it hit the inside reef, sucked dry and threw—totally unridable and looking to be some 60 feet on the faces.

The beach was filled with big wave surfing legends who just stood there and watched. The Eddie Aikau contest? Meet director George Downing called it off without the slightest hesitation. Jay Moriarty, who had a spot on the alternates list, said, "I was just in awe. I'd never seen anything like that before. The whole ocean came alive and put on a show. You guys ain't going surfing today. You're just going to watch."

Kenny Bradshaw couldn't believe the Aikau was even a possibility. "You'll notice nobody's out," he said. "You can't *get* out."

Nevertheless, everyone was stealing glances at Brock Little, the man generally expected to charge the hardest at big Waimea. "Sure. If someone else is going to paddle out," Brock said later, "then I'll paddle out, probably to my doom. I'm kind of cocky in that manner. I don't give a shit. But it was crazy to even consider it."

"It wouldn't be a contest," said lifeguard Mark Dombrowski. "It would be people running for their lives."

"Outside Logs is the call," said Brock. "Biggest and best ridable waves in the world. Bigger than Jaws. It's gonna be unreal."

With his mind on Outside Log Cabins, Brock appeared to be in eminently good hands as he arrived at Haleiwa Harbor—the only remotely safe place to attempt a launch—with ocean safety mainstays Brian Keaulana, Terry Ahue, and Mel Pu'u. But this swell had everyone freaked out. A state-mandated order forced closure of the harbor, and even Keaulana, considered to be Hawaii's top all-around waterman, wasn't allowed to go out there.

"I had to respect Brian and Terry, because they were dealing with their bosses," said Brock, whose tow-in partner, Mike Stewart, was stuck in California. "If it had been just me and Mike, fuck it, we would have gone out there, anyway."

Stewart confirmed that, saying, "Throw me in jail later, but I'm out there. I would have launched at frickin' Leftovers, if I had to (the Leftovers-Alligators area is where Todd Chesser died in 1997). But I'm out there. Brock and I have been waiting five years for this. Missing that day—I'm just sick."

Brock was beside himself. Deep down, he wanted to drag Keaulana's crew up to Sunset for a tow-in launch. But the traffic was insane; it seemed that everyone on Oahu had turned out to watch the surf. Knowing that Keaulana was leaning heavily toward Makaha, Brock jumped in a truck and headed for the west side.

About an hour later, Brock's three-Ski crew hit the water at the Waianae lifeguard substation. The group included Keaulana, Ahue,

Ken Bradshaw towing in with Dan Moore at Maverick's.
PHOTO BY LAWRENCE BECK

Pu'u, lifeguards Cunningham, Mike Hart, and Kawika Foster, and Ronald Hill. I took the wheel of Cunningham's rig and embarked on a most promising journey: tooling around the west side on one of the biggest, cleanest days of the last 25 years, the ultimate Big Wednesday.

I figured Brock and the boys had headed up to Kaena Point, and I was hoping to catch at least a glimpse through my binoculars. As it turned out, they stopped short of Kaena and had a tremendous tow-in session at Outside Makua Cave, a spot that to Keaulana's knowledge had never been ridden. But I'll never forget what I saw at Kaena: indescribably beautiful 40-foot waves, monstrous and peeling, blue-green against the late-afternoon light. Even from a mile's distance, they came majestically to life. Forget anything you've seen at Jaws or anywhere else; if challenged, these would have been the biggest waves ever attempted.

"I think if it had been just Brock, Brian, and Mel, they would have gone out there," said Cunningham. "But we had a lot of baggage, myself included. Not everyone in that crew was ready for waves that big. We made the safe call at Makua, and those guys just went off."

Not that Brock enjoyed it much. Back on land, he was still stewing about leaving the North Shore—and he hadn't even heard what went down with Bradshaw, Noah Johnson, Aaron Lambert, and the rest of the dozen-odd surfers who experienced Outside Log Cabins. In fact, this was the day that North Shore surfers pushed the tow-in standards up a full notch, especially Bradshaw and Dan Moore, who racked up the most mind-blowing tow-in session ever enjoyed on the island of Oahu.

Moore is a largely unknown but highly competent strapped-in surfer and, like Bradshaw, a top-notch driver. Asked if he had any regrets about his underground status, Moore said, "I suppose if I'd wanted it, I could have made some sort of name for myself, but I didn't put the time and energy into promoting myself. It wasn't a priority. I'm just out there because I love to do it. Not to make money or anything else. I'm still a full-time contractor. Unless it's macking. Then I don't go to work."

This marked the third straight winter that Bradshaw and Moore were tow-in partners, and their experience really paid off. "Phantoms was the only place to launch that day, and it was sketchy at best," said Moore. "I've never seen it closing out like it was, from Revelations all the way through to Kammieland. There was no getting around it. You were gonna have to jump waves—it was just a matter of where and how many. Ken and I must have sailed 12 feet in the air going over one. The whole thing was just unbelievable. But we weren't the least bit nervous about the situation. All the elements came together, and we were mentally prepared for it."

And so it was at Outside Log Cabins, the ultimate Oahu location for outer-reef perfection, that Moore towed Bradshaw into the largest wave ever ridden on the North Shore. Nobody even disputed the notion—it was just that apparent. Bradshaw's wave was in the mythical 40-foot realm, a cut above most of the waves ridden that day. And he didn't just survive it. He carved a huge bottom turn and pulled up into the hook before easing onto the shoulder, where Moore picked him up on the Jet Ski.

Bradshaw caught two other waves in the 35-foot range and maybe 20 others at around 25 feet, pretty much the minimum size for this mythical break between Waimea and Pipeline.

As for his own surfing, Moore said, "I took one doughnut. I did a face plant down in the pit, probably a 25-footer, and it gave me a good spanking. Then I went back over the falls and it spanked me again. But it was a great session considering how many waves we got—I'd say 25 or 30 apiece. On the way back to shore, Ken and I couldn't stop congratulating each other. We knew how much we killed it. It was a pretty touching moment."

Another North Shore contractor, veteran big wave rider Bill Sickler, watched his old friend Bradshaw from the hills above Pupukea that day.

"Ken got a stand-up barrel that was approaching 35 feet," said Sickler. "Had to be the most beautiful wave I've ever seen. Glassy and peeling, like Backdoor blown out of proportion. Ken was surfing beautifully. The gods were smiling on him. He couldn't do anything wrong."

As Bradshaw recalled it, "Dan and I surfed three hours, had lunch, then went back for a two-hour session. It was a little bumpy in the morning, but it was so big and hollow, it was okay. The afternoon session was velvet. Totally still, mind-blowing, massive. I felt like I was slicing through butter on my 7' 10" at 45 miles an hour. My biggest wave was in the morning, but I got another 30-plus wave in the afternoon. Aaron Lambert came up to me and said, 'As long as I live, I'll have that view in my mind.' And Dan was like, 'That's it! That was fuckin' beyond cartoon!' He was like a little kid."

Bradshaw and Moore weren't the only ones making history that day at Outside Log Cabins. As Peter Mel later said, "Everybody was going off . . . on the biggest waves ever ridden. If anyone tells you the stories of that day are an exaggeration, they're wrong."

"I had some exciting moments," said Cheyne Horan, "but the best was going up to the top and snapping back as the lip was coming over on a 30-foot wave. Those were the biggest waves I've ever surfed in. If you saw someone coming off a huge bottom turn out there, it didn't even look real. It felt like the whole planet was breaking."

"I reckon the first wave I caught was 30 feet, and that's being modest," said Ross Clarke-Jones. "It was surreal out there. I got like four waves, and on the fourth one Tony put me in a little deep. We were going as fast as we could, and when I let go I was going faster than Tony, but neither of us were going fast enough. That Ski just couldn't outrun the wave. It collected me and Tony and we both got smashed.

"I popped up screaming, where the fuck is Tony? I couldn't see him anywhere and then I saw this patch of purple floating around. It was the seat of the Jet Ski. I finally saw Tony a little farther out than me. Tony and the Ski were getting dragged to shore with the Ski full of water when Aaron Lambert came to the rescue. He towed Tony and the Ski back outside into the channel.

"I was so pissed off that I lost my board and that we might lose the Ski. Tony and I had spent almost 10 grand on the thing. Kawika Stant and Shawn Briley got there with a bigger Ski and they towed us through Haleiwa Harbor. That was incredible in itself. The waves were closing out between Avalanche and Puaena Point and I was thinking, 'Oh my God, how are we going to get in?' It was a mad ride but we made it."

"This is only like the third time Aaron and I have done it together in any kind of size," said Noah Johnson, "and we're really unorganized. We just use the Skis to get us on the waves and then ride them like normal. And if we fall in the pit, we're going to take a few waves on the head. We're not counting on the Ski to pick us up afterward. We haven't done it enough to be totally sure of doing that. We don't even have a sled on our Ski right now. We're trying to head in the direction of the Maui guys, where we get rescues down.

"I pulled Troy (Alotis) into a crazy closeout, backside. I think I put a little warble on it with my wake, and I wish I hadn't done that. He would have had a much better chance. But I didn't think he was going to pull in. I was going, 'Whaaat?' It was heavy. The whole day. It was probably the most amped I'd ever been in my life. We were jumping up and down, high-fiving each other on the Ski. It was crazy.

"I guess the whole North Shore was watching, yeah. It was kind of weird thinking about that. It's been the buzz and the talk and everything. It was like the biggest playground you could ever have handed to you. Our faces were all cracking from smiling. I still can't believe it actually came together. I've just been running around in circles getting ready for the next one. But it's a bummer. I'm starting to realize that it may not happen again in my lifetime."

"It was such a pleasure to watch Noah Johnson out there," said Bill Sickler. "I've never really seen him before. I knew he charged, but made it look like he'd been out there a hundred times before. He'd go over behind the peak of these waves, and the driver, too, and they'd start bombing parallel across, full blast, so deep it was unbelievable. I saw Noah disappear in the tube for about 3 or 4 seconds, in the top half of the wave, and come out of a wave well over 30 feet. Later he had to straighten out on one, and the thing just crushed him. He had to go underneath the next wave, easily the biggest wave I've ever seen someone go under. A 35-foot set, easy. There was so much whitewater frothing, I was beginning to wonder if he could get a breath if he *did* come up. And shit, he jumps back up on the tow handles and heads out for another one.

"And Ross Clarke-Jones is just exceptional. He's like Brock, just the best there is. He caught the first one that I saw and my god, he cooked. He's peaking right now, he's right at that age. He's kind of like Bradshaw used to be—and obviously still is."

Sickler paused for a moment. "I can't believe I'm throwing out 30 feet and 35 feet like it's nothing. Most of us, guys who've ridden Waimea Bay for years, can count the number of 25-footers we've caught on one hand. It's just a whole new dimension out there."

Tow-in surfing, ridiculed for years by purists, is now considered fully legitimate. Even old hands like Sickler, Ricky Grigg, and Peter Cole are marveling from a distance. It's flat out the only way to ride waves in the 30-plus range. The possibilities are mind-blowing, a fact not lost on Kenny Bradshaw.

Bradshaw dropped into a funk following his historic session at Outside Log Cabins, "kind of like a postorgasmic depression," as he put it. But a month later, Bradshaw rediscovered the old stoke. It took something dramatic to restore his motivation, and it wasn't the North Shore, where the month of March unfolded with mostly medium-range surf. It was the notion of towing in at Jaws, at Maverick's, any new frontier he could find.

"There are so many places out there," he said. "I've never been out at Jaws, but I think those guys are ready for me to come over. There are other places in Hawaii that I want to go experience. I started thinking about Maverick's and that whole north coastal area, just a bumper land waiting to be discovered. That started motivating me. It was great. I got over that emotional depression and got back to living life again."

Bradshaw is deadly serious about towing in at Maverick's. It became evident this winter, when three separate 30-foot swells pounded Northern California, that you'll need a Jet Ski, foot straps, and a shortboard to get anywhere near the peak of that wave. As it happened, some tow-in history was written at Maverick's on January 30. Santa Cruz surfer Perry Miller and his partner, Doug Hansen, arrived late in the afternoon and had a lively session.

"I saw some video of that and it was fascinating," said Bradshaw. "On big days, the peak at Maverick's is this mythical, impossible thing that everybody runs away from. Towing in, getting in super early, you could negotiate that part of the wave. It would be unbelievable. Dan (Moore) and I really want to do it. We'll be there . . . count on it."

There are no photos of Bradshaw's ultimate wave on Big Wednesday, the bomb he caught that morning. Not a single snapshot. And here's why: Bradshaw didn't alert the media that day. He didn't call the magazines, collar some personal photographer, or announce his intentions to the world. He just went surfing. Just as he's done for 25 years.

RETROSPECTIVE

20 YEARS OF BIG WAVE RIDING

Ricky Grigg

When all is said and done, what does a lifetime devoted to riding big waves really mean to a person? The following piece by big wave icon Ricky Grigg seeks to answer that question. We leave him to tell his own story, but it's worth noting the common thread running through the testimonies of many great adventurers: the profound appreciation for having lived to experience the natural world on its wildest terms and to have shared the experience with others whose hearts pounded to one beat.

‡   ‡   ‡

On the morning of February, 17, 1983, Peter Cole called me at work and said, "Waimea Bay is huge. Let's go surfing." As luck would have it that day, my work could wait. In 20 minutes I was speeding to meet Peter by 1:00 P.M. at the Bay. The view awaiting me was indeed awesome: long clean lines stretching to a horizon cloaked in mist, a buildup from hours of pounding surf. Off the point, a set perhaps 40 feet high was pouring into the Bay. The first wave sucked out over the takeoff. Lunging forward, it bowled into an enormous, makable, curling wall. We imagined ourselves tucked into the tube. The wave broke, shooting a gigantic plume of whitewater into the air. It was clean to be sure, actually surfable, but impossible to get out or, for that matter, back in! We decided to drive west to Makaha, where we knew there was at least a small chance we could ride. When we arrived at 2:30, the channel was closing out. Fred Hemmings, Carl Heyer, Ace Cool, and Joe Teipel had been out in the morning, and it was big, a solid 20 feet. Larry Goddard walked up and announced it was now 25 feet and still rising—the biggest Makaha he had seen since 1969. The sets were zippering off the point at 25 miles an hour. That was Larry's calculation of how fast we'd have to slide to ride a wave through the treacherous bowl. It was hardly "fun surf," but in 25 years Peter and I had never seen Makaha so big.

We paddled out.

Although riding truly monster Makaha was a first for Peter and me, we'd both ridden colossal Hawaiian surf a thousand times. Despite that, it was unique for us to paddle out, and out, and out, and finally reach the lineup—and find ourselves all alone. We were definitely scared, no question about it. Disoriented, too. This was a quarter mile farther out than either one of us had ever been at Makaha. Peter reached the lineup first and yelled back over his shoulder, "Waves couldn't possibly break farther out than this!" As I paddled up, Peter started to laugh nervously and added, "Where is everybody? Do you think we are screwed up?"

"Yeah, Peter," I agreed, "I think we are a little bit screwed up." But before we could wonder about it, a set loomed on the horizon. We paddled straight out, furiously, for a full three minutes—but to no avail. A mountain of water, perhaps 30 feet high, was already curling over. We stood up on our boards and dived for the bottom.

I remember going down about 25 feet before feeling the concussion. Opening my eyes, I could see enormous boils of whitewater coming down in huge plumes. I picked a hole between two of them and squirmed for the surface. In spite of a couple more close-outs like this, we both made it through that day fairly unscathed—but certainly not without a certain feeling of humility and respect for the ocean. No doubt about it: The ocean had beaten us handily.

In fact, after 25 years the score stood something like 50/50. Peter had lost effective sight in one eye and I had incurred two hairline fractures in my neck. But the fact is we're still stoked. Perhaps we're no longer in charge of the situation as we previously were, but somehow we're still drawn into it for the thrill, the beauty, and the fun.

As I look back now, after all these winters, several memories really stand out. There have been lots of changes—certainly the surfers and obviously the boards. But also more subtle things like changes in depth at certain spots, due to shifts in sand, or changes in a reef due to catastrophic storms, like the great waves of 1969. And there are the legends, and the surf heroes who have come and gone. And there's been the media, the beach hype, the contests, the crowds and thrill seekers. The North Shore has remained a place of colorful lifestyles, but also it has been a private place where an individual

Fred Van Dyke and Paul Gebauer in the old days at Waimea Bay. PHOTO FROM VAN DYKE COLLECTION

can feel seclusion and freedom, where one can connect with the ocean at its finest hour, during the full fury of 30-foot Waimea, or during a summer calm, in crystal clear water over a coral reef.

One of the most interesting changes has been in regard to big wave riding. In the early days, the biggest goal was the biggest wave. At first, surfers were satisfied just to make the wave, just to survive. Surfers like George Downing and Buzzy Trent established this early period of surfing history and perhaps rode some of the biggest waves. I recall an early Bud Browne movie, with Buzzy at Makaha skipping down the face of a 30-foot mountain—and making it. Later that day a wave broke on him and broke his leg.

Gradually, in the 1960s big wave riding became more a matter of performance. Control and speed became more important than wave size per se, although size still mattered. Hotdogging big surf slowly caught on. Radical bottom turns, off-the-lip cutbacks, arches, and total in-the-tube lock-ins. Then, in the late 1960s, boards began to shrink and the maneuvers got hotter. The '70s were a decade of increasing performance. The biggest waves were no longer the best; it became more a matter of quality, of fine tuning skill and equipment.

Today, in 1985, big wave riding is a dying art. Most of the top-name surfers are into high-performance twin-fin or tri-fin boards in the 6- to 8-foot-length category. To ride a truly big wave, say over 20 feet, you need a full-on gun, 9 to 11 feet long. To me, the challenge to future greats will be to apply what has been learned in high performance—on smaller to medium-size surf—to the heavies once again. To some extent this is already happening with new gurus like Ken Bradshaw, Charlie Walker, and Bobbie Jones. These and others are beginning to shred Waimea like it's never been shredded.

And then there is the Kaena Point myth: that someday, someone will ride a 40- to 50-foot wave out there and survive to tell the world about it. I call it a myth because all I've ever heard is people broadcasting that they are going to do it. First there was Charlie Galento, who made headlines by promising, promising. Then there was "Wildman" Jim Neece, who in 1974 mysteriously disappeared, several days before the great waves came. Of course a few have actually ridden Kaena on smaller days: 15 feet, perhaps even 20. Flippy Hoffman and Jeff Johnston were first. And now there is Ace Cool, who caught a monstrous wave at Kaena last year, and who is gearing up, perhaps more seriously than anyone ever, to tackle Kaena at 40-plus. It will take a boat, a survival kit with a mini aqualung, a 12-foot board, and tremendous training. Will Ace Cool do it? I hope so, but I wouldn't bet on it. Kaena is ridable at 40 feet perhaps only once every ten years. Ace may end up doing more pushups than any surfer in history.

But what else in 25 years? We've had lots of good years and lots of not so good. The biggest were 1958, 1969, 1974, and 1982. These roughly correspond to the so-called El Niño years. El Niño is an oceanwide phenomenon that is caused by a breakdown in high pressure, particularly in the South Pacific. In such years, winter storms in both hemispheres in the Pacific advance closer to the equator and bring with them immense surf. People who live on the beach in Malibu, California, will long remember the winter of 1982 to '83 for its El Niño surf. El Niño occurs every 5 to 8 years but not with any regularity or predictability.

What about the surf itself? Surfers are forever arguing about whether or not the surf used to be bigger. Many say that Waikiki used to be 20 feet quite often. Well, in my 25 years, I've rarely seen it over 15 feet—and that's pushing it. Maybe the real old-timers had it better, or maybe they are just better storytellers. In any case, in 25 years, the surf really hasn't changed in any consistent way on the North Shore. There have been "runs" of good or bad years, but it's not getting any bigger or any smaller.

There have been, however, some small changes in the way certain places break. At Waimea Bay, for example, there is more sand in the middle of the Bay and a little less just outside the takeoff. The result is an even steeper takeoff than before and a longer wall. It is harder now to get out, and harder to get in, because waves roll all the way through inside the Bay. In balance, the Bay seems a little harder to ride now. Sunset is the same: still a game of who can jockey best. And Pipeline is still the most horrifying wave to ride in the world. There are one or two surfers who die there every year, usually from hitting the bottom.

On the beach things seem to be much better: fewer drugs, more mellow vibes, and all-in-all a cleaner lifestyle. So what's new besides these memories? First, memories are just fine: of friends riding incredible waves, like my friend Peter Cole, and many others. Their names run together and form a virtual history of the sport. Buzzy Trent, George Downing, Jim Fisher, Pat Curren, Greg Noll, Fred Van Dyke, Jose Angel, Tommy Lee, Sammy Lee, Paul Gebauer, Kimo Hollinger, Mike Doyle, Midget Farrelly, Fred Hemmings, Joey Cabell, Nat Young, Jeff Hakman, Mike Milles, Eddie and Clyde Aikau, Felipe Pomar, Barry Kanaiaupuni, Mark Richards, Shaun Tomson, Randy Rarick, Jock Sutherland, Reno Abellira, Paul Strauch, Gerry Lopez, and a new breed of high performers who are now taking their turn at Waimea and Sunset.

And the lineup at Waimea really is a meeting ground. Even today.

How many times have our bodies tingled with adrenaline, pumped with a magic joy after 25-foot drops, of free-fall wipeouts, of hitting the bottom, of making it and not. Eddie and Jose are gone, lost at sea in separate tragedies. But they are still out there in spirit, part of a certain brotherhood.

And when the Pacific rages and mammoth waves roll into the North Shore, as they do once, twice, or half a dozen times each year, our telephones will ring and there will be a voice that says, "Let's go surfing." And as sure as the sun also rises, we will keep on surfing. And there will be a new generation out there to ride, to join that brotherhood, and to know the thrill of conquering and being conquered in big surf. Looking back over all of those winters, all I can say is that it's been one hell of a ride.

BIG WAVE RIDING—JUST FOR THE FUN OF IT!

Peter Cole

*P*eter Cole's name is peppered throughout the history of big wave surfing, and most every mention describes the same event: Cole paddling out beyond everyone else, waiting for the absolutely biggest wave and nailing it cold. During a recent conversation with Fred Van Dyke, I asked if Cole was still surfing and Fred said, "Hell, yes. The guy's nearly 70 and he still paddles out in huge Waimea, out past everyone, and he just sits out there waiting for the set of the day. He might wait out there two hours but he'll pick off the biggest wave and ride it all the way to shore. And that's his day. Of course, sometimes he wipes out. And he never wears a leash. You ought to see all the young guys diving for their lives, trying to get out of the way of his board, which is this huge bastard that's long as a station wagon and weighs about 70 pounds." "Damn," I said. "The old fart must swim pretty well to be pulling that off." "Peter Cole?" Fred answered, "Swim?!" He almost sounded offended. "Peter Cole's like a dolphin, man. He can swim circles around all those kids. Even now." And the legend grows.

‡   ‡   ‡

It has been a 25-year stoker riding the large North Shore waves, since the time Ricky Grigg and I arrived in the Islands together in the fall of 1958. Rick had come over to attend graduate school in marine biology at the University of Hawaii. I had come over to teach mathematics at Punahou School. Ricky and I had just completed a winter of surfing together at Steamer in Santa Cruz.

At Santa Cruz that winter there were many days when Ricky, Bill

228

Peter Cole, a living legend. PHOTO BY BUD BROWNE

Bullis, Rick Paleager, and I would be the only ones in the water. The three of them would come down from Stanford on weekends and stay with me on East Cliff Drive near Pleasure Point. Five years earlier I had graduated from Stanford and was teaching in Santa Cruz. It seemed then, and of course much more now, that Rick and I had followed almost exactly similar paths—separated by five years, but the same events: first learning to surf at Malibu, then attending Santa Monica High School, lifeguarding the Santa Monica beaches, attending Stanford, and finally arriving in Hawaii in 1958 to ride giant waves on the North Shore. This was the beginning of what has become a 25-year adventure together.

Even after 25 years we still manage to stay out as long as ever, particularly when there is quality big surf. We have a common and simple goal: to have fun. To be sure, our surfing at Waimea has slowed down a bit—we still paddle out and get exciting rides, but the desire to take off on the very largest wave is rarely there. Younger surfers have replaced us in this arena. However, the camaraderie we share with all the surfers out there is the same as it has always been.

Many changes have occurred over the last quarter of a century—most obviously, surfboard designs and surfing styles. One of the most interesting changes has been in surf-height communication. There are currently three or four radio stations announcing several times daily the surf heights along Oahu's shores. In contrast, back in the '60s, milling around in the Punahou teacher's lounge, I can remember calling various sources for surf information. First I would call Klausmeier, at Makaha. A relatively accurate assessment could be calculated by dividing the Klausmeier estimate by two and subtracting three. I would then call the Haleiwa army beach lifeguards. It turned out that my most reliable source was Colleen Harlow, who is married to surfer Warren Harlow. In those early years, they lived at the Point at Waimea Bay. Colleen would always respond, "Now, Peter, you know I can't tell you how many feet the waves are." I would counter, "Don't worry about feet, Colleen, just tell me how many refrigerators you could stack up the face?" Converting refrigerators to feet always produced the most accurate estimates!

Rick and I have watched many good surfers come and go. What has contributed most to our 25-year stoke is both our approach to surfing and what we do outside of surfing. Our lives have involved the usual activities of raising children, enjoying our families, furthering our education, and working on projects at our jobs that both interest and challenge us. For both Ricky and I, surfing is simply our primary source of recreation. It is an outlet in which we can relax and escape the pressures of demanding jobs. We surf mostly during late afternoons and on weekends. Only on rare occasions will we take time off from work. Most of the old-time surfers who still ride North Shore breaks juggle their surf time with a variety of other chosen activities.

We enjoy doing well within our own capabilities and have no illusions that we can perform the antics of the current crop. I am aware of the humorous spectacle I present to the younger surfers sitting inside as I approach them from the Point on my 11' 6" gun. I couldn't care less. I'm having a ball. Too many surfers have quit because they are no longer numero uno. Surfing is an individual sport. Surfing is fun, and surfers who do moderately well have just as much fun as those who are recognized as the best.

I cherish my time in the water at Sunset. In particular, I remember the last big day of a recent winter. The normal crowd had been riding Waimea most of the day. Sunset looked ridable but no one was out. I watched it carefully for a good hour. Just then Ken Bradshaw drove up in his bus, and not more than five minutes later Ricky arrived. We all decided to go out together. I entered the water first, was immediately joined by Ricky and followed by Kenny and Beaver. Both Kenny and Beaver had guns slightly over 10 feet. The waves were uneven and not of particularly good quality, yet we were all sharing the same enthusiasm that has prevailed for the last 25 years. We were surfing for the fun of it: We were happy; we were refreshed from the week's headaches; we were stoked for the next opportunity to catch a wave; we couldn't possibly imagine 25 years without it.

BIG WAVE SURFING TIMELINE

Ben Marcus

January 18, 1778 Captain James Cook, aboard the *Resolution*, sights the first Hawaiian Island, Oahu. He lands at Kauai and Niihau then sails north to explore the Bering Sea. Returning the next winter, he lands on Maui and on the Big Island, where he first sees a man riding waves on a piece of wood. Cook is killed by angry Hawaiian natives on February 14, 1779.

1917 Duke Kahanamoku rides a giant wave on the South Shore of Oahu, steering a 16-foot surfboard from Castles to Canoes, a ride of over a mile.

December 22, 1943 Woody Brown and Dickie Cross get caught outside on a big day at Sunset Beach on the North Shore of Oahu. They paddle down coast to Waimea Bay and attempt to paddle in through closed out surf. Brown makes it, Cross drowns, and the Waimea Bay legend begins. "It was a few days before Christmas and I remember having to go to Mrs. Cross and tell her that her son had died," Woody Brown recalled.

November 27, 1953 An Associated Press photo of George Downing, Buzzy Trent, and Wally Froiseth riding a giant wave at Makaha is run in mainland newspapers. The photo inspires a stampede of surfers heading for Hawaii. "I saw that photo, quit my teaching job and headed for the Islands," said Fred Van Dyke.

November 7, 1957 First day at Waimea. Greg Noll, Mike Stang, Harry Church, Bing Copeland, Del Cannon, Pat Curren and a few others put aside their kapu fears and surf Waimea Bay for the first time. Opinions differ, but many say Greg Noll and Pat Curren shared the first wave.

Winter, 1964 Greg Noll rides/drags a banana-yellow, 70-pound elephant gun to outside Pipeline and catches one of the most famous waves in big wave history. He takes a hell-bent-for-leather ride on a giant wave at

Outside Pipe, makes it a lot farther than he should have and finally falls at the end.

February 20–21, 1965 10- to 12-foot surf at Punta Rocas for the Peru World Contest. Felipe Pomar beats Nat Young by one point and the world wakes up to the fact that there are big waves to be ridden outside of Hawaii.

December 4, 1969 The swell of '69. A humungous Pacific storm fills nearly the entire North Pacific and sends a tremendous swell straight at Hawaii and California. On Oahu, Greg Noll turns away from closed-out Waimea Bay and drives around Kaena Point to Makaha, which is bigger than Noll or anyone else has ever seen it. Noll paddles way outside, ponders those big, black ones thundering around the Point, then drops into what is considered by most to be one of the biggest waves ever ridden.

January 17, 1972 Huge Monday at Pipeline. Gerry Lopez, Rory Russell, and James Jones are all victimized by 15-foot surf at Second Reef, leaving Owl Chapman, Jock Sutherland, Sam Hawk, and Gary Speece all alone in perfect, backlit Pipeline. Owl is the standout with his drop knee, hood ornament stances in the giant barrels.

October 3, 1974 At La Isla, Peru, a huge earthquake creates a tidal surge that sucks Felipe Pomar and a friend out to sea. Pomar claims to ride a tidal wave to make it back to shore.

Thanksgiving, 1974 The Smirnoff Pro is held in giant surf at Waimea Bay. Reno Abellira wins it, beating Jeff Hakman by half a point.

Winter, 1975 Half Moon Bay resident Jeff Clark overcomes his fears and paddles out at a giant reef off Pillar Point Harbor. He surfs Maverick's mostly alone for the next 15 years.

September 21–26, 1975 The Monster from New Zealand. A giant storm in the southern hemisphere sends one of the biggest south swells in history toward the California coast. It rages for a solid week, bringing some of the biggest summer surf California has ever seen.

February 4, 1977 James Jones attempts to tube ride Waimea Bay. On his first try he is drilled by the lip and pushed through his board feet-first. He drives 40 miles to Honolulu, gets a backup board, makes it back to the Bay and successfully drives through the hook of a 20-footer. Jones proves that Waimea is a wave to be surfed, not just survived.

January 1, 1980 Operation Avalanche. Dale Hope, Tommy Holmes, and Aka Hemmings borrow a boat from the Outrigger Canoe Club and attempt to ride 20-foot-plus Outside Avalanche. The wave starts well but ends in a wipeout with Hope breaking his arm.

Evan Slater and Steve Dwyer doing a dance at Maverick's. PHOTO BY LAWRENCE BECK

Easter, 1981 The Rip Curl 3GL Easter Classic is held in huge surf at Bells Beach. Most pros are undergunned in heavy offshores and 15-foot surf. Simon Andersen introduces a new invention, the Thruster, to the world, beating Cheyne Horan on a 6' 6" tri-fin in the final.

January 5, 1985 Alec "Ace Cool" Cooke attempts to helicopter surf Outer Reef Pipeline. Dropped from a helicopter, he catches three waves, gets closed out on two and earns a place in history.

January 15, 1985 Mark Foo coins the phrase "The Unridden Realm" on this giant day at Waimea Bay. Challenging a giant day at the Bay, Foo, James Jones, Ken Bradshaw, Alec Cooke, and J. P. Patterson get caught inside a wave Jones describes as 48 feet, and Bradshaw calls the biggest wave anyone has ever had to deal with. Bradshaw swims around the Bay twice before getting in. Cooke and others are rescued by helicopter. Foo attempts to ride a 25-foot wave and gets creamed. In a December 1991 *Surfer* magazine article, Foo identifies The Unridden Realm as anything 35 feet and over and believes that these waves are just too big and massive for any one man to ride. He says that towing into these waves behind a boat or a Jet Ski would be possible, but wonders, is that surfing?

December 9, 1986 Waimea Bay is giant for The Billabong Pro. Pro surfers Gary Green and Bryce Ellis refuse to paddle out, while Mark Richards returns from retirement to dominate the day, catching one of the biggest waves of his life.

Super Bowl Sunday, January 31, 1988 Brock Little, Ken Bradshaw, and Darrick Doerner challenge a giant day at Waimea Bay. Riding a 9' 6", Doerner catches a wave that many consider one of the biggest ever ridden. Brock Little is one of the believers.

January 21, 1990 The second Eddie Aikau Invitational is held in huge, perfect 25-foot surf at Waimea Bay. Keone Downing wins the contest but Brock Little, Kerry Terukina, and Richard Schmidt make history with death or glory surfing in giant conditions.

January 22, 1990 A day after the Eddie Aikau contest, Jeff Clark lures Santa Cruz surfers Dave Schmidt and Tom Powers from Ocean Beach, San Francisco to Maverick's and gives the first outsiders a look.

January 23, 1990 Two days after the Eddie Aikau contest, Brock Little flies from Hawaii to Mexico to join Mike Parson on a huge day at Todos Santos. The era of the Jet Stream Jet Set is born.

November 10, 1990 Bloody Big Saturday The ASP Tour gets the biggest contest surf since the Bells Beach contest in 1981. Margaret River is 15-feet-plus and Barton Lynch beats Jeff Booth in the final.

Winter, 1991 Buzzy Kerbox and Laird Hamilton experiment with catching waves using Kerbox's Zodiac as a tow boat. They catch one giant wave at Phantoms, almost get creamed, and realize their 40-horsepower engine isn't enough.

January 29, 1991 Richard Schmidt rides a huge wave at Maverick's but gets creamed on the inside section. A sequence of the wave is run in a *Surfer* magazine article titled "Cold Sweat." Maverick's has been exposed to the world and the entire surfing world stands up and says, Holy shit!

Winter 1992 With a 60-horsepower Mercury attached to the Zodiac, Laird Hamilton and Buzzy Kerbox spend the winter pioneering tow-in surfing at Outside Backyards and other North Shore locations. Their friend Darrick Doerner isn't interested at first, but after watching them from his lifeguard perch at Sunset Beach and experiencing a big day at Outside Laniakea, Doerner becomes a believer.

Winter 1992–1993 Laird Hamilton and Buzzy Kerbox take the Zodiac and a WaveRunner back to Maui, where they try their tow-in techniques at an outer reef near Piahe, a place that had been christened Jaws. Joined by friend Mike Waltze, they tow into a giant wave at a venue that had previously only been sailboarded.

December 19, 1994 A series of Pacific storms sends a week's worth of huge, perfect west swell directly at Maverick's. On this morning, 19-year-old Santa Cruz surfer Jay Moriarty paddles off a boat and into history. Taking off on the first wave that comes his way, Moriarty is held up in the lip and launched into the most spectacular wipeout caught on film. He survives, the photo makes the cover of *Surfer* and Jay and Maverick's are instant legends.

Winter 1993–1994 Team Tow In—Laird Hamilton, Buzzy Kerbox, Darrick Doerner, Pete Cabrinha, Mike Waltze, Dave Kalama and others—team up for an all-out assault on Jaws. A sequence of Pete Cabrinha and Laird Hamilton nearly colliding on a giant wave makes the September 1994 cover of *Surfer* magazine. That ride is featured in Bruce Brown's *Endless Summer II* and also *Wake Up Call,* a video by cinematographer Dave Nash which introduces tow-in surfing to the world.

December 23, 1994 Mark Foo and Ken Bradshaw fly to California from Hawaii to get a look at this Maverick's place. Joined by Brock Little and all the Maverick's regulars, they surf a big, clean 15- to 20-foot day. Foo performs well before digging a rail and wiping out on a solid wave in the bowl. He disappears from sight. A few hours later, a crew of surfers coming in on a photo boat discover Foo's drowned body. Foo is the first experienced big wave surfer to drown and the fact that it was a Hawaiian in California waters makes it that much more mysterious. The resulting media frenzy puts big wave surfing and Maverick's in the world spotlight.

December 23, 1995 Experienced California big wave surfer Donnie Solomon drowns at Waimea Bay, exactly one year to the day after Mark Foo drowns at Maverick's. Solomon is sucked over the falls after trying to duck dive through the back of a huge wave.

February 13, 1997 On this day, Hawaiian big-wave surfer Todd Chesser is supposed to fly to Maui to stage a stunt wipeout and drowning on a big wave for a Hollywood movie called *In God's Hands*. Ironically he blows off the job, stays on Oahu and drowns for real. Chesser is killed while paddle-surfing with two friends at Outside Alligators, a reef just west of Waimea Bay. Considered one of the fittest, most experienced big wave surfers in Hawaii or the world, Chesser's drowning in his own backyard sends shock waves through the surfing world. He is the third experienced big wave surfer to die in three years. Chesser was adamantly opposed to tow-in surfing, but some surfers speculate that if a Jet Ski had been around at Outside Alligators that day, Chesser may have been rescued.

January 28, 1998 Biggest Wednesday at Log Cabins. One of the biggest winter swells in many years hits the North Shore of Oahu. Waimea Bay is closed out and too big for the Eddie Aikau competition, sending the world's best big wave surfers scattering for calmer water. A platoon of surfers make it past Condition Black restrictions and the shorebreak to find giant, perfect bluebirds breaking at Outside Log Cabins. The resulting tow-in session makes history as Ken Bradshaw is towed into what many consider the biggest wave ever ridden. The session is also recorded by an IMAX team and is featured in the IMAX film, IMAX Xtreme.

Although not as well covered, this day is also historic at Jaws. Buzzy Kerbox gives witness: "Jaws was very, very heavy that day, but for some reason it keeps getting forgotten. Although the swell direction wasn't perfect it was the biggest day ever ridden out there. Laird Hamilton, Dave Kalama, and I all rode huge waves that raised the bar for big waves at Jaws. Ken Bradshaw did ride a monster on Oahu but I believe that some at Jaws were just as big. Guys survived errors at Logs that would have been fatal at Jaws."

Anyone want to argue with that?

February 16, 1998 Todos Santos produces giant surf for the First Annual Reef Brazil Big Wave Team World Championship. It's death or glory all day long, with two dozen of the world's best big wave surfers taking big drops and bigger beatings. Halfway through the event, Taylor Knox bags a giant wave, barely makes the drop, and ends up winning the $50,000 K2 Challenge for the biggest wave of the El Niño winter. Brazilian Carlos Burle wins the contest.

New Year's Day, 1999 The Quiksilver Invitational in Memory of Eddie Aikau goes off in 20-foot surf at Waimea Bay. Conditions are slow at first but improve with the tide. In the first heat of the second round, Noah Johnson bags a legitimate monster and goes on to win the event and $55,000.

March 22, 1999 Sarah Gerhardt, a 24-year-old Ph.D. candidate and resident of Santa Cruz, CA, rides three waves at Maverick's and breaks down one of the last bastions of men's surfing, the Maverick's Mens Club. Along with other women such as Layne Beachely, Gerhardt is helping pave the way for female big wave surfers of the future.

CONTRIBUTORS

Erik Aeder is a photographer based in Hawaii.

Lawrence Beck is a fine-art photographer who resides in Pacifica, California. His works range from African dunescapes and wildlife to jazz musicians, Mediterranean landscapes, and, of course, big waves at venues in California and Hawaii. He has been published in numerous magazines and newspapers, and exhibits his work at several galleries in the San Francisco area and beyond. He is currently launching a photo safari operation in southern Africa. Visit his website at www.primitive.com or e-mail him at lbeck@primitive.com.

Bud Browne is widely recognized as the pioneer of surf-film making. Throughout the 1950s, 1960s, and 1970s he released 17 films, including *Locked In, Gun Ho!,* and *Cavalcade of Surf.* He has recently transferred several of his most classic films to a video format, and they are available from Hillcrest-Retroart Distributing, 800-248-8057.

Peter Cole began surfing in 1944. At Stanford University, where he received his B.A., he was an All-American middle distance freestyle swimmer. In 1958 he moved to Hawaii to teach math at the Punahou Academy in Honolulu; that same year he won the Makaha International Surfing Championships. He is currently a supervisory computer specialist at the headquarters of the Commander-in-Chief of the Pacific Command in Hawaii. Cole says he has "tried to surf every good swell at Sunset Beach from 1958 to the present day." He lives with his wife Sally and has three sons.

Ken "Skindog" Collins, 31, was born and raised in Santa Cruz, California, and is regarded as one of the most talented big wave surfers in the world. An accomplished surfboard airbrush artist who works for Pearson Arrow Surfboards, Ken is among the young crew who first tackled the amazing surf at Maverick's. In addition to Pearson Arrow boards, he reps Counter Culture clothing and Black Flys sunglasses. Friends claim that Skindog has "more energy than a power plant." He lives with his wife Annoeskia in Santa Cruz.

Alec "Ace Cool" Cooke is a resident of Hawaii and one of the pioneers of extreme big wave surfing. An indigenous part of the Hawaiian scenery, he writes a regular column for the *North Shore News* called "Surf News by Ace," and is currently putting together a book called *Twenty Years of Surf,* a collection of *North Shore News* surfing articles written by himself and Mark Foo. From 1978 to 1990, he issued a surfing report three times a day on several Hawaiian radio stations. For the last ten years he has lived in his house on the North Shore near Chun's Reef. To obtain copies of *Twenty Years of Surf,* call 808-641-7038.

Mark Foo was born in Singapore in 1958. His mother was a first-generation descendant of a prominent Manchu family, part of the imperial clan that ruled China during the Ching Dynasty. His father's father was the first Chinese-American to graduate from medical school in Michigan. Foo was widely recognized as one of the world's premier big wave surfers before his death in 1994, and his accomplishments helped propel the sport into the national spotlight. He is survived by his nieces and nephews, and his sister Sharlyn, who lives in Hawaii and runs Mark Foo Backpackers.

Hank of Hank Fotos is a surfing and bodyboarding photographer based in Hawaii.

Rob Gilley is a photographer and photo editor at *Surfer* magazine.

Ricky Grigg is equal parts distinguished oceanographer and big wave surfer. His detailed and thought-provoking studies of coral reefs are respected the world over, as is his surfing ability and love of the ocean. He began surfing near Santa Monica, California, with Buzzy Trent, long before he became a standout at Waimea Bay and an innovator at Sunset Beach in Hawaii. In 1967, he won the prestigious Duke Kahanamoku contest at Sunset Beach against a fierce field of competitors including Greg Noll, Mike Doyle, Jock Sutherland, and Eddie Aikau. After finishing his education at Stanford University and Scripps Institution of Oceanography, Grigg moved to Hawaii where he began his long oceanography career. His biography, *Big Surf, Deep Dives, and the Islands: My Life in the Ocean,* is available from Editions Limited in Hawaii, 808-735-7644.

Gardner Heaton graduated *cum laude* from Cornell University in 1991, with a degree in Anthropology/South Asian Studies/Nepali Language. He works as a professional mountain guide for EXUM Mountain Guides in Jackson, Wyoming, and as a freelance illustrator and artist.

Derek Hynd, 42, is one of surfing's seminal figures. Educated at Sydney University in Australia, he has been involved in the sport since 1977 as a professional surfer, highly respected journalist, coach, film maker, and market innovator. He was the driving force behind Rip Curls landmark '90s campaign The Search (along with Doug Wambrick). His film of the 1998 A.S.P. World Tour, *Pro Land,* is regarded by some as the archetypal portrait of the sport. Future projects include an upcoming surfing series, Inside Surf (Sky Sports); a grassroots series of surf/surf music culture Search STOMP (Channel 4 U.K.); a sequel to *Pro Land;* and an alternative world tour of pro surfing. His ultimate goal is to do justice to the life of Roger Erickson in print and film. He has a six-year-old son, Lochlan.

Phil Jarratt is a writer, editor, and publisher based in Noosa Heads, Australia. He has written about surfing for 30 years and has been North Shore correspondent for *Surfer* magazine, editor of *Tracks,* and is currently editor and publisher of *The Australian Surfer's Journal*. He and Jeff Hakman have been friends for 25 years. *Mr. Sunset: The Jeff Hakman Story* is available by mail order from The Blue Group for $45, including postage. Fax: 011-61-7-5449-0188. E-mail: bluegroup@peg.apc.org.

Bruce Jenkins, 51, has been a member of the *San Francisco Chronicle* sports staff since 1973 and a columnist since 1989. He has covered numerous major sports events and has won many national awards for his writing. In 1992 he was nominated for a Pulitzer Prize for his columns on the Barcelona Olympics. Jenkins has written two books for North Atlantic books: *Life after Saberhagen* and *North Shore Chronicles*. He is a contributing editor to *Surfer* magazine and is currently senior editor at *SurferGirl* magazine. He resides in Montara, California, with his wife, sports photographer Martha Jenkins, and their daughter Molly.

Buzzy Kerbox moved to Hawaii and started surfing at age 10. He turned pro at 18 and traveled the pro circuit from 1977 to 1983, finishing in the top 10 six years in a row. He has won two major competitions: the 1978 World Cup at Sunset Beach, and the 1980 Surfbout competition in Sydney, Australia. In 1992 Kerbox helped pioneer tow-in surfing with Laird Hamilton, then moved to Maui and began towing into Jaws (Peahi) in 1994. At 42 years old, he is still active in Masters events and paddleboard racing; he is the reigning Masters champion in the over-40 division.

Brock Little, 32, has been a professional surfer for 14 years. He lives in Hawaii.

John Long's instructional books have made him a best seller in the outdoor industry, with over a million books in print. His recent instructional book, *Advanced Rock Climbing* (Falcon Publishing, coauthored by Craig Luebben), won the 1997 Banff Mountain Book Festival award for Best Mountain Exposition. His award-winning short stories—known for taut action and psychological intensity—have been widely anthologized and translated into many languages. A legendary performer in the sport of rock climbing, Long's achievements include the first one-day ascent of the 3,000-foot face of El Capitan in Yosemite. Long's other adventures include a Baffin Island–North Pole expedition; a coast-to-coast traverse of Borneo; discovery and exploration of the world's largest river cave in Papua New Guinea; the first descent of Angel Falls in Venezuela; and the first land crossing of Indonesian New Guinea, one of the most primitive regions in the world. He splits his time between California and Venezuela.

Gerry Lopez was born and raised on the beaches of Hawaii and has been surfing since the age of 10. He has made a career of surfing, both as a professional surfer and as a surfboard builder. In 1972 he started Lightning Bolt Surfboards and these boards became the most recognized brand in the 1970s. In 1980 he sold his interest in Lightning Bolt and turned his attention toward surf exploration in Indonesia, windsurfing in Maui, and building a home on the beach near Pipeline. The son of a career newspaper editor, his passion for writing began with a weekly surf column in the *Honolulu Advertiser;* he went on to be a regular contributor to numerous surfing publications. He currently lives in Bend, Oregon, with his wife Toni and his 10-year-old son Alex. He is still building surfboards and taking surfing trips around the world, and has also taken up snowboarding.

Ben Marcus, 38, grew up surfing near Santa Cruz and moved to Southern California to work at *Surfer* magazine in 1989. He claims he is better at writing about surfing than actually doing it. After 10 years at *Surfer*, he moved back to Northern California and claims he will most likely never go south of Point Conception again.

Sam Moses is a renowned sportswriter who worked for many years on the staff of *Sports Illustrated* magazine.

Greg Noll is a surfing legend if there ever was one. Nicknamed "Da Bull" for his ability to plow through tons of whitewater without so much as a wobble, Noll was a pioneer big wave surfer on the North Shore of Hawaii for many years and has perhaps done more than anybody to glorify and institutionalize the sport. In the 1960s, he was one of the premier board shapers, and he also produced several classic surf movies during this period. Later, he ran a shrimp trawler in the Pacific Northwest out of Crescent City, California, before returning to surfing as an entrepreneur in the '80s and '90s. His book *Da Bull: Life Over the Edge* is recognized as a true classic of the genre. It is available from North Atlantic Books.

Dave Parmenter is well known in the surfing community as a surfer who writes, rather than as a writer who surfs. While traveling on the world professional surfing circuit, Parmenter began writing features, and his work has appeared in a number of surfing magazines, including *Surfing, Surfer, Australian Surfing Life*, and *Surfer's Journal*. Parmenter, currently a surfboard designer, splits his time between San Luis Obispo, California, and Makaha, Hawaii.

Mike Parson runs a surfwear company called The Realm based in San Clemente, California, along with five partners (www.realmsurf.com). He still competes in surfing competitions and, when not competing, watches the water for good swells so he's ready to go on a moment's notice. He is grateful to Taylor Knox and Alister Craft for riding waves with him at Todos Santos, Randy Laine for his rescue efforts, and his dad for introducing him to surfing.

Clay Rogers is a photographer based in Hawaii.

Jason Smith, 29, is a contributing editor for *Surfer* magazine and an associate editor for the *Los Angeles Times* Calender Live! He has been surfing 17 years, beginning in the cold waters near Santa Cruz and eventually relocating to Southern California, where he is ecstatic to have shed his neoprene wetsuit. He has recently completed the first of several screenplays he is writing, and is poised to begin the Herculean task of schmoozing it toward production. Like Jay Moriarty, the focus of his contribution to this book, Smith was a protege of Rick "Frosty" Hesson and benefits from Frosty's profound and oblique wisdom every day.

Skip Snead, 29, is the editor of *Surfer* magazine. He grew up in Upland, California, and has been surfing since he was five years old, traveling the world in pursuit of beautiful waves. He started the Aerial Surfing Tour in 1996 and pioneered the "Flowrider" wave machine in Norway in 1994 through 1997. He hosts a radio show one day a week in San Diego called The Surfing Mag Airshow. Snead has almost been killed 10 times in motocross, snowboarding, skating, and traffic accidents, but has yet to break a bone. He lives with his wife and daughter in Newport Beach, California.

Mike Stang, originally from California, migrated to Hawaii in 1957 to become a pioneer big wave surfer on the North Shore. He surfed Waimea Bay with Greg Noll on the day when the first waves were ever ridden there, and was a major player in many other groundbreaking events.

Fred Van Dyke is a native San Franciscan who moved to Hawaii as a young man to pursue his dream of riding big waves. He is passionate about many things, including health and fitness, fishing, hiking, jogging, swimming, skiing, and surfing. For 30 years, he taught English at Punahou School in Honolulu. He has written four books: *Thirty Years of Riding the World's Biggest Waves; Riding Huge Waves with Ease; Once upon a Wilderness;* and *Two Surf Stories for Children.* Along with his wife Joan Marie, he now he divides his time between the beaches of Hawaii and the mountains of Montana.

Les Walker is a photographer for *Surfing* magazine and contributes to many other publications. Visit his website at surfphoto.com.

Matt Warshaw began surfing in 1969 in Southern California and competed professionally in the early '80s. From 1985 to 1990 he was managing editor and editor of *Surfer* magazine and has published numerous articles on surfing in publications around the world, including *Surfer's Journal, Esquire, Outside,* the *San Francisco Chronicle,* and the *Los Angeles Times.* His credits also include writing several television shows about surfing, and a book called *Surfriders: In Search of the Perfect Wave* (Collins). He is currently writing a book on Maverick's and big wave surfing, due out from Chronicle Books in the spring of 2000, and is also working on *The Encyclopedia of Surfing* (Harcourt Brace). Warshaw lives, writes, and surfs in San Francisco.

COPYRIGHTS AND PERMISSIONS

GLOSSARY

angling: going sideways or riding the wave along the unbroken portion of its length, ahead of the broken portion

ASP: Association of Surfing Professionals

backside: surfing with your back to the wave

beach break: where waves break over a sandbar

big: as in, riding big Waimea; makes a distinction between surfing a spot when the waves are small, or surfing it when the waves are big—two very different undertakings

blown out: condition of waves tor n up by wind

bluebirds: beautiful waves

bodyboard: a bodyboarder lies chest-down on the board and rides the waves, rather than standing up

Boneyard: rocky, shallow, dangerous area at a surf break

closed out: condition of a wave that breaks all at once, making angling impossible

crest: top of a wave

curl: breaking part of a wave

drop: the act of catching the crest of a wave and riding high speed down the face of it

dry suit: waterproof suit designed to keep the user completely dry when immersed in water

duck diving: diving under a wave to avoid its full force as it breaks

goofy foot: the natural preference for keeping your left foot back as you ride a surfboard

gremmies: grommets

grommets: small surfer kids

gun: a surfboard nine feet or longer for riding big waves

hang ten: placing all 10 toes over the nose of a moving surfboard; usually associated with long board surfing

haoles: Hawaiian word for outsiders or whites; pronounced HOW-lies

hellmen: big wave surfers

impact zone: where the waves break

inside: the area "inside" the breaking waves; also may refer to smaller waves breaking closer to shore than the bigger waves breaking further out

Jet Ski: personal watercraft used to tow into and maneuver around waves

kook: inexperienced or disrespectful surfer

K2 Big Wave Challenge: a contest run during the 1997/1998 El Niño winter that awarded $50,000 to the surfer who got photographed surfing the most radical big wave

lefthanders: waves that break from the peak to the surfer's left; also called "lefts"

lineup: area outside breaking waves where surfers sit on their boards and wait for waves

lip: very tip of cresting wave curling or plunging down

locals: surfers who frequent a certain spot

lull: period of time when "sets" of waves are not coming in

mackers: big waves

menehunes: mythical Hawaiian leprechauns that fix or create problems, depending on their mood; also used to refer to surfing contest categories for young kids

outside: the area "outside" the breaking waves; may also refer to waves breaking further out from shore than the smaller waves breaking closer in

overgunned: choosing a surfboard that is too big for the size of the waves

peak: the portion of a cresting swell that breaks first

pearl: when a moving surfboard nosedives due to weight too far forward

pit: the bottom of a wave

point break: where waves break around a point of land

pop up: the single motion of standing up on your surfboard, from belly to feet

reef break: where waves break over an underwater reef

reforms: waves that have broken once and reformed to break again

regular foot: the natural preference for keeping your right foot back when riding a surfboard

righthanders: waves that break from the peak to the surfer's right; also "rights"

riptide: the river of water, headed back out to sea, that forms after waves break

rogue wave: a wave that is much bigger than the other waves that day

sea: waves of all wavelengths within a storm, forming a chaotic surface

sets: waves arrive at a beach in sets, with lulls in between

skeg: a type of fin on a surfboard

snaking: catching a wave in front of another surfer who has caught the wave closer to the breaking part of the wave

soup: whitewater

stall: when a moving surfboard slows due to weight too far back

stick: surfboard

swell: smooth, deep-water waves formed by the marching lines of wind-inspired energy that travel across the open water

switch foot: when a goofy foot rides regular, and vice-versa

trim: being balanced fore and aft, and side to side, on your surfboard, so as not to nosedive or stall as you paddle or ride; trim encourages maximum thrust through the water

trough: bottom of a wave

tube: a type of wave that breaks top to bottom, with the crest of the wave plunging out and down to the base of the wave, forming a hollow tube

undergunned: choosing a surfboard that is too small for the size of the waves

watermen: extremely proficient ocean swimmers and surfers

wave height: the vertical distance from the crest to the trough of a wave

wave length: distance between two successive wave crests

WaveRunner: personal watercraft used to tow into and maneuver around waves

wet suit: neoprene suit (usually between two and five millimeters thick) that holds a small amount of water close to the skin, creating a warm pocket of water that in turn keeps the user warm

whitewater: the broken or spent part of a wave that has peaked and toppled over

Zodiac: personal watercraft used to tow into and maneuver around waves

Fred Van Dyke says goodbye to another board after a wicked wipeout in Waimea Bay.